AFRICAN LITERATURE:

Gender Discourse, Religious Values, and the African Worldview

T0339878

AFRICAN LITERATURE:

Gender Discourse, Religious Values, and the African Worldview

SAFOURA SALAMI-BOUKARI

AFRICAN HERITAGE PRESS

New York • *Lagos* • *London*

AFRICAN HERITAGE PRESS

NEW YORK
PO BOX 1433
NEW ROCHELLE, NY 10802
USA

LAGOS
PO BOX 14452
IKEJA, LAGOS
NIGERIA

TEL: 914-481-8488 / 855-247-7737
FAX: 914-481-8489
customerservice@africanheritagepress.com
www.africanheritagepress.com

First Edition, African Heritage Press, 2012

Library of Congress control number: 2011941393

Salami-Boukari, Safoura

Cover Design: Dapo Ojoade

ISBN: 978-0-9790858-5-7
ISBN: 0-9790858-5-3

DEDICATION

To both my late grandmothers, Nana Tikpaba Donyi
Whose lessons I will never forget, and
Nana Amissotu Salami, daughter of
M'ma Halima, a Konkomba princess descendant of warriors,
A widow who single-handedly raised her seven children
To my late mother El-Hadja Abiba Kouna Ogamo
"Fofana Adjate, N'gom Takoni Sim'be Taya!"
Who would repeatedly state:

"May God give us a resourceful and prosperous child
Who has a vision in life, no matter the gender.
The girl I have is worth a good man!"
For my father and Yaya, the pivotal men in my life
Who inspired my emotions and without whom
I would not have succeeded in my endeavors.

To all those who helped carve the stature I have today,
I am thankful
To the Most Gracious and Merciful
Almighty,
I am grateful.

TABLE OF CONTENTS

Acknowledgments

I want to thank my professors at the State University of New York at Buffalo, Ruth Meyerowitz and Masani Alexis De Veaux, now respectively, former Chairs of American Studies and of Women's Studies in the Faculty of Arts and Sciences. I owe this work to my foremost instrumental teacher and mentor, Professor Mensah Nubukpo, Dean of the Faculty of Arts and Human Sciences at the University of Benin, former Minister of Higher Education and Scientific Research in Lome, Togo. Could I have undertaken the challenge of proving myself had it not been for my friend and mentor, Dr. Akrima Kogoe, Professor of Educational Sciences and Research at the University of Lome (Togo), and Director of the International Airport of Lome? I am indebted to him.

My sincere gratitude goes to the other faculty of American Studies, Sociology, and History, especially to Professors Elizabeth Lapovsky Kennedy, former Director of Women's Studies, and Monica Jardine in the Department of Sociology, whose team-taught introductory course in "Cross-Cultural Studies of Women" and the Sociology course on "The World Economic Systems" opened another window in my mind, and inspired me to undertake this study. My thanks also go to Professor Peter Ekeh, former Chair of African American Studies and my professor in Education, at SUNY (Buffalo), Professor Mwalimu Shujaa, former Dean of Liberal Arts at Medgar Evers College in New York City, now Provost and Executive Vice Chancellor at SU, Baton Rouge (LA) for stimulating my interest in Black Studies and cultural identity. I owe thanks to Drs. Nadine Lockwood, and Nah Dove, my friends and "Sisters in Kemetism." I am grateful to the needed support Dr. Catherine Bankole gave me during her leadership as former Director of the Black Cultural Center and Research at West Virginia University. My thanks are extended to Professors Amachree in the Department of Sociology, and Abdul-Rasheed Na'Allah, former Chair of the African American Studies Department and Professor of Comparative Literatures at Western Illinois University, now Vice Chancellor of Kwara State University, Nigeria.

I am thankful to the instrumental and decisive assistance Professor Chimalum Nwankwo, Professor of English and World Literatures at North Carolina AT&T State University (NC) gave me in the final stage of this project.

To my different students in AAS 281 "Literature of the Black World," AAS 381 "Modern African Literature" and AAS 491 "Seminar in African American Studies: African Women Writers" whose questions, and passion for knowledge prompted me to present this book in the format it is, I am thankful. To Dr. Judith Stitzel, founder and former Director of the Center for Women's Studies at West Virginia University, thank you for believing in me and planting the seed of a writer's urge in me at our first encounter.

This work could not have materialized had it not been the students contributing to its inception and shaping, especially, in inspiring my formulation of the Essay and Discussion questions on each chapter, in the last part of the book. Thus, *African Literature: Gender Discourse, Religious Values and the African Worldview* serves as a support document to satisfy the students' curiosity through a discussion of peculiar topics such as tradition, modernity, religion, female circumcision, colonialism, gender perception, male/female relationships, marriage, violence, and women's activism, just to name a few. It is a pedagogical tool, which provides a contextual background for a better understanding of African literature. The end questions on each chapter will stimulate critical thinking and discussion as well as broaden the readers' exposure to African cultural practices and the colonial influence as a leitmotif in Modern African literature.

My ultimate thanks go to my brothers in Kemetism, Professor Tanure Ojaide, Drs Salau Abdul Razak, Jose Pemienta-Bey, and Joseph Quarshie, "brother Gany" in France, "Tonton Souley," and the belated former UN journalist, Dermane Traore Abdou for their unshakable moral support and encouragement for me to pursue my life path. This work has materialized and is here presented to the reader with its strengths and flaws. Take it and read it keeping in mind the efforts came from a writer whose linguistic hybridization includes French, as the first language.

Preface

This book, *African Literature: Gender Discourse, Religious Values & the African Worldview*, is a significant contribution and service to the study of African literature. Safoura Salami-Boukari's vision encompasses the interests and needs of a broad spectrum of readers.

For students and the general reader outside the discipline, Boukari's methodology offers a foundation for the understanding of African literature not just by women but by male writers too. Both in subject matter and rendition, the book answers a call which scholars and teachers in the discipline have been suggesting and recommending over the years, that is, the issue of context. It is a folly and a disservice, and indeed somewhat of a deception when cultural materials are presumed to exist in a vacuum bereft of the elucidating context of cosmology and culture, ontology and history. The epistemological dynamic, the great foundry of the deep psychology of structural formations and the politics of the organization of those formations including their perpetuations are just too weighty for one to sweep over with an all too familiar pretence of universality, or in today's predominantly single-gendered political parlance, the so-called globalism. In most workable systems of thought, it has always been particulars first before the invocation of the single or general umbrella. Such an approach serves well our efforts to make sense and meaning out of all cultural productions. This issue is particularly important and virtually urgent when the item being studied is African literature, an area where over the years, people continue to settle very quickly into the strange convenient melding of stereotype with presumption, and presumption with spurious hasty conclusion.

Boukari's study reverberates with stubborn old questions. How do we resolve the insider/outsider interpreting conundrum? Why do readers from different parts of the world read, interpret, or understand foreign literatures the way they do? What drives peculiar critical reactions, canon formations and such issues which determine the survival of cultural productions or their continued adoption as useful bolsters for a people's self-definition or indeed self-preservation and self-determination? Students new to this area will find good attitudes or approaches to such common questions in this study of African literature by women and men. That a woman raises such gender neutral questions in a work that skirts or creates its own bit of gender controversy makes the study even more intriguing and interesting. Boukari does none of the old familiar feminist grandstanding about evil men destroying good women. She is occasionally careful to promote a more extenuating position that endorses a Womanist/feminist posture with gender compromise as objective. This gender compromise that the author coins as the "Kemetic Paradigm" is developed in an upcoming study.

Scholars and teachers of African literature will also find Boukari's work affirming and enriching the old issue of the degree of permutation of anthropology in literary criticism. When the anthropological lens comes to bear on African literature, common wisdom endorses cautious deployment. Invoking the names of reputable anthropologists such as Ifi Amadiume, Boukari endorses that caution as long as the approach enhances or augments authorial vision and perspective. No harm is done if the aim is to deepen the recognition of our awareness of the complexity of difference or the role of relativity in the study of culture. Anthropology should not be in literary study or analysis for mere end-closed validation of the modes of human behavior which the works appear to reflect, depict or explore. It becomes a choice between reading literature as social tract and reading literature as a veritable probe of the depths of the human condition in question.

A key strategy in this important work is Boukari's use of Chinua Achebe's Igbo world as a fulcrum for hoisting into clearer view other cultural circumstances where a wedding of literature and history similar to what we find in *Things Fall Apart* produces significant moments in the reading of national consciousness. Some of Boukari's examples are contemporaneous with *Things Fall Apart*, and some come after. By and large, such a comparative stance continentally universalizes human destiny, the vicissitudes of African peoples and their ways as those ways collide with Western imperial irruption. Her choice of materials for this particular exercise is eclectic, from the works of Egypt's irrepressible and prolific Nawal El Sadaawi to Algerian Leila Abuzeid, Senegalese Mariama Ba, and Nigerian women writers. The textual analyses are quite incisive and elucidatory and the critical eye is compelling and steady. Scholar, student and general reader will find the whole work rewarding in what it asserts and affirms.

This is no one-dimensional feminist study. Its compass is broad and engaging, the style free of academic affectation, with clear and jargon-free diction. In sections where men and women writers are compared, there is neither truculence nor phony adversarialism, just simple down-to-earth expression of disagreement or difference. Women writers against men balance the picture, fill up absences or reinstate erasures of presence in agency and thought. The overall result is generally an ennobling vision of society where judgment is left to the subjectivity of the reader, man or woman.

—CHIMALUM NWANKWO
Chair and Professor of English and World Literatures
North Carolina A&T State University
Greensboro, USA

Introduction

This book is a product of my experience teaching "Modern African Literature" and specifically "Selected African Women Writers" at the State University of Buffalo, New York (SUNY at Buffalo), and "Literature of the Black World" at Western Illinois University. The book was also driven by a need for foundational material beyond the assigned traditional textbooks. I have found it increasingly necessary to provide information to enable better understanding of the relationship between cultural factors and the impact of colonization on people's behavior. Though this material is designed with non-African students in mind, other teachers and scholars in the discipline are likely to find it useful. My inter-disciplinary perspective will also be beneficial to departments engaged in Non-Western Literatures in English Departments, Women's Studies, Multi-cross-cultural/Diversity Studies, and African/Black Diaspora Studies. General Education students and teachers may also find pertinent information/discussions on sensitive and controversial issues such as gender perceptions, male/female relationships, traditional versus modern marriage, polygamy, female circumcision, religious rituals, suicide, and body modifications like tattooing, piercing, and so forth.

The adoption of a comparative methodology to discuss the literary elements and cultural aspects of a few African novels provides a critical thinking approach as well as an opportunity for students to learn, analyze and synthesize the information. This approach prepares students to better understand the difference between classical British writers like Shakespeare or Thomas Hardy and American materials like Samuel

Langhorne Clemens (Mark Twain) or Robert Frost, and even post-colonial literary genres, particularly in the African literature of the 1960s.

For a rewarding use of this book, and considering the focus of our discussion, prior or parallel readings of a few West African novels would be helpful. A few titles, which are referred to and commonly studied in classes, include *Things Fall Apart* by Chinua Achebe, *Efuru* by Flora Nwapa, *So Long A Letter* by Mariama Ba, *The Concubine* by Elechi Amadi, *Anowa* by Amah Ata Aidoo, *Male Daughters, Female Husbands* by Ifi Amadiume, *Second Class Citizen* by Buchi Emecheta, *Death and the King's Horseman* and *The Lion and the Jewel* by Wole Soyinka, *Purple Hibiscus*, or *Half of a Yellow Sun* by Chimamanda Ngozi Adichie, *Year of the Elephant* by Leila Abuzeid, and *The Prophet of Zongo Street* by M. Na Shehu Ali, among others. Depending on the course title, African American and Caribbean writers are added to the list of readings.

In that vein, *African Literature: Gender Discourse, Religious Values and the African Worldview*, a revised and expanded version of *Gender and Cultural Issues in Igbo Society*, is designed to help students enjoy the selected readings while fulfilling their general education, multicultural, or course/subject requirements. While *Gender and Cultural Issues* had only three parts, *Modern African Literature* has six, with an expansion on excision/female circumcision/Female Genital Mutilation (FGM), examination of "Religion in African Literature," "Relationships: Marriage, Polygamy & Monogamy," "Leila Abouzeid: A Pioneer Moroccan Woman Writer," in North Africa, and Discussion/Essay questions.

It is important to mention the diversity existing among modern African writers, a distinction fostered by the Western European colonization. Hence, different regions of Africa inherited the linguistic and cultural legacies of the different European countries which occupied them. As a result, the variety of denominations, such as Francophone literature for the countries colonized by the French, Anglophone literature for countries colonized by the British, Luxophone literature for those colonized by Portugal, and so on. For the purpose of sampling stories written in the post-colonial era of the 1960s, and keeping in mind an objective reading selection, the focus will be thematic discussions of re-curring themes of gender and culture, including character depictions. Though the focus is on the Nigerian woman writer Flora Nwapa's first book, *Efuru*, other African writers will be discussed in comparison or juxtaposition in order to draw parallels and broaden the scope of our the-matic study. Examples are such writers as Kenyan Ngugi Wa'Thiongo, in the discussion of female circumcision; and Moroccan Leila Abouzeid, in dealing with the impact of social constructs and patriarchal dominance coupled with a religious misinterpretation of the family code in North African countries. While Nawal El Saadawi is well known as an Egyp-tian revolutionary writer for her advocacy regarding justice and women's rights in North Africa, espoused in more than fifteen books in English, Leila Abouzeid hails from Morocco, another Arab country colonized by France and therefore speaking Arabic and French. She has published quite a few works, including *Year of the Elephant, Return to Childhood: The Memoir of a Moroccan Woman, The Last Chapter: A Novel,* and *The Director and other Stories from Morocco.*

Considering the multi-faceted treatment of the different themes il-lustrated in the works discussed, the structural division, and the critical approach used, this textbook does not only provide students with essen-tial thematic information furthering their understanding and analysis of African literature. It also opens a window into experiencing a different cultural immersion for those in the mainstream population who are in-terested in diversity, African culture, and a global world vision.

The style is designed to make it accessible to a heterogeneous student audience in General Education, Multicultural studies and Humanities in Arts and Sciences. The textbook was initially prepared as a supporting document for students who might have been exposed for the first time to non-Western literature, in general, and to African literature, in par-ticular. However, the overwhelming positive feedback and suggestions to include it in the required readings led me to take a closer look at the African concept of gender and its intersection with some salient socio-cultural issues raised in the selected academic readings. As such, the work is meant to foster understanding of human diversity, knowledge of our common features, and appreciation of African literature as an important part of a global world literature. Therefore, the material is presented to the reader as part of the instructor's efforts to provide additional tools for the students' better understanding of the cultural background and historical context surrounding the stories they read. Moreover, the multicultural exposure adds to the readers' critical thinking skills and personal knowledge assessments, based not only on social but also on environmental factors.

Despite the emphasis put on the dynamics of gender in Igbo society, a multidisciplinary perspective guides the overall discussion in this book, a collection of essays divided in six parts.

Thus, the first part of this study will lay the ground for discussing some Igbo cultural beliefs and practices in a traditional setting, in the pre-colonial, colonial and postcolonial eras, from the nineteenth century to the 1950–60s. The second and third parts will highlight cultural and gender intersections such as religious and secular beliefs/practices illustrated throughout Flora Nwapa's *Efuru*. The fourth section presents a comparative approach in which character delineation, both in Nwapa's novel and in other works of some West African writers are discussed. Parts five—African Women's Voice: Critical & Comparative Perspectives—and six—Reflection on Arts & Activism—revisit some salient issues which were discussed in the previous sections while using simultaneously a comparative approach to consider how they are expressed in contemporary African society and their correlation in today's American society.

The comparison of Flora Nwapa's writing with other Igbo and African women writers such as Ama Ata Aidoo and Buchi Emecheta is discussed by using a thematic analysis alongside the historical contexts of their works. A few examples include, Ama Ata Aidoo's *Anowa*, Buchi Emecheta's *Second Class Citizen*, Ifi Amadiume's *Male Daughters, Female Husbands*, and Mariama Ba's *So Long a Letter*. Answers will be provided to such questions as: What place did the traditional African woman occupy before encountering the Western civilization? What impact did colonization have on West African women in terms of economic power? How did the Igbo social division of labor shift from an egalitarian status to a predominantly patriarchal one? Why has it become almost impossible for women in general, and especially African women, to participate in the national/international public arena today?

Some might object to the interrogative statement above considering that a few women have made their way into the political leadership. One should consider the global demographic predominance of women, their socioeconomic contributions, as opposed to the actual privileges, power, and wealth they have in the *per capita* stratification.

A different set of questions which ultimately arises with a focus on Flora Nwapa's *Efuru* should be kept in mind in the critical analysis of the different literary references throughout the book. For instance, where does Flora Nwapa stand in West African post-colonial literature of the 1960s? What is the relationship between her writing and other women's writings in other parts of Africa during that time? What other connections can be made between Nwapa's *Efuru* and West African male writers' novels? To what extent are Flora Nwapa's novels reflective of, and comparable to other West African women's experiences and writings today? How does Flora Nwapa's novel, *Efuru*, delineate the heroic place of African women in general? To what extent is Nwapa's novel a pioneering work that clears a path for other African women writers? What recurrent themes are prototypically common African features? Which ones are universal and stand for global considerations?

In the course of this discussion, such themes as tradition versus modernity as the result of the colonial impact; the persistence of secular beliefs and ritualistic practices such as female circumcision; the presence of the medicine-man, called "*Dibia*"; and gerontocracy, the leadership of the elders as guardian of the community sustainability are explored. Other aspects which are also examined are the gender division of labor, beliefs about men and women, and symbols of tradition as presented by Chinua Achebe in *Things Fall Apart*, and Flora Nwapa in *Efuru*.

Africans have now been acknowledged to possess a literary tradition traced not only to oral communication through Griotism, but also to the hieroglyphic writings in Ancient Egyptian civilization. The modern African literary canon is also a fertile ground to explore because of its inheritance of Western values. Modern African literature based on Western European norms only came to life in the late 1950s and in the 1960s, during the independence era preceding the end of the direct European colonization of most African countries. Hence, the necessity to produce historical European influences in writing the first literary genres which became common as a result of the Europe-Africa's second contact, characterized by the conquest and domination of strategic African societal life.

For a better understanding of the dynamics of gender and culture in the approaches of male and female African writers to different sociopolitical or economic issues, it is necessary to highlight the fundamental factors which influenced and molded the thinking and choices of those first intellectuals. Dealing with gender roles in Igbo society is enlightening as it uncovers the socio-cultural and religious realities of a particular group of African people. The term "gender" refers to the social, cultural and historical construction of male and female roles, which though "related to biological roles are not coterminous with them."[1]

If the above insight can, in a way, apply to any group of people, the cultural study of Igbo society serves as a model for applying the definition of gender as well as exploring other implications. In that light, this study will help us understand why African women occupy a nearly invisible spot on the world sociopolitical and economic scenes. The socio-cultural and historical background of Black women in general has proven to be diametrically opposed to the apparent negative and alienated image that is presented of them. Going back to the past, literatures have significantly illustrated how African women and people of African descent have occupied a central role in their communities.

---

[1] Monk & Momsen, p. 14, 1994.

Despite the physical and mental traumas they experienced with European contact, Black women have always managed to survive discrimination and hardship while taking care of their families and contributing to their communities' sustainability through their socioeconomic and political achievements. Apart from the continent, Africans are in the Diaspora, meaning locations outside of the African continent where they originated, namely in the United States, Europe, South America, and the Caribbean Islands. The women in our discussion are the Black women who remained on the continent and who experienced colonization through contact with European countries in the nineteenth century. Consequently, the discussion will turn around gender issues within the context of African culture, while simultaneously using a comparative approach to European-based concepts and social constructs of gender. As the concept of gender is directly related to socio-cultural and economic factors, the following discussion will logically involve a treatment of practices and religious beliefs governing the social behavior of men and women in a particular geographic area of South-Eastern Nigeria, and in a defined time span. In this respect, "gender roles" will be discussed in the Nigerian Igbo traditional setting during the postcolonial era. That is also called the post-independence era—the 1960s—when the majority of colonized African countries got their nominal freedom from domination by European countries, namely, Britain, France, Spain, Germany, and Portugal.

The methodology used in the following study is an interdisciplinary one, combining historical and anthropological approaches, even if the focus of discussion is mainly on literary works and thematic analysis. As mentioned earlier, the study is divided into six interrelated parts. Some historical facts will be necessary in the first part to place Flora Nwapa's *Efuru*, in its African literary context. After retracing the general beliefs and practices which constitute the conceptual framework in Part Two, the following sections explore some literary aspects, such as the thematic treatment of religion in Part Three, and comparative character delineations in Part Four. The fifth Part simultaneously points out specific thematic treatments of socio-cultural issues, and recurrent themes in the novel. It also tackles comparative or contrasting aspects of Nwapa's work with regard to other contemporary African writers, both women and men. Part Six—the conclusion—explores African women writers' artistic creativity as well as focuses on the writer's role not only as an ambassador, but mainly as an activist and a promoter of social change within a global context.

Flora Nwapa's first novel, *Efuru* which retraces the legacy of Igbo traditional life and culture was published in 1966, a few years after Nigeria's independence from British colonial rule. It is a fiction dealing with the past period when Western representation had not yet endangered the peaceful African life and altered secular and religious traditions. So, in the first part of this study, "Historical Background & Methodology," it is important to lay the historical background for the discussion of *Efuru* and the works of other Igbo writers, such as Achebe's *Things Fall Apart* and Elechi Amadi's *The Concubine*. Both Nwapa and Amadi share some common features as Igbo writers. Through the components of their works such as the rural setting, and traditional culture beliefs and proverbial references, it is easy to pick the similarity in the literary genre which reflects that both writers belong to the same generation and have an identical educational background. The second part, "Socio-cultural Issues in Igbo Society," deals with Igbo traditional beliefs and world vision with examples on beliefs about women, traditional practices such as excision, male/female relationships, flexible gender roles, and others. This section also focuses on the recurrent issues pertaining to contemporary African women's predicaments, such as juggling gender in the Igbo traditional social arena, marital status, polygamy, economic contribution and background political activism. Apart from these pervasive aspects, in Part Three—Religion in African Literature & Impact in today's Society—a particular scrutiny is given to the impact of religion in traditional African people's lives, with a comparative approach to Christian religious concepts and perceptions of indigenous belief systems through an analysis of Obinkaram Echewa's novel, *The Land's Lord*, and the exploration of two pivotal characters, Father Higler, a German deserter who became a Christian missionary sent to Igboland, and Old-Ahamba, a traditional Igbo leader. The discourse in the fourth part, which is mainly a comparative study and characterization, involves touching on secondary characters in the novel. The following Part Five, "African Women's Voice: Critical & Comparative Perspectives", highlights the Nigerian woman writer, Flora Nwapa, in a male-dominated literary world and it provides a comparative approach to other African women writers such as Mariama Ba in *So Long A Letter*, Buchi Emecheta in *Second Class Citizen*, Ama Ata Aidoo in *Anowa*, and others from North Africa. Leila Abuzeid is included in the study to serve as a sample reflecting the diversity and multifaceted scope of the British and French colonial influences on the lives and intellectual productivity of Africans, in general. The closing section, Part Six: Reflection on Arts and Activism, deals with the woman writer as promoter of social change. The last part highlights the African women's standpoint and also raises consciousness for self-discovery, self-definition, and self-appreciation as a full human being, not inferior or superior to man, but just different. Thus, *African Literature: Gender Discourse, Religious Values and the African Worldview* is a mixture of sociocultural issues and commentaries with a global and critical perspective.

PART ONE

Historical Background & Methodology

The Historical Context of West African Literature in the 1960s & the Study Structure

We cannot deal with the contextual African literature without referring to the socio-historical background that shaped the characteristic features of that literature. According to Bill Ashcroft (1989) *The Empire Writes Back: Reading Postcolonial Literature*, more than three-quarters of the people living in the world today have had their lives shaped by the experience of colonialism. The remark is pertinent as it is easy to see how important this shaping has been in the political and economic spheres of disenfranchised countries.[2] The general influence of colonialism on the perceptual frameworks of contemporary peoples is often less evident. Literature offers some important ways in which these new perceptions are expressed. Christine Ramsay took a cue from Ashcroft in her work "Canadian Narrative Cinema from the Margins: 'The Nation' and Masculinity in *Goin' Down the Road*,"

> Postcolonial writers try to create an authentic language that gives voice to those that are silenced . . . the perception of figures of a text as metaphor imposes a Universalist reading because metaphor makes no concessions. . . . It is in their writing, and through other arts such as painting, sculpture, music and dance, that the day-to-day realities experienced by colonized peoples are significantly encoded.[3]

---

[2]Ashcroft, Bill, *The Empire Writes Back: Reading Postcolonial Literature*, Routledge, London, 1989. The disenfranchised are countries that seemingly got their independence and freedom to operate without the intervention of European colonizing countries such as France, Britain, Spain, etc. Addition is mine.

[3]Christine Ramsay, Ashcroft Summary, *Reading Postcolonial Literature*, "Canadian Narrative Cinema from the Margins: 'The Nation' and Masculinity in *Goin' Down the Road*." Canadian Journal of Film Studies/revue Canadienne D'Etudes Cinematographiques, Vol. 2 #2-3 retrieved July 1st 2011.

The different influences that colonized African peoples inherited from their interactions with Europeans in their African native land are not in doubt; that ruling period of European countries such as Britain, France, Portugal, and Spain in the late nineteenth century is called the "colonial era." Though the term "post-colonial" might better stand for the historical period beginning from the Europeans' official departure from the conquered territories in Africa and elsewhere around the world, it is used to cover all the culture affected by the imperial process from the moment of colonization to the present day. So, the term "colonial" is generally used to determine the period before independence and "post-colonial" for the period after independence, although the reality has proven the continual involvement of Western countries in the socio-political and economic lives of their erstwhile colonies, up to the present. Consequently, the pre-colonial era refers to the ancient traditional or indigenous life before the arrival of the Europeans. As most African countries became independent in the 1960s, all the literatures written from that period of time up to the present are considered "post-colonial literatures."

In the context of African countries, like in other patriarchal societies around the world, men were the first to write after colonialism ended. Many people felt the need to express feelings internalized during the colonial period. Most writings were created to inform the world about the African past, and as such were either nationalistic or expressions of ancient traditional world-views. Novels such as Achebe's *Things Fall Apart* and Elechi Amadi's *The Concubine* are stories of a "lost innocence and romanticized past of Africa," as many critics noted. One would agree with others to say that often these first post-colonial books exhort an era of prototypical heroism and open-heartedness, of simple integral living, and of adherence to rigid moral codes of conduct imposed by a culturally well-grounded society with a holistic world vision.

C. L. Innes noted in her work, *Chinua Achebe* (1992), that when the British took control of Nigeria in the late nineteenth century, they assumed that together with trade in palm oil they brought enlightenment and progress to a people they deemed to have no valid social, religious, or political institutions, and no history of their own. She further explains that the beliefs and shrines of the Igbo, like those of other people in Africa, were dismissed as mere superstitions and 'fetishes,' and the British failed to acknowledge any system of government which did not fit their preconceived notions about chiefs and emirs. In 1900, the British imposed their administration upon the Igbo by dividing Southeastern Nigeria into areas ruled by District Commissioners, and appointed selected Igbo to act as warrant chiefs, clerks and messengers to assist them, a system resented by the Igbo not only because it was an alien imposition violating their own more democratic structures, but also because those who accepted the appointments were men without status conferred by the villagers and without allegiance to their own communities. They were regarded as contemptible collaborators. While the decentralization of Igbo society contributed to some of its more admirable qualities and sustained the independence of small communities, it also made organized group resistance to the imposition of British rule more difficult. But neither could there be any surrender on the part of the Igbo as a group, so the British were embroiled in endless village-to-village skirmishes in Igboland.[4]

Nwapa's *Efuru*[5] came in the same line of the first African novels written in English, after Amos Tutuola's *The Palm-Wine Drunkard* (1952), and Chinua Achebe's *Things Fall Apart* (1958). Along with the end of British colonization, such inherited Western cultural remnants as modern education and the advantages of a scientific age infiltrated African traditional life. Far from spreading the supposed good news, the alien rule that was practiced by some missionaries was known to be marked with strangeness and terror. The irreparable outcome of these practices was the decline and death of Africa's heroic age that contemporary Griots are still chanting about. The emergence of Third World literature and the many works written by men from the late 1960s up to

---

[4]C.L. Innes, 1992, *Chinua Achebe*, Quoted in a note to the author by Achebe himself, pp. 6–7.

[5]Based on their novels set in traditional Nigerian societies, Nwapa and Amadi seem to have been to the same "School of Thought" following Achebe's footsteps as both writers' works: *Efuru* and *The Concubine* were published in 1966.

now, and the absence of women writers from the literary forum, led the women writers of Africa to be unheard voices. Not until recently has an interest in women writers arisen following the struggle of women writers to be heard. They tried to express their voices through these two outstanding creative writers: Flora Nwapa in Nigeria, and Ama Ata Aidoo in Ghana. In women's literary works we notice quite explicit diverse images of African women, whereas in men's writings those images are shown either ambiguously, or represented in a distorted manner.

The discussion of the changes in West African women's social status today cannot be fully understood without referring to their socio-historical past and in relationship with the coming of Western colonizers, and subsequently the change in people's consciousness. Since Africa as a whole is a vast continent, and cannot be dealt with simplistically as if it were one country with a variety of cultures, a study of the Igbo society will serve as representing the general pattern of beliefs and customs in the Eastern part of Nigeria.

There are many reasons to study Flora Nwapa's pioneering work, *Efuru*. The main element that led me to scrutinize Nwapa's novel was the outcome of my previous research on religious syncretism.[6] This earlier comparative study, which centered on Chinua Achebe's *Things Fall Apart* and *Arrow of God*, and Obinkaram Echewa's *The Land's Lord*, reflects the pure male perspective in the characters depicted in their works. The female representation has been superficially dealt with. Throughout the study of these two writers I pointed out that in spite of the artistic qualities that are apparent in the work of Igbo male writers, there is a blatant weakness related to the paucity of strong/positive female characters depicted. The absence of female characters in men's writings reflects the "apparent little" role women are supposed to play in patriarchal societies. This gender-based attitude is more or less explained in that men were the most privileged and most educated, and subsequently spoke for all with the coming of the Western culture.

---

[6]Boukari-Salami, Safoura (1990), *The Socio-Religious Factor in the Fiction of Chinua Achebe and Obinkaram Echewa*, Master's Thesis, University of Benin, Lome-Togo (Unpublished).

Having inherited Western European cultural concepts and deep-rooted patriarchal behaviors, many African egalitarian societies progressively lost their deference to the woman as a productive/reproductive creature who used to be revered and viewed as a source of union and comfort. As anthropologist, Ifi Amadiume states clearly in her book *Male Daughters, Female Husbands* (1987) that the socio-economic and political status of Igbo women deteriorated with the coming of Europeans. The European arrival in Africa not only brought about changes in the cultural life of the local people, but it also created a spiritual disequilibrium in the church followers. In this respect Echewa's characterization of Philip in *The Land's Lord* (1976) is significant, for the author displays the tribulations of Philip, acolyte of a traditional God. The spiritual damage that European missionaries brought to indigenous peoples is poignant, as Philip's dilemma closes with the most outrageous tabooed act when he commits suicide.

One starts wondering why few women are characterized as protagonists in different plots presented to the reader by Igbo male writers such as Achebe, Amadi and others. Why are women represented in small numbers and given minor roles at important socio-political and religious gatherings in today's society? Does this mean there have never been women leaders in Igbo traditional societies? As a woman reader who was expecting to identify with the writer and/or his/her works, reading Achebe's *Things Fall Apart* and Echewa's *The Land's Lord* left me thirsty for information about women's experiences at the particular period in which their stories were narrated. My expectations were only partly fulfilled after coming across Echewa's other novel, *I Saw the Sky Catch Fire*, in which a female character depicted highlighted the missing characteristics of female power and the essential binary complementarity of both genders for a balanced world. Another element that aroused my curiosity and interest in studying women's writings came from a general socio-cultural behavior that favors men, and puts them in a privileged social position.

In Africa, though women do the maximum work at all levels, they are placed at the lowest rung of the social ladder. The apparent image that is projected of the African woman is that of a totally subjugated and enslaved being. She is generally referred to and portrayed as a character unable to participate or contribute in global political and economic issues. Yet, social history and personal observation teach us the woman's pivotal role in the family structure, the community, and society as a whole. When reading women's writings, women could find elements to quench their thirst for knowledge, representation, and identification with the female perspective. They can identify with the writer's subject of discussion and find partial or full answers to interrogations pertaining to their personal lives or environmental experiences.

Despite the large number of women of African descent constituting the majority of African literary scholars nowadays, the pivotal role of African women is still not yet acknowledged for its value. And though Nwapa's later novels position her as a post-modernist writer, and more specifically as a pioneer of African Womanism, her work has partially gone into deep freeze on the world scale. Thus, this study will not only highlight the genius of her literary creativity from African women's standpoint, but it will also focus on Nwapa's emergence as the prototypical African female voice, through her use of socio-cultural elements and characterization. The intention is also to point out how socioeconomic factors and some cultural beliefs, such as gender roles and title-taking, contributed to the empowerment of women in traditional society.

In choosing to study *Efuru*, I thought of providing the reader an exposure to historical factors which helped to shape the modern African woman since the pre-colonial times. Furthermore, the ultimate goal is to explore how fiction is partly intertwined with reality in most African women's writings. Since this pattern is traced through African American women's literary production, one might notice the similarities and say that African and African American women write about human emotions and their daily struggle for survival. Not only do these two groups of women write about their own experiences and emotional feelings, they often deal with universal women's issues that are profound and have no geographical or racial boundaries. Such topics tackled are male and female issues, woman to woman relationships, marriage, sustainability, production and reproduction, gender discrimination, and violence/abuse in all its forms: physical/mental, economic disparities, sexism and rape, sexual preference, ageism, and disabilities, just to mention a few. Though these topics are often intertwined with different socio-historical conceptual frameworks, they share some commonality in essence and concerns about the survival and improvement of the human race. Patriarchy, which means the rulership dominated by men, is a social structure that we have been living under for a long time in all societies. In Africa, this situation has been so much stressed and internalized through European education that we tend to believe the sexual division of labor and gender roles are a given and take them for granted. As a result, society assigns specific roles to women and men. According to the Western traditional concept of gender roles, the man is supposed to provide for the family and the woman is to take care of the home and make children. These traditional ideas which are not foreign to other societies have been reinforced and are noticeable all over the world now.

Unlike the general Western conception of gender with its ingrained male superiority in which men are the "bread-winners" as opposed to women's role as homemakers, many indigenous peoples had a more egalitarian conception of men's and women's socio-political and economic roles. Though men and women were viewed as complementary in many African societies, colonization and Western cultural influences strengthened latent patriarchal tendencies. As a result, from the middle of the nineteenth century the sleeping African patriarchy awoke and overshadowed women's efforts to climb up the social ladder.

In some traditional Igbo societies, a woman's socio-political status was egalitarian despite the distinctions and apparent boundaries existing in some gender roles. In the pre-colonial period, women used to work mostly side by side with men in activities outside the home such as farm work. But with the European contact and the development of economic needs coupled with change in the minds of people, some women turned to different activities, like trade, rather than remaining in farming. The introduction of foreign goods on the local market created new needs and a sense of competition that was not known before. They (the women) who used to control their own markets started losing their power as the new administrative establishment took over by levying taxes and even changing market days to match their interests, including the official work days.

The interest in Nwapa is stimulated by personal experiences and a purely feminist/womanist inclination for justice restoration in dealing with gender distribution of rights and property. First, Nwapa is one of the very first African women writers to take up the challenge of creative writing in English. Second, she tries to deal with issues that are mostly neglected by male writers. In the 1960s, the major themes in African literature in English were more about post-independence issues than slavery and colonialism. For instance, Achebe's *No Longer at Ease* (1960) and *A Man of the People* (1966), T.M. Aluko's *Chief the Honourable Minister* (1966), and Ayi kwei Armah's *The Beautyful Ones Are Not Yet Born* (1968) were works mostly dealing with post-independence. They also highlight the socio-political situation with its evils, such as corruption and selfishness, just to name a few. Aspects of the inhuman cruelties of slavery and the frustrations generated by colonialism were still fresh in people's minds then. Therefore, almost all male writers tried to recreate, on the one hand, those past days of horror and humiliation that European colonizers brought to native African people in a more or less obvious way. On the other hand, some male writers created a romanticized image of the past to defy the negative stereotypes circulated then, mostly by outsiders who misunderstood and unconsciously or intentionally looked down upon Africans.

Prema Nandakumar (1971) points out that, though their novels should be considered primarily as works of art, African writers like Achebe and Nwapa had to deal with the anthropological past or the sociological present in their writings. Their writings refer to the African milieu, African customs and manners, Africa's days of glory and years of degradation. Besides, "the writers unconsciously hark back to their past to reassure themselves of their African identity. The hurt to the pride of race, and the damage to human self-respect poison the very springs of consciousness, and whether in prose or in verse the [African/Asian] writer finds himself inescapably held by this terrible vice from the past." This critic went so far as to illustrate an extreme form of African writers' glorification of their past by quoting the following lines from an article in the Nigerian nationalist paper *Daily Service*:

They (the Africans) know that they are Hannibal crossing the Alps when snows were young. They remember that they are the little black bambino, the pet of the Italian church. They are Krishna, the Black Christ of India. They observe portraits of Black Virgins strewn all over Europe. They reminisce over paintings in the caves of Austria, of Germany, of Spain, of Portugal, of France. They know their warm Negro blood flowered in the veins of Cleopatra and that Caesar fell in love with her just the same . . .

They know that these and more are no dreams . . . They know that if they once built pyramids on the Nile, fought with Caesar's battalions, ruled over Spain and dominated the Pyrenees, they the same very black people can be great again and be slaves no more.[7]

Though the general themes related to male and female relationships, such as the gender division of labor, with men expected to go farming and women caring for the family are common issues discussed in *Efuru*, Nwapa has portrayed an innocent, pure traditional world in which the heroine plays what Ifi Amadiume called "flexible gender roles." After reading Amadiume's *Male Daughters, Female Husbands* (1987), based on

---

[7]Iyengar, "Two Cheers for the Commonwealth" pp. 28–9 quoted by Nandakumar (1971) in "An Image of African Womanhood" *Africa Quarterly*, p. 141.

gender and sex in an African society, we cannot help but realize that Flora
Nwapa's heroine Efuru is faced with issues similar to those Amadiume
highlighted in her anthropological work. Not only are both writers
Igbo, they share a similar socio-historical and cultural background despite their different approaches to gender in the same society. For example, while dealing with thematic issues such as traditional cultural
beliefs, economic activities, sexual and gender problems, or colonization, Nwapa adopts a literary approach using a realistic fiction in which
idealized characters act, whereas Ifi Amadiume makes use of anthropological methods in ethnography and history to describe it. Her explanation of the structured Igbo society thus sheds light on the versatility and
complexity of gender roles, which were based on multi-layered cultural,
political and economic factors.

Overall, the different sections highlighted in the discussion of the
multi-faceted socio-historical structures and literary topics in African
society cannot be brought to a conclusion without grappling with the
epistemological and ontological foundations behind the different works
mentioned above. Thus, the last part of this book, "Reflection on Arts
and African Women's Activism" re-visits not only the theoretical background of modern African literature, but also its role as a social regulator
as well as its use to reach out to the outside world. One cannot but
acknowledge African women's huge contributions in helping to establish the place of African literature on a global scale in the international
literary arena.

PART TWO

Sociocultural Issues in Igbo Society

Beliefs about Men & Women

The Igbo people share a common language (although there are differences of dialect in various regions) and common religious beliefs and practices. A number of anthropologists and commentators have asserted that they also worship a supreme deity, Chukwu, the Creator, but in recent years this assertion has been challenged by Donatus Nwoga.[8] Looking at the contemporary status of West African women in general, the remarkable thing is their subordination in a male-dominated society. Certain points raised in this chapter will be partly related to the historical heritage that teaches us that there had been whole and prosperous kingdoms in Africa which even traded with Europeans before being invaded and finally destroyed. If African people were able to survive through the ages before colonization, it is logical that they certainly had a sound philosophy and a scientific approach which guided their lives. What kind of beliefs governed Igbo male and female behavior in the pre-colonial period? How was the sexual division of labor defined? How were gender roles perceived in traditional Igbo society? What sort of relationship did men and women have regarding gender spheres in terms of economy and power? Who was the bread-winner? The next paragraphs will deal with a few writings on the issue and, simultaneously, give answers to each of the above questions.

According to Adiele Afigbo (1996), roles were shared by men and women in Igbo cosmology. Historic pre-conquest Igboland was not one of straight-line dominance by men. It was rather a world founded on complementarities. As the author puts it clearly in the Igbo language:

---

[8]Donatus Nwoga, *The Supreme Deity as a Stranger in Igbo Religious Thought*, in C. L. Innes, 1994, p. 5.

Ihe di abua abua
Nwoke na Nwanyi
Elu na Ala
Ehihe na Anyasi
Ututu na Mgbede
Aka-nri na Aka-ekpe
Onwu na Ndu
Ihe oma na Ihe ojo.[9]

The translation of the above lines is basically about the philosophical thought that duality and ambivalence exist in every creation. The equivalent ideas are as follows:

Things come in doubles
Male and female
Heaven and Earth
Day and night
Morning and evening
Right and left
Life and death
Good and evil[10]

According to Ifi Amadiume, though there were certain matters considered to be exclusively female spheres in traditional society, the division of labor was such that no clear-cut gender distinction was in the value judgment of those roles. Igbo society was described as the one in which "a dual-sexual management and governance" were practiced. The remarkable harmony and order were created via "in-between" areas,

---

[9]Afigbo, Adiele, (1996), "Igbo Women: Why Mgbafo Philosophy is more important than Plato's" *African People's Review*, Sept–Dec.

[10]This is a translation I got from a friend of Igbo background with whom I was taking EOP courses at SUNY Buffalo.

which brought men and women together and allowed an egalitarian interaction in the socio-political domain.

In the description Afigbo makes of pre-colonial Igbo society, one would be tempted to say that these in-between areas of interactions were also an opportunity for men to take the lead while women voluntarily sat behind. We will notice later in the description made of Igbo society that the women's spheres would gradually be eroded, and ultimately, be replaced by men, with the coming of the Europeans who brought along with them their patriarchal culture in which women could only be valued through their husbands. Based on the Victorian ideology of the cult of "true womanhood" which perceived women as home-makers and men as "bread-winners," the former were considered inferior and thus, relegated to the less important roles in some social arena, mainly political, religious, and economic. Another reason why women sat behind in the in-between areas was related to the Igbo cosmic vision of things. One should not be misled and think that women sitting behind men meant a hierarchical position of men's superiority over women.

The apparent factor which might lead the untrained mind to think that women were, in a sense, inferior to men, is the contemporary male appropriation of power in almost all African social, political and economic domains. However, one should keep in mind that gender boundaries were often blurred due to role reversal or flexibility in many traditional societies. For example, it was not uncommon to see women plough fields just as men, and conversely, for men to do household chores such as cleaning, cooking, or babysitting while women were away for other chores. What is common in Igbo domestic life of the past is while men participated in kitchen chores, they were limited to those of them that demanded energy, namely pounding of fu-fu or palmnuts, climbing of vegetable trees like the uha tree whose leaves were used to prepare the soup. Men baby-sat occasionally to enable them to appreciate their children for a while. This gender role reversal which Ifi Amadiume qualified as "flexible" gender roles is also perceived in the Bassar (Togo) culture as "Nimpi Ninja" meaning literally, "Woman-man" especially when women take over male roles in not only providing for the family but also in performing other traditional male activities. In that regard, a majority of us remember how our grandmothers and mothers would be at the market all day long and still manage to have the food ready for the household during the day and in the evening. This was feasible through a genuine organization and distribution of labor among close or extended family members.

Nevertheless, in today's society, because of engrained patriarchal ideologies and male dominance coupled with prejudice, it has become rare to see men operate freely in certain spheres reserved for women in mainstream African societies. Though the trend is once again changing for educated families in urban areas where household chores have engendered an egalitarian division of labor between men and women out of necessity, the traditional gender roles are still deep-rooted in people's minds. According to the Igbo, "If two (individuals) are riding a horse, one must sit behind." This proverb is relevant as it can apply to different situations men and women may find themselves in. For instance, during public gatherings or religious rituals, particularly naming ceremonies and wedding celebrations, women would sit in the back rows. This rear position may be misleading, especially in the coastal societies. Some people might think that the women's sitting behind was significant of their secondary position, or inferiority, based on the modern social stratification. But this position does not equate to a social classification of genders, it simply reflects a separation of spheres with interchangeable roles depending on circumstances. A similar idea would be that there cannot be two captains commanding the same ship at the same time; there is always a need for one leader. However, the Igbo world was fluid and dynamic in that men's and women's gender roles were/are not rigid. The Yoruba and Igbo illustrate that dynamic through a poignant metaphor: "Living is like watching a masquerade. You cannot do it by standing in one place."

Adiele Afigbo (1996) argues that the domains that called for purely feminine management and governance were vast, and so intricate that they gave women an opportunity for leadership, to come to the top of the social ladder, just as their male counterparts. The author goes on to point out that "some women achieved such complete dominance over their husbands that the children of the marriage came to be known by the name of their mothers. This is a good observation that can also be verified in other ethnic groups like the Hausa in Northern Nigeria, who name children after their mothers, especially when such mothers are affluent and independent. Not always because of wealth, their militancy or their leadership attributes could make them so powerful that their children are identified with their own names rather than those of their fathers. What the author is not explaining here is that those women were so powerful because of their resourcefulness, which allowed them economic freedom, and subsequently, the possibility of acquiring titles, known as "Ekwe" titles.[11] One should argue, though, that reaching the highest and most respectable level in African society does not necessarily mean that the women have to dominate their husbands, since there were/ are unmarried affluent women, or submissive and understanding married women capable of rising high on the social ladder. This point will be explored further in the section dealing with "Gender and Economy." In addition to these ideas, many Igbo writers made an interesting point related to the Igbo world vision. The Igbo, according to Afigbo, tended to view the coming into being of each of its constituent communities as the coming of the primordial egg, which is perfect in all essential aspects and whose development is nothing more than the gradual unfolding of this primordial perfection.

Among the many writers who have dealt at length with the traditional Igbo society and culture regarding these ideas is anthropologist

---

[11]Ifi Amadiume, 1987, *Male Daughters, Female Husbands* by Billings & Sons Ltd, Worcester, pp. 42–3.

Ifi Amadiume, whose outstanding book, *Male Daughters, Female Husbands* (1987), mentioned earlier, also scrutinizes colonization and the transformation of the Igbo women's socio-political and economic status today. Reference to historical facts in Amadiume's book highlighted that the post 1900s period saw the invasion of the Igbo hinterland by the British. This period was followed by the violent suppression of indigenous institutions, the imposition of Christianity and Western education, and the introduction of a new economy, including a new political system through the nomination of Warrant Chiefs. Perhaps further readings of Adiele Afigbo (1972) *The Warrant Chiefs: Indirect Rule in South Eastern Nigeria 1891–1929* might help for historical references about Aba women riots and the British Indirect Rule system over taxation and census, which then were new to Igbo people. These new institutions carried along with them cultural ideologies which affected not only the structural position of Igbo traditional societies, but also women's socio-economic positions in other parts of the entire subregion. According to Amadiume's sources, British colonial domination introduced more rigid patriarchal concepts of gender roles. Whereas in the past, more flexible indigenous gender concepts allowed men and women access to power and authority, the new Western concepts introduced through colonial conquests carried strong sex and class inequalities supported by gender ideology and constructions: a woman was always a female regardless of her social achievements or status.[12] In this particular context, the status of a woman as a female should be related to her biologic constitution, and reproductive abilities, as a mother and nurturer. Though men contribute to conceiving babies, women are naturally structured to carry the pregnancy through its term and deliver the baby because of their natural reproductive and physiologic endowments.

---

[12]Ibid, p. 119.

The Anthropologist pursued that the flexible gender system of the Igbo traditional culture and language meant that biological sex did not always correspond to ideological gender, and women could play roles usually monopolized by men. They could even be classified as "males" in terms of power and authority over others. In this respect, the concrete example of the Ekwe women is more than edifying. The word "Ekwe" is an honorific title, which allowed women in the Igbo society to rise to higher socio-economic, political, and religious strata. As a consequence, in the traditional Nnobi society that Amadiume describes, roles were not rigidly masculinized or feminized before the arrival of the Europeans. To use her words, "no stigma was attached to breaking gender rules." The author contends that the presence of a goddess-focused religion does nothing but favor the acceptance of women in status and roles of authority and power. Amadiume supports Afigbo's earlier argument about the dual sexual management of socio-political and cultural matters. Another aspect to consider is the idea of balance and cohesion within the traditional order, alongside the possibility of merged male and female spheres. Further information on the reciprocity and the twin-lineality of gender and sex roles is widely explored in Oba T'Shaka's phenomenal book, *Return to the African Mother Principle of Male and Female Equality* (1995), where the author's discussion not only enlightens us on the historical foundation of the female principle, but also provides us with a prototypical twin-lineal community organization for contemporary society based on the vision of the just society, "where all just males and females are equally empowered to govern every phase of society."[13]

A comparative approach to these traditional indigenous beliefs leads to extending these ideas to a similar situation noticed in women's roles in African American and some Native American societies in the United States. Proceeding with the discussion based on the writer's

---

[13]Oba T'Shaka, 1995, *Return to the African Mother Principle of Male and Female Equality*, V.1, p. 322.

anthropological findings, the preexistence of a relatively egalitarian gender distribution of roles in some matrilineal societies undoubtedly had an impact on Black women's resistance and survival strategies in the U.S. Black women's different forms of resistance throughout the slavery period and their continuous struggles for survival were inherited from their holistic past on the continent. For example, the women's equal and flexible roles are reflected through the necessity for them to head their families in the absence of their men. These are factors which help us understand the strength and endurance of women of African descent on the continent or in the Diaspora. Reference to David Sweetman's work, *Women Leaders in African History* (1984), gives a few names, such as the Kahina of the Maghreb, Hatshepshut (Eighteenth Dynasty) of the Ancient Egyptian civilization, wore an artificial beard in her regent role of Queen for twelve years. Others were the Candaces of the Kemetic and Meroeic era; Amina of Zawzau from Hausaland (present Northern Nigeria), Yaa Asantewa of Ghana, Dona Beatrice of Congo, Queen N'zinga of Angola and others. It is revealing that all these women fought wars against invaders and reigned over societies which were very much established and structured.[2]

According to some writers, including Ifi Amadiume, the Western culture and Christian religion brought by colonialism carried rigid gender ideologies, which aided and supported the exclusion of women from the power hierarchy. Obviously, this gender-oriented social system characterized by strictly masculinized and feminized roles has led Africans to where we are today, with an acculturated modern society, where most young people, some well-educated, are still searching for their identity. The worst scenario is the one where the social environment fosters macho behaviors, which end up being detrimental to the individual. That colonization brought about tremendous changes in the structure of African societies is quite evident, but looking at these arguments from another angle and using a critical approach, it is easy to blame the colonized for the inability to develop the necessary technology which would allow competition in order to keep up with the scientific progress of the

Western world. In addition, African societies were subject to internal transformations due to normal evolution, which also helped quicken the collapse of traditional socio-cultural values. Today, the challenge is to find constructive ways out of internal and external socio-cultural, economic, and political factors that hold us down as women. In a highly patriarchal society such as today's Sub-Saharan Africa, where the majority of women are still illiterate despite their resourcefulness, the task remains for the few educated to initiate actions as well as raise consciousness at the grass-roots level.

From Amadiume's study (1987), the ideology of gender regarding the socio-cultural system of "Nnobi" in the nineteenth century shows that roles were neither masculinized nor feminized. The dual gender role that Afigbo dealt with in theory by the notion of re-incarnation is given significant illustration in Amadiume's book. The "flexible" gender role is explained as the women's ability to play interchangeably a male/female gender role according to circumstances. Challenging the inherited orthodoxies of social anthropology, she argues that in pre-colonial African society, sex and gender did not necessarily coincide.

Moreover, many other researchers dealing with the Igbo society assert that women could play roles usually monopolized by men, and then be classified as males for the purposes of power. That power was created through women's economic resourcefulness and the existence of a strong goddess-focused religion. The contemporary African women's situation finds its roots in the nineteenth century when Europeans invaded Igbo land and subsequently reorganized the existing traditional socio-political order to fit their Western world vision. In some cases European administrators stripped former traditional rulers of their political and strategic roles in their respective communities, and replaced them with ordinary individuals who seized the opportunity to become affluent. This method of ruling, known as British "Indirect Rule," totally disrupted traditional social organizations and structures that had sustained the Igbo people's equilibrium. Unlike the British rule in countries like Nigeria and Ghana, the French practiced the politics of assimilation, through which the colonized people were expected to behave like the French, speak the French language well enough to procure a relatively decent administrative job, and help protect the interests of France. As a result, the traditional socio-political organizations were maintained and strengthened, with a sense of cooperation between colonial representatives and established native rulers.

That economic changes in colonial times undermined women's status and reduced their political role, while patriarchal tendencies, introduced by colonialism, persist today to the detriment of women is not in doubt. Critical of the chauvinistic stereotypes established by colonial anthropology, the writer stresses the importance of recognizing women's economic activities as an essential basis of their power. This last point will be fully developed in the section dealing with "Gender and Economy" as illustrated through the characterization Flora Nwapa makes in her novel. Within the pre-colonial Igbo society of Nigeria, women were highly involved in marketing and were the authorities within the marketplaces.

Other interesting elements mentioned are mostly related to the subsistence economic activities under-girding their lives. During the pre-colonial era, the three main cash crops in Igboland were palm wine, whose production and sale was controlled by men; and palm nuts and palm oil, whose production and sale were controlled by women. The latter were extremely important for women because of the many useful marketable products such as brooms, oil, soap, fuel, and light which women were able to sell and kept the proceeds. Other products which women controlled included various livestock and poultry. These patterns are still apparent in today's rural African societies where life seems to stand still for centuries because of the slow changes and transformations at different stages of human life. For instance, the daily rural activities are still carried out with the same rudimentary means, the ritualistic practices known as customs are still performed with the same ceremony.

Rites of Passage & Ritual Practices: Female Circumcision (Excision)

Some graphic and uncommonly descriptive language is used in this section for the purpose of accuracy and an objective approach to the sensitive issues that female circumcision represents. Critical thinking requires caution in dealing with cultural matters as well as the presentation of true facts to allow a neutral viewpoint. The objective in discussing this apparently barbaric practice is to allow a close look at it, which not only allows comparisons with certain contemporary and modern rites, but also enables the reevaluation of the old practice in its entirety. Female circumcision, also referred to as excision, is a tradition that is found in different cultures in Africa, Asia, and even some parts of South America. Just as young boys went through wrestling and other physical and mental initiation rites to become men, the girls, apart from the household duties, had to be circumcised. Thus, in Flora Nwapa's *Efuru*, at the beginning of her stay with Adizua, Efuru has to undergo this customary ritual. Here again, the denomination "circumcision" or "female genital mutilation" would depend on whether the speaker put the practice in a socio-cultural context or whether, as an outsider, s/he gives a judgment of value and looks at the practice as a barbaric mutilation of innocent females. Our critical insight would prevent us from being too judgmental of what we fail to understand and prompt our sensitivity towards the offense our quick reaction might cause to the people concerned.

Considering the religious basis for female circumcision, Lighfoot-Klein (1989) reveals that excision and infibulations are practices done by followers of different religious denominations, including Muslims, Catholics, Protestants, Copts, Animists and non-believers in the various countries concerned. However, there is no foundation in the respective religious scriptures for this practice; rather, it is how these religious texts have been interpreted that counts. For example, according to Toubia (1995), circumcision is not mentioned in the Qur'an, although it has been often carried out by Muslims who thought that it was required by the Islamic faith. Another scholar, Dorkenoo (1994), pointed out that

Muslim law, which governs the lives of believers, originated from two sources: the Qur'an and the tradition of Sunna, recommendations of the Prophet Mohammed. In addition to these two sources, Muslims are governed by the *Igtihad*, tenets in the school of Muslim law throughout the centuries.

In most African countries the practice of female circumcision is noticeable in Muslim communities. Does it have something to do with religion? The answer is no. However, there has been a tremendous influence of Arabic tradition on some practices so that at times Arabic culture is confused with Islamic principles. Even though some polemicists argue that the aim of the surgery is to suppress the woman's sexual pleasure, it would be difficult to buy into that interpretation and believe that all the perpetrators look for is to prevent women's eroticism, and as a result, inflict pain. Could we consider this a sadistic behavior seeking to inflict pain upon young innocent girls when we consider that most often mothers are present to help the young girl endure it without too much fear? When we put ourselves in the minds of the people who still practice this rite, it is apparent that they do not see it as a bad thing, but rather they see an ethical and even a certain 'aesthetic' value in doing it not only to conform with tradition, but also to elevate the girl's self-esteem among her peers who might have been already circumcised. The question is why would women's sexual pleasure be reduced, or even suppressed at times when at birth both men and women are given an equal sexual potentiality? In Igbo society, the rationale for the removal of the clitoris is that it facilitates childbirth.

According to some Igbo rules, the operation should occur before the girl gets married or pregnant. According to other people, the cutting of the clitoris is a prior painful physical experience which later helps the young girl to overcome the pain women undergo during childbirth. If this was the reason behind the practice, then one might understand the usefulness of the initiation. Nevertheless, this understanding and meaningful justification should not be seen as an excuse or a support for the practice of female circumcision. Understanding why people are doing it does not necessarily mean one agrees with the practice. On the contrary, as researchers/learners, it is helpful to seek to understand the reasons behind cultural customs which may look odd to the untrained mind or to the outsider and thereby mislead them into hasty and unfair judgment of the unknown.

Returning to Nwapa's novel and scrutinizing the eponymous protagonist Efuru's case, one realizes that she accepted the torture of circumcision in order to prove that she too was courageous, and therefore was a woman, as were many others around her. In the minds of the women, this is the first experience of childbirth. But we should not overlook the physical pains that women endure during this operation. It is as much painful as the pleasure and the joy one expects to gain after the surgery. Nwapa gives us an eloquent illustration: "Efuru screamed and screamed. It was painful. Her mother-in-law consoled her. 'It will soon be over, my daughter, don't cry'" (*Efuru*, p. 14).

Meanwhile Efuru's husband was in his room. He felt all the pain. It looked as if he were the one being circumcised. One of the neighbors said to the other: "Efuru is having her bath. Poor girl, it's so painful." But it is important to point out that this was going to be the beginning of a new life for Efuru. After the operation, people would look at her with new eyes, with respect. All the rituals before and after the operation were testimonies of its importance in that particular society. Nwapa provides an illustration of the rituals: "The woman gave instructions. She prepared a black stuff and put it in a small calabash and left it outside the room where Efuru was lying," and said, "Sprinkle this on the feet of all the visitors before they come into the room. It will be infected, if it is not done . . . If anything goes wrong, send for me," she added (*Efuru*, p. 14). The event is so significant that it has an impact on Efuru's diet, and on her mother-in-law's social behavior in the village:

She was to eat the best food . . . She was simply to eat, and grow fat. And above all she was to look beautiful. The cam wood was used in dyeing her cloth . . . She ate whatever she wanted to eat.

She did not eat cassava in any form. Only yam was pounded for her. She ate the best fish from the market. It was said she was feasting. On market day her mother went to the market and bought her the best. She too rubbed some cam wood on her hands and feet to tell people that her daughter has been circumcised (*Efuru*, p. 15).

Thus, during her stay in Adizua's house at the beginning of her union with him, Efuru has to undergo this customary initiation that is excision, or female circumcision. Through the above lines, we learn the traditional perception of female beauty. The relativity of beauty is significant in that the African view of a beautiful woman is somehow different from the Western standpoint. Whereas contemporary Westerners like slender women with a mannequin shape, Africans prefer theirs with more flesh on the body, with roundness. We understand why Efuru had "to eat and grow fat." Good looks still matter in the choice of a wife, or an in-law. Though the traditional African customs have changed, and younger generations tend to prefer skinny girls/women, a large number of people of African descent appreciate plump women, and like to eat good food, which is part of socialization. Sharing food and drink is the primary symbol of welcoming someone in your house. In places where preparing food and drinking is no longer as easy as it was in the past, people would present cola nuts, just like in some Igbo societies.

Coming back to female circumcision, which opponents and most Westerners call female genital mutilation (FGM), Nigeria is not the only African country where this practice has been the norm. It has also been practiced in many other parts of Africa, including Sudan, Burkina Faso, Cote D'Ivoire, Togo, and Senegal, just to name a few. This practice, which may be considered a monstrous act against the woman's right to control her own body, is tightly linked to people's cultural beliefs and still has a great impact on their daily lives, especially in rural communities. Unlike the normal and innocent portrayal that Flora Nwapa gave of female genital cutting in *Efuru*, in the mid-1960s, contemporary women writers have gone far to denounce that secular practice as another aspect of women's exploitation and subordination. Alice Walker called it "the sexual blinding of women." Circumcision is not without its detractors, as some would say. More and more people are raising their voices against it today. One argument used to combat circumcision is the high risk of death due to hemorrhage and/or infection. The supporters of the practice, on the other hand, consider it a fundamental element of their culture. In the movie "Shackled Women: Abuses of a Patriarchal World," Taslima Nasreen, author of *Brides Are Not for Burning*, and others speak about diverse topics of women's rights abuses such as dowry deaths, FGM, child prostitution, the *hijab* (veil) wearing, the Islamic *Zina* (adultery) Law, and others.[14]

In the struggle to end female genital mutilation, Egyptian advocate for women's rights and social justice, and Medical Doctor, Nawal El Saadawi voices her take on the practice in her article, "Changing a Social System into a Divine Law."

Female and male genital mutilation (FGM and MGM) are not characteristic of any society or any religion or any country, or race or color, or ethnic group. Like the oppression of women and poor classes, they constitute an integral part of the political, economic, social, cultural, and religious systems preponderant in most of the world—west and east, north and south, Jewish, Christian, Islamic, Hindu, and others. FGM and MGM were born of development in history that led one class to rule over another and men to dominate women in the state and in the family unit, which together constitute the core of the patriarchal class relations.[15]

---

[14]Women's Studies in Film for the Humanities and Sciences,Fall 2010 catalog, p. 49.

[15]Nawal El Saadawi, The Struggle to End the practice of Female Genital Mutilation: Changing a Social System into a Divine Law, in *African Women Writing Resistance: Contemporary Voices*, Edited by Jennifer Browdy de Hernandez, Pauline Dongala, Omotayo Jolaosho, and Anne Serafin, University of Wisconsin Press, Madison, Wisconsin, 2010, p. 192.

At this point we are left with two alternatives: getting rid of circumcision or improving conditions for its practice. But given the cultural foundation of circumcision, is it easy or even possible to get rid of it? To what extent are people prepared to drop or lose what they consider an important element of their culture? It seems that they will be more likely to accept an improvement of the conditions for the practice of circumcision. On the other hand, to what extent are the detractors of circumcision prepared to accept such a compromise whereby they feel themselves becoming guilty accomplices?

These are unanswered questions because of the complexity of the problem and its relationship with the mores and beliefs of the people concerned. In the next segment of the discourse, mention would be made of a critical perspective, by which is meant some other works that have already dealt with the same topic, and try a comparative approach with Flora Nwapa's position. In an interview she granted Tobe Levin at the 1980 Frankfurt Book Fair, Flora Nwapa felt that Western media tended to exaggerate the extent of the problem. However, in the same year (1980), she wrote Levin a letter in which she admitted the need to revise her point of view. In fact, she realized that the practice of female circumcision was more prevalent and the consequences graver than she had imagined. Nevertheless, her fiction presents the earlier attitude, accepting female circumcision as an integral part of a vital culture. This was acceptable in those days when nationalism and a search for an authentic identity were in vogue. The author deserves particular credit in having unconsciously opened a painful door for future male and female writers to explore.

As it is said in *Efuru*, "having a bath" is a euphemism for clitoridectomy, and the ritual 'purification' is so important that one baby's death was attributed to the mother's fear of the razor. Since Nwapa presents traditional society in a realistic way, her portrayal of attitudes favoring genital mutilation is, to some extent, entirely appropriate and understandable. Tobe Levin confirms this position by stipulating that Nwapa's compromise is reflected in the manner she scrupulously avoids oversimplification by showing how humanly concerned the midwife and the neighbors are for the health and comfort of the initiate, thus denying both the danger that the operation can represent for Efuru, and the fact that certain operators are inept—especially when it is stated that, one circumcision practitioner is known who has caused numerous casualties in the communites. Yet one can perceive the disturbing aspect of the narrative in the following passage. When asked how she was feeling after having gone through circumcision, Efuru replies, "It is much better now. It was dreadful the first day." The only consolation she gets is the usual resigned response: "It is what every woman undergoes. So don't worry" (*Efuru*, p. 15). Here, the author seems to share this essential attitude as she describes the festive context of the operation as though compensatory. We are presented with a picture of Efuru feted and coddled from one to three months. After her operation, her relatives and neighbors are shown to relish the special situation of happiness culminating in the offer of gifts in the marketplace. We are given to understand the attitudes of women themselves, a kind of solidarity in adversity without any significant attempt to challenge or question the very essence of a practice which causes them pain. The description of the women's or mother's sadistic attitude toward the circumcised individual is not so apparent in Nwapa's *Efuru* as in the first part of Egyptian El Saadawi's *The Hidden Face of Eve* (1980), or Walker and Pratibha's *Warrior Marks*.

In *The River Between* (1965), Ngugi takes a similarly complex approach to the problem of circumcision and even goes further. According to Levin (1986), *The River Between* is the only fictional work which elevates female circumcision to the position of central thematic importance. Ngugi presents female circumcision as a battleground in the clash between conservative tribal elements and the patriarchal church. The plot is based on events of the 1920s and 1930s, marked by growing national sentiment in Kenya. That period was marked by the creation of two oppositional groups, the Young Kikuyu Association led by Harry Thaku, and Kenyatta's Kikuyu Association dedicated to removing British colonialism and restoring the traditional values eroded under white rule.

In that revolutionary fervor, Jomo Kenyatta, who would later become Kenya's Head of State, gave the definitive male view on female circumcision by asserting that "not a single Gikuyu worthy of a name wants to marry an unexised woman because that operation is the basis of all moral and religious instruction" (Jomo Kenyatta, quoted in Gourld, 1975, p. 105).

In response to this nationalist situation, many males opted for excommunication and expulsion from Presbyterian schools, which were against the excision propaganda, rather than see "their" women freed from the knife. In this regard, resistance to the abolition of female circumcision is clearly, in part, an oppositional gesture against colonialism. An interesting aspect to notice is that Ngugi places the rebirth of the rites within the context of land expropriation, the composition of taxes, and forced labor to pay those taxes. In any case, Ngugi's novel deals with female circumcision not from a feminist, but solely from a humanist, progressive, and chauvinistic standpoint. Nevertheless, as readers, we are led to understand that male insistence on female rites is displaced importance and deconstructive in that there is no logical relationship between the facts. The question that comes to the mind is, "What does land repossession have to do with female circumcision?" An attempt to answer this question conjures up a gender related question: Why are men in Ngugi's story not using their own circumcision as powerful enough to fight against colonizers? Here, the objectification of women is blatantly highlighted in that their sexuality is used as a political weapon. Hence, the practice of circumcision, seen from a male perspective, could serve any purpose that the creative writer would like as well as divert the focus of socio-cultural and political struggle against the European invaders to women who, in this case, are used as scapegoats to bear the brunt alone.

On the one hand, one cannot help but think of the egocentricity of men involved in the entrenched traditional practicing of FGM as practically saying, as long as their own privileges are not in danger, they are ready to sacrifice the opposite gender, women. Nowhere is this gender bias or misogyny more vividly apparent than in N'gugi wa'Thiongo's novel, *The River Between*. Ngugi has tried to show, for example, how male advocates were wrong in viewing circumcision as a pure source of cultural integrity from which strength could be drawn in preparation for battles ahead to repossess the land. It appeared that without the removal of the women's clitoris, without purity, the female sexual energy would threaten the tribe with destruction, just as in Flora Nwapa's *Efuru*, where the death of a baby is attributed to the mother's fear of the razor, meaning here, circumcision. The rite of circumcision is so culturally embedded in some societies that girls who escaped it were referred to as "Irigu" and considered outcast or unworthy. According to Ngugi,

> There was a new edge to the songs. Uncircumcised girls were the objects of cutting attacks. Everything dirty and impure was heaped on them. They were the impure things of the tribe and they would bring the wrath of the ancestral spirits on the ridges. A day would come when these Irigu would be circumcised by force to rid the land of impurity (Ngugi, *The River Between*, p. 21).

Here, it is clear that not the white British colonizers, but the deviant African women are to blame for the apocalypse. Looking at this, women are assigned a new symbolic role to play in their society. As critic Judith Cochrane has put it so well in her discussion of Ngugi, they become the "guardians of the tribe," an ascribed status not of direct advantage to them as a group. On the contrary, these women are excluded from the development process by the importation of Western-style sexism and pushed out of the economic field in which they had been sovereign. In this respect, women have been systematically disempowered and abused, as illustrated by the figure of Waiyaki, a schoolteacher whose nightmare symbolizes the failure of his own attempt to marry an uncircumcised girl. "They were pulling her into pieces, as if she were a thing of sacrifice to the god of the river, which still flowed with life as they committed this ritual outrage on her" (*Ngugi*, p. 120).

To some extent, female circumcision is an outrage committed against women because it deprives a woman of her most delicate, most precious, and most important sexual organ. Moreover, there are other disgusting and inhumane manners in which this operation takes place in some societies. For example, El Saadawi (1980) shows how female circumcision is a real nightmare whose traumas are felt forever by women. Another example is the worst situation, where not only is the clitoris cut off but also other parts of the female sex are operated on. This is seen in some parts of Africa, like Sudan and Egypt, where labial excisions and infibulations are practiced. For example, when a married woman or her partner needs to travel, her labia are sewn together in such a way that sexual intercourse is impossible. This practice is mainly meant to "protect" and prevent the woman from committing adultery. Gender discrimination comes into play here, shown through the double standard of actions taken to prevent the woman from free ownership and disposal of her body. Why are similar measures not taken to prevent the traveling man from sexual intercourse wherever he would be? Why is he allowed to go unprotected against sexual temptation? Not to extrapolate a lot from our subject matter, one realizes that the same social behaviors are relevant in today's society when we are dealing with HIV/AIDS, which disease is easily transmitted. Although some might argue that the contamination risks are equal between men and women, the reality is that women find themselves more vulnerable than men, not having control over their partners' movement and relations.

Going back to the risks following female genital cutting, not only does excision prevent the woman from enjoying sex, it may mutilate her by depriving her of her reproductive abilities, and even jeopardize her life forever. Some writings and films portray the unmitigated horror of female circumcision. Regarding the paradoxical socio-cultural context and the perpetuation of this practice, it is necessary to comment on a few aspects at this point. The setting in which female circumcision is practiced shows a completely single-gendered environment. The women are the ones who most likely perpetuate this custom by which they are at the same time victimized and suffer physical and mental trauma. How then could one possibly understand what is going on in those women's minds? Psychoanalysis of the adult women performing the ritual might provide a viable answer. Generally, during the operation, the girl's mother or a close relative is always there to assist, but usually in a "passive" way. She is present but helpless because of the social constraints. Taking into account the atrocity of the operation we may wonder what reasons can be given for this apparently criminal practice perpetuated on women, and by women themselves. The ready answer to the question may be that "it is tradition," as some people like to justify it. But this is a simplistic answer. One would concur that tradition should be respected, perpetuated and transmitted to the younger generations, but not at the cost of female welfare and dignity. This practice raises divergent opinions in and outside Africa because of its socio-cultural background and its danger to women's health and lives.[16]

Considering the well-grounded socio-cultural impact on people and the tremendous power of gerontocracy on the younger generation, the rites have been accepted without too much resistance. Had female circumcision been without risks and not involving the female genitals, nobody would have cared about it. Otherwise, the polemics would have no place, for nobody can claim to explain the tradition of a society she/he does not belong to. In this respect, Levin attests that

---

[16]One way of better understanding African traditions in order to create a basis for mutual respect as different people is through open-mindedness, which allows critical thinking when handling information we receive. Literature and especially fiction writers provide a wide range of issues, whose complexity and approaches might help reconsider sensitive topics as well as secular practices, namely excision. There are male writers as astute as Somali novelist Nurudin Farah (*From a Crooked Rib*, 1970), who demonstrates a high degree of feminist awareness in dealing with the problem of infibulations. Others, like Amadou Kourouna (*Les Etoiles des Independances*, 1968) and Yambo Oluguem (*Bound to Violence*, 1971), are African male authors who previously criticized the inhumane rite, or rendered the initiates' state of mind during the experience through the use of stream of consciousness.

Tradition can also be invoked with pride where the customs in question are innocuous. In international struggle to extend Human Rights to women, the need to distinguish between beneficent and malicious practice has become more acute than ever, for if our aim is the eradication of dangerous rites, Western activists must learn to enter the value system of the circumcised to avoid the counter-productive approach based on ignorance and indignation alone. (Davies, 1986, p. 208)

When practiced in healthy, sanitary conditions, female circumcision is linked to the spiritual healing of the individual and provides a kind of harmony with a specific cosmic order that only the people concerned understand. In the same line of ideas, the Association of African Women for Research and Development (AAWORD) in Dakar, Senegal, has warned feminists against viewing African societies exclusively in terms of female oppression and insists that "solidarity can only exist alongside self affirmation and mutual respect."[17] As a matter of interest, Buchi Emecheta has also expressed moderate views on the subject. In an unpublished taped conversation with Sigrid Peicke, in January 1983, she doubted the efficacy of Western feminist intervention in the campaign for total eradication of excision. What happens when the sanitary conditions fail, during and after the operation? This is the aspect that Nwapa has failed to point out in *Efuru*.

In the struggle for womanhood, selfhood and the right to dispose of one's body, many Africans on the continent, in the Diaspora, and

---

[17]Tobe Levin, 1986, "A Statement on Genital Mutilation" in *Third World: Second Sex Women's Struggle & National Liberation* by Miranda Davies, editor Zed Press, 1983, p. 217, quoted in Carole Boyce Davies and Graves, *N'Gambika*. AAWORD charges the Western Press with extreme insensitivity in the handling of this theme. A plethora of media tracts on the issue are guilty of "aggressiveness, ignorance, or even contempt." Hence, effect has been achieved through sensationalism, violating "the dignity of the very women to be save(d)." Finally, certain Western campaigns have drawn on "the latent racism" present where ethnocentric prejudice is so deep-rooted (p. 219).

particularly in the United States and Europe have organized in associations and undertaken actions to raise people's consciousness. In the process, some prominent African American writers such as Alice Walker have published polemics that might divert the genuine and positive intention of the author's mission, that of consciousness-raising, education, and possible social change.

In Alice Walker and Pratibha Parmar's collaborative work, *Warrior Marks* (1993), female genital mutilation is presented to the reader as a shocking subject. But considering the extent of the practice affecting one hundred million of the world's women, circumcision is an issue that needs attention for its pervasive worldwide practice and relationship with health risks that threaten women's lives. The Kasinga case really aroused the American public's attention and led most media to condemn certain traditional practices that should be revised, if they are to continue for a long time.[3]

Advocates of granting Ms. Kasinga asylum argued on another front that clitoridectomy, or excision, is female mutilation, a fundamental human rights violation, and according to some, the Immigration and Naturalization Service should recognize it as such by granting Ms. Kasinga political asylum. Surita Sandosham argued in the *Daily News* (May 2, 1996) in support of the Kasinga case, answering "Yes, it's brutal persecution" to the rhetorical question "Genital mutilation: grounds for asylum?" Dan Stein responded with "No, it will open the floodgates." To support his argument, Stein pointed out that, clearly, in the societies where circumcision is practiced it is not viewed as torture, punishment, or any other form of persecution. In addition, it is not a governmental practice. Considering that sexuality and rituals related to it are traditionally private matters, one could assert that circumcision is not a governmental issue. However, the contemporary inter-relatedness of the personal and the political has led to the government's involvement in cultural practices that used to go unnoticed. To prevent the relatively high death rate and risks of lifelong sexual or reproductive disability, some African governments, such as Togo, Benin, Mali, Niger, Burkina Faso,

Central African Republic, Djibouti, Egypt, Ghana, Guinea, Ivory Coast, Senegal, and Sudan have passed laws or decrees prohibiting FGM, and others have designed policies prohibiting certain risky traditions such as female circumcision (See WHO notes further in supplement #1). Understanding the viability of an individual story, sorting the problem out for a case study, and coming up with an appropriate solution would be better than politicizing and over-emphasizing/over-generalizing in order to present an agenda. This should be deplored. Western feminists have often appropriated underrepresented groups' cases to serve short-term agendas, whereas real help would require an honest and long-lasting collaborative struggle for the empowerment of the needy and less represented.

The reality is that it is quite easy to stay outside and pretend to have the solution for all problems, but once faced with the realities from within, things become more complex. Three to four decades ago, Ms. Kasinga's case would have been meaningful and right in space and time as the practice was widespread. Her case could be generalized to young women in Tchamba, and furthermore, to a large part of the African continent and accepted as something normal. But some would argue today that the practice is something barbaric and obsolete that raises questions and polemics about contemporary African women's experiences. Is female genital cutting totally eradicated because of modern development and some governmental laws banning it? The answer to this question is probably no. It is not just because the normal dissemination of information takes long to reach the people concerned, who unfortunately often reside in remote rural areas. But it is mainly out of the deep-rooted beliefs surrounding female genital cutting. Though the practice is receding, its eradication cannot happen overnight. How do we explain the perpetuation of the practice in big cities and across the oceans outside the African continent, in Europe and the United States? More recently in 2008 *New York Times Magazine* published an article on female genital cutting in Indonesia which projected the triviality of the practice by showing the picture of women performing female genital cutting in schools where young girls were lined up and circumcised. They were simply given some milk to drink and presented with small gifts as a sign of reward for their courage during the operation serving as an initiation, a rite of passage into respectful female spheres.

Even though the Kasinga case has generated a great deal of interest and a final solution through the granting of "cultural asylum," a lot of discussions initiated around this issue were partly due to the wide contribution of the media, and some other agencies which dramatized and perhaps over-generalized the situation in other parts of the world. The book entitled, *Can They Hear You When You Cry?* (1997), issued during the whole Kasinga controversy, has certainly found a large readership among some feminist advocates looking for hot topics to quench their thirst for new women's issues in the United States. But, do they happen to look at the issue from different angles or at least put it in a cultural context before rushing into subjective conclusions? An objective treatment of any women's issue must be approached with a critical thinking methodology, which allows one not only to know how certain things are done, but also, and mainly, to understand why they are done, and only after that, to help provide solutions for improvement or eradication, in the case of female genital cutting.

A document on the Mali-net, a Malian website, in 1996 is another poignant and factual piece that highlights current discussions about the secular practice of female circumcision. In the same stream of concerns, Celia Dugger presents a striking depiction of the ongoing debate around female circumcision. In her October 1996 article, "Genital Cutting in Africa: Slow to Challenge an Ancient Ritual," she lays out different opinions justifying the cultural enclosures that prevent people from stopping the practice. When discussing an ethnic group in Ivory Coast, the writer argues that the tradition of female genital cutting is woven into the everyday life of the Yacouba people there, just as it was for hundreds of years for ethnic groups in a wide band of 28 countries across Africa. In Man,[18]

---

[18]Man is a small village in Cote D'Ivoire where the rite of female genital cutting is still practiced secretly because of the government's prohibition.

it is part of a girl's dreams of womanhood, a father's desire to show off with a big party and a family's way of proving their conformity to social convention. She goes on, "after the rite, the girls are showered with gifts of money, jewelry and cloth. Their families honor them with sumptuous celebrations where hundreds of relations and friends and children feast on goat and cow."[19]

The description by Dugger (1996) is so similar to Flora Nwapa's depiction of Efuru in the Igbo society that we have the impression of a static society, regardless of the three decades of difference between the fictional account and the reality of the present African society. But in the last few years, many African countries have begun measuring the prevalence of female circumcision as part of national health surveys or in such a research as surveys of birth control. In the Ivory Coast and Central African Republic, two out of five women have been cut. In Togo, it is one in eight. In the Sudan, the only country that already had a reliable national estimates, it is nine out of ten. In Mali, it is 93 percent.[20]

Considering these figures and some comments by international researchers, there is every reason to say that women in most African countries are nearly as likely to accept this ritualistic practice as their mothers and grandmothers, although this may be changing. Looking at the same figures from another angle also suggests the differences in the extent of the practice between countries. A survey has shown that in the Sudan the prevalence of the practice has dropped from 96 percent to 89 percent over the course of the 1990s, and there has been a shift toward a less severe form of genital cutting. In Togo, a survey found that half of the mothers who had been cut wanted to spare their daughters. While three-quarters of women in Mali favor continuing the practice, the majority of people in the Central African Republic want to end it. Reasons for the decline of the practice in many places are family-planning programs,

---

[19] Abdi Wardere (Original Document) *Genital Cutting in Africa: Slow to Challenge an Ancient Ritual* forwarded to PHN Africa Missions @G. PHN.MLIST@AIDW, Oct. 11/96 with comments by Joyce Holfeld@G.PHN. OFPS@AIDW.

[20] Ibidem: Malinet Website.

social health organizations' campaigns for mass consciousness-raising, and some women's sad experiences of death and traumas.[21]

Contrary to the simplistic treatment that we have in Nwapa's *Efuru*, the wide range of scholarship after the 1970s deals with the complex aspects of excision. In literature as well as in film, the rite is more and more presented in its outrageous aspects not only to raise consciousness of international constituencies, but mainly to urge decision-makers to ban it. The poignant images taken from the film version of *Warrior Marks* are significant graphics meant to shock the spectator. There is a constant stream of consciousness from the narrator which runs throughout the book and which leads to some interrogations. As Walker puts it emotionally,

> "I think of these young girls as little birds whose fragile bodies have been bashed, whose wings have been clipped before they can discover the power of their own souls and their erotic selves. They have been irrevocably wounded by traditions that cause them much pain and deny them the freedom to fly, to flourish. The circumciser's knife had eradicated a source of fundamental pleasure for these girls. The knife had cut deep into their souls, putting out the sparkle in their eyes as the psychological and psychic scarification took root. They have been robbed of something so primary. But for now, questions passed at random through my mind: Would they ever experience the pure pleasure of a clitoral orgasm? How many of these girls will develop infections? How many of them will experience excruciating pain every time they menstruate? How many of them will decide not to perpetuate this mutilation on their daughters, and how many will keep the tradition going? When will the cycle of violence and humiliation end?"[22]

---

[21]Ibid: Malien website.

[22]Walker, Alice and Pratibha Parmar, 1993, *Warrior Marks: Female Genital Mutilation & the Sexual Blinding of Women*, Harcourt Brace & Company, New York, pp. 176–177.

The differences between what women want, and what they are able to accomplish reflect a huge gap amongst them. The tremendous influence of gerontocracy on younger generations is one of the reasons why women's desire to stop the practice can hardly materialize. Parents insist on the rite so that their daughters can be marriageable. Another reason is a common thread in all forms of cutting: the psychological impact of having achieved something special. Let's take, for example, the motives behind tattooing and body–piercing in modern American or European society. Not to go in-depth into this area, the justifications given to these so-called "cool" practices are almost the same from the young people's perspective. They tattoo to look like their peers, to look beautiful, to prove their maturity, endurance, or affiliation/belonging to a particular group, be it a fraternity, sorority, or sports team. Some say, for example, they tattoo to rebel against their parents, to commemorate/immortalize an emotional event, the loss of an important person, or other experiential events.

For a member of a group which has established a habitual practice, that in a way has become a ritual, tattooing could be seen as a rite of passage, an initiation that allows transformation and provides the individual with a pass for membership in a particular cultural, or sub-cultural, organization. The person who does not participate in tattooing or piercing, while the rest of the group does, is likely to be viewed as an outcast, as out of fashion, and subsequently, may feel frustrated, rejected, or ashamed when everybody exhibits the different/exotic designs on their bodies. In light of this, tattooing or piercing one's body is done for the satisfaction of a code of conduct in a group context, or for a personal fulfillment that certainly provides a kind of pleasure. One should note that though the pleasure, satisfaction or sense of achievement often occurs after the preliminary pain endured during the actual operation, at the specialist's shop, the bar, or simply at home, sometimes disappointment follows. It is not uncommon to see tattooed people go back to the tattoo shop to have their tattoo removed when they start feeling uncomfortable with the design.

Considering the pain and scars inflicted on the body, would we deny that the body is being mutilated in this process of seeking pleasure and beauty? Could we stop for a while and think about the number of people who subject their bodies to multiple surgeries to repair unwanted or outdated tattoos? How about those who feel uncomfortable with their natural faces, and decide to trade them for something else by going through plastic surgeries, or those who willingly suffer atrocious and traumatic mutilation of their body parts to lose weight? In an analysis of the physical pain inflicted on the body let us also consider the sadomasochistic setting, where one would draw a certain pleasure through enduring or inflicting pain. In other words, when we narrow the picture down to our contemporary practices of plastic surgery, tattooing or piercing different parts of our body, one realizes that the ultimate satisfaction of the individual supersedes the pain and is worth the sacrifice. Could we have the courage to judge these practices as savage, barbaric, or otherwise, after realizing how close these archaic behaviors are to our own?

Even taking into account not only the physical scars, but also the psychological traumas that may result from female circumcision, as opposed to tattooing and body piercing, which some advocates defend as bringing about a personal sense of happiness. Do we still have the right to blame other people for choosing the body part they want to perform their initiation on? Some would say female genital cutting is not the same. What about piercing the nipples, the tongue, and other parts, such as belly button and sexual organs, which are meant to be the most sensitive and erotic parts of the body? Furthermore, think about the branding that a lot of youngsters enjoy going through to prove their masculinity, to show that they are capable of enduring pain to belong to a club or fraternity, as part of personal self-expression, or as a sign of loyalty.

Though Nwapa has not dealt with the drawbacks of the practice in presenting circumcision as an integral part of the Igbo culture, reference to recent works on the issue shows the intricate network of patriarchy underlying this practice, and the patronizing, self-congratulating attitude of some Western feminists towards indigenous cultures and practices. Some claim their advocacy without ever wanting to understand what is going on in traditional people's minds or without considering the environmental/

group effect and shaping of people's mentality based on external and internal influences. For instance, in *Warrior Marks*, the song[23] that Alice Walker reads during the documentary film shown in California shows that the dancing women sing about becoming men in order to undergo circumcision. According to Walker, women literally abolish themselves as women and take on a male persona in order to participate in the ritual.

This ritual song also reveals how deeply rooted patriarchy perpetuates this violence by turning women into heroes for withstanding the terrible pain of the mutilation. Perhaps this frantic dancing is a way for women to numb themselves. The complexity of this web of denial and distancing demonstrates women's ability to embody, embrace, and reinforce patriarchal power. Unfortunately the phenomenon of "colonizing" and oppressing one's own kind is not new or unique nor is it rare.[24]

Walker's idea of the women's heroism is quite revealing inasmuch as it illustrates the prototypical traits shown in the traditional hero image, wherein the actor transcends the natural and human behaviors through courage and extraordinary deeds. Those deeds elevate the individual from his/her simple and natural functions to the uncommon and the special. Here we could also refer to the symbolic mask that women have to wear as a shield not to project cowardice or a fragile woman's image to the public spectator. Thus, the women have to move beyond and transcend the traditional gender categorization and prove their courage, as they are being elevated to a higher state of mind, just as men can be, by showing their courage and not crying/screaming from the pain involved in this process.

Economic realities underlying the practice of female circumcision in rural areas lead women who have no way to survive without a husband to

---

[23]From *Moeurs et Coutume des Manjas* by A.M.I Vergiat (Payot, 1937) quoted by Alice Walker in *Warrior Marks*, pp. 178–9.

[24]Ibid, pp. 178–9.

submit to the risks. Considering this prevalent situation of female genital cutting, Ellen Gruenbaum, a medical anthropologist at California State University, San Bernardo points out that people do know the health risks. They have seen people get sick. On rare occasions, a girl will die. But you will not change people's minds by preaching to them or telling them they're primitive. They undertake the risks for reasons important to them.

This is a significant remark that helps outsiders to understand that in matters of culture there is no appropriate judgment of value, and no other individual can understand what is going on in the minds of the people concerned. A relativistic approach is more helpful for understanding that which is different from one's customary knowledge. But are we obligated to keep or perpetuate rites and practices which undermine and endanger the physical and mental health of women?

Other queries come to mind: How many of the women who undergo the rite really feel that they are being used or mutilated? How many are of an age to reasonably protest or stand against the perpetrators? Who are the manipulators? What interests do men and women have in encouraging the practice? These are a few questions that are necessary to explore in order to fully understand the politics surrounding the perpetuation of customary practices.

Before bringing this chapter to a close, reference to the socio-cultural background in which female circumcision is practiced is worth grappling with for a better understanding of the environmental impact on people's social behaviors. We could say that it is a very sensitive and sometimes political issue, which is indirectly related to the development of the society concerned. Though circumcision in the Kikuyu ethnic group (Kenya) was used as a political weapon against the British religious establishment, it usually has nothing to do with the political authorities of a country. If Ms. Kasinga's story is true, then female circumcision is not a practice that can be blamed on governmental authorities and stopped overnight.

Although the practice is judged by many as outrageous and even criminal, it is so embedded in the people's minds and so intertwined with diverse socio-cultural beliefs that its total eradication may take a long time to materialize. Therefore, the first consciousness-raising should be at the individual and family levels. But is this an easy task when the target group lives in remote and often inaccessible areas? Perhaps it is helpful to mention the Western feminists' appropriation of some lucrative international issues, considering that Ms. Kasinga's story resulted in a book publication, a comfortable shelter for her in the U.S., and the production of a documentary which is widely advertised in women's studies arenas.

It is important to come back to the rhetorical question that opened this discussion. Shall we preach the abolition of female circumcision while thousands of women are still being victimized, or shall we promote hygienic and sanitary means to lessen the risks of physical and mental trauma? The situation's complexity is such that the people practicing circumcision do not view it in terms of physical mutilation, as opponents have labeled it. What is most important to them is the benefit of circumcision for the individual and the society. But are there any benefits when the initiated person has part of her body cut off, when she undergoes pain and carries an irremediable mark? Could we carry on the ritual without cutting? Here an alternative solution may become a common ground. The final remark is the one Alice Walker makes regarding the criticism that might arise from her book or film. She says: "Do we care about African children, or are we like the midwife who says she doesn't hear the little girl screaming when she is cutting her? Are we expected to be deaf?"[25] The answer to this question is, certainly not. What could we do about it? Perhaps raising people's consciousness about the dangers of the practice might be the first step to eradicating it in the long run.

Women should not be expected to be insensitive to other women's suffering around them, or elsewhere in the world. Though one is often centered on oneself out of human egocentricity and greed, the poverty that drives women to continue practicing some archaic rites has tentacles

---

[25]Ibid, p. 215.

which indirectly affect women in developed countries as well. Removed from its geographical context and put in a global concept of violence against women, female genital cutting (FGC) is comparable to the other multifaceted ways of subjugating women. Perpetrating and perpetuating the practice is another facet of the violence, abuse, appropriation, and objectification of the female body to better subjugate us. It is incumbent on each individual, women, men and teenagers included, to contribute in their location to an individual or a mass consciousness-raising. In this light, I concur with Pratibha Parmar's hopeful statement about the future:

> I believe *Warrior Marks* is part of an ongoing project to speak out against the violence directed at women across the world. We need to be willing to transcend all our differences without ignoring them, to build new communities that bring us nearer to our Utopian ideals, to continue to redefine our ideas about womanhood and feminist politics, and to embrace concepts of justice and equality, while at the same time recognizing the complexities of our diverse identities.
>
> The future looks hopeful. (Walker, p. 97)

According to her, there is cause for hope when we learn that mothers in different parts of the continent are encouraging their daughters to fight against the practice. Not only mothers, but also fathers and husbands are joining in the awareness of the dangers and the resistance to the practice. In their efforts to change attitudes and break down the local resistance built up over the centuries, these women should be seen as pioneers in their local social transformation.

Other cultural aspects of similar importance in traditional and contemporary societies are worth considering through fiction. Without modern medicine and its sophisticated technology, how did traditional Igbo people manage to sustain their physical, mental and spiritual health before the coming of Westerners? How have people of African descent managed to keep themselves in a relatively good health when they have no *Dibia* to resort to? This last question will lead into touching on survival strategies of African Americans and other people of African descent in the Diaspora who have devised means of survival during and after their forced or voluntary migration to different parts of the world. The focus of this discussion will remain on continental African women and their current predicaments, struggles and triumphs through their own survival strategies and activist involvement.

One should point out that another perspective on the Western feminist attitude towards the issue of female genital cutting is fully analyzed and discussed by articulate scholars, particularly Oyeronke Oyewumi's *African Women & Feminism: Reflecting On The Politics of Sisterhood* (2003), in which she compiles articles highlighting the complexity of feminism and the role the self-congratulatory and patronizing position of some European and American feminists play in damaging the work of well-intentioned activists. It is one of the first collections written by continental African women, who are well aware of other women's discourses. For example, Nkiru Nzegwu's article "O Africa! Gender Imperialism in Academia" raises the pertinent issue of the perpetuated patronizing attitude observed in academia and warns in her own words:

> Our white female colleagues and feminist 'sisters' must learn that solidarity is not built on other women's backs, with people of color relegated to the subordinate status of servers, and cleaners. They need to learn from strategists the art of being one with others if they seek a viable women's movement.[26]

L. Amede Obiora's article, "The Little Foxes that Spoil the Vine: Revisiting the Feminist Critique of Female Circumcision," is another piece

---

[26]Nkiri, Nzegwu, 2000,"O Africa! Gender Imperialism in Academia" in *African Women & Feminism: Reflecting on the Politics of Sisterhood* edited by Oyeronke Oyewumi, Africa World Press, 144.

worth mentioning. It is a Biblical juxtaposition of images of beauty and destruction. The imagery in the title speaks of how ill-conceived strategies to end female circumcision may undermine rather than further feminist goals. More precisely, it is invoked by the author to capture the insidious and far-reaching negative implications of well-meaning efforts to stem the practice. Within a broader historical and sociological context, the article traces the emergence of the Western feminist campaign against female circumcision in order to illuminate the limitations of its reductionist approach to a deeply embedded cultural phenomenon.

Primarily informed by Alice Walker's 1997 best-seller, *Possessing the Secret of Joy*, the critique emphasizes the subversive dangers of studied sensationalism. Enunciating the virtues of contextualized analysis and bottom-up solutions, derived in collaboration with (not in alienation of) grassroots initiatives, the article calls attention to the need for connections between altered perceptions, material empowerment, and social change.[27] Here, the issues of authority, ownership and representation are suggested. Who has the authority to speak and represent a culturally autonomous group of people? Can an individual, either member of a community of an outsider, claim to be knowledgeable enough, to the point of becoming an expert, to represent and speak for a different group of people in a different geographical location? In this particular case, one should note the sensational character of some feminist scholars' work and its negative boomerang effect. The risk is that instead of drawing readership and empathy, the work may adversely do nothing else but offend, and turn off the subjects concerned in the issues raised.

Cultural Violence

One cannot discuss female genital cutting without associating it with the issue of violence against women and measuring the different forms

---

[27]Ibid, p. 197.

it takes in our real lives. While FGM/FGC (Female genital mutilation/ female genital cutting) may appear too far removed from some of us and we may look at it as "their culture," assault on women has been one of the most pervasive current issues of violence, as is experienced and witnessed in our homes and neighborhoods. Violence in all its forms, physical or mental, battering, and abuse in all its forms, whether economic, emotional, or verbal abuse, including sexual assault and rape, all of which women are subjected to, do nothing but traumatize and endanger not only women's well-being, but have a direct impact on the stability and life of the family as a whole.

In Buchi Emecheta's *Second Class Citizen*, Francis and Adah's example is unfortunate. The issue of violence is pushed to the extreme when we reach the violation of basic common morality in Francis's behavior, as he not only fails to take responsibility for his own mediocrity and failure to succeed in his education, but he also blames his wife for all his inabilities and tries to keep her down through belittlement and the destruction of her intellectual property. Francis burns Adah's manuscript of the "Bride Price," which the author euphemistically terms "killing her baby." Another aspect of abuse is illustrated through *Second Class Citizen*'s protagonist, Adah, who is "incapacitated" by multiple child births and her husband's refusal to cooperate in her choice of family-planning and use of birth control, and overburdened by work to support a whole family, first in Nigeria and later abroad, in England. By extension, and in opposition to another male character depiction in African American Harlem Renaissance writer Zora Neale Hurston's best seller, *Their Eyes Were Watching God*, Tea-Cake transcends the social norm of the 1920s–1930s and lavished love and understanding on his wife, Janie.

Moving away from Nwapa's generation of the post-independence writings of the 1960s to Buchi Emecheta's generation of the 1970s, and focusing on the new generation of young African women writers, one must mention the Igbo woman writer, Chimamanda Ngozi Adichie. Her groundbreaking first novel, *Purple Hibiscus*, deals with re-occurring themes of culture, tradition versus modernity, relationships, family, education, class, and abuse, which are taken to a relatively complex level where the abuser ends in tragedy. Compared to the mild level of violence in Flora Nwapa's *Efuru* and Emecheta's *Second Class Citizen*, Papa's (Eugene's) anger is not based on poverty or the partner's fault, but rather apparently on a blind religious fanaticism which reduced him to a captive of a static notion of reality.

Violence against women takes the form of physical abuse when the wife is incapacitated and cannot defend herself because of pregnancy. In addition to the emotional and physical abuse of his wife, Eugene's violent reactions terrorize his children in the house. A fake goodwill benefactor, devout Christian, and respected Igbo native, Eugene combines all the paradoxical and contradictory characteristics of the lovable public figure he projects to his community and society, and the abusive father and brutal husband he is to his close family. The abuse is pushed to the extreme in which he becomes a constant threat to the freedom of movement and expression of his children, Kambili and Jaja. The emotional abuse of his family culminates in its destruction and Eugene's tragic death by poisoning. Though the family collects the pieces to continue surviving later without the father, the scars of an iron-hand upbringing and the fear that the children have developed, have in a way overshadowed any parental love they might have experienced from time to time. Preventing the children from visiting their grandfather because the latter has maintained his traditional beliefs and practical indigenous life is another aspect of a recurring theme in present day African life. Some Christian or Muslim converts are comfortable rejecting their traditional values along with family relationships whereas the majority of people navigate between faiths, combining and taking advantage of different trends.

Adichie's depiction of Aunt Ifeoma is poignant in the sense that she stands out as a counter-weight to her brother Eugene's disrespect and ruthlessness towards their father, who symbolically represents the old Igbo traditions and belief in ancestors. Her characterization allows an escape for Kambili and Jaja to socialize with the outside world of teenagers. Though other pressing themes such as domestic violence and the religious blinding of communities are worth discussing, one would rather devote another study effort to deal with those aspects of contemporary African literature typical of the aftermath of the independence era. From that angle, Adichie has moved further in dealing with gender and other intertwined issues of class and bigotry embedded within her Igbo society, regardless of the current apparent emancipation and economic growth. Her character delineation of young Kambili is testament of the genius that will undoubtedly be exhibited in future writings and exposure to the public.

Pushing the discussion further and in reference to the famous African American woman writer, Alice Walker, and Pratibha Parmar (1993), one might ask why the producers of the film and book *Warrior Marks* failed to deal with other issues, such as the burning of women or female infanticide in India, poverty and others. Is their treatment of FGM (Female Genital Mutilation) not another contribution toward strengthening stereotypical concepts and as such, perpetuating the existing negative images of women in different parts of the world, namely those of African and Asian women?

On the one hand, the ways in which the media and foreign feminists approach the issue are offensive to those who are not even members of the communities practicing FGC. On the other hand, somewhere along the way, the issue of female circumcision should be discussed in order to find possible remedies and avoid irreparable mistakes. Why do Africans always have to be presented on the darker side? This cry of indignation and anger that might come from people who think an outsider has no right to criticize African culture could be perceived as a legitimate interrogation, as it reflects one's self-victimization, including a negative reaction resulting from a blind and chauvinistic pride. This parallels other concerns regarding who has the authority to speak for and represent a group of people rooted in their traditional culture, and living their relatively harmonious lives before the interference of outsiders.

Regardless of emotional feelings and judgment of value, which different groups of people have about female genital cutting, the truth of it is that its practice is detrimental to women wherever they are. Stories and myths souring the practice of circumcision are built on the reality and the traumatic experiences many female human beings have undergone throughout generations.

It is true that an outsider can never penetrate the psychological impact, and the scope of the ritual. But the outsider's reaction might have a positive impact on catching what was missed from an insider's perspective. To borrow Patricia Hill Collin's term, "Outsider within" in feminist research methodology, what if s/he is an "outsider within" who is a participant-observer, someone who can identify better with the situation or has expertise in the field by being at the same time able to understand, and to distance her/himself to better see, compare and finally reevaluate the practice? Thinking of the reaction people had at the publication of Walker and Parmar's *Warrior Marks* (1993), and the premiere of their film on female circumcision in 1995, outsiders' reactions can help us reexamine some secular practices that have blinded our whole integrity as women with senses and full human beings. These leads provide a stimulus for going back to the Kasinga case and pointing out the positive roles the media publicity, including the Human Rights Advocates and feminist involvement, have generated. Today, more and more people are aware of the practice and its health and death threats to women's human right to life, for which countries took official steps banning it. *U.S. State Department (25 February 2009)—Togo: Country Report on Human Rights Practices—2008* revealed the current governmental efforts to sensitize people and the pervasive perpetuation of FGM in that country.

According to the U.S. Department of State country Report on Human Rights Practice, penalties for practitioners range from two months to five years in prison as well as substantial fines. Further, the research found that the law prohibits FGM; however, according to UNICEF, FGM continued to be perpetrated on approximately six percent of the girls. Although no statistics were available, the government and NGOs believed the practice had decreased significantly in urban areas since the 1998 anti-FGM Law was passed but continued as previously in rural areas. Most cases occurred where victims usually were unaware of their rights. Traditional customs often took precedence over the legal system among certain ethnic groups.[4]

The Togolese Ministry of Feminine Promotion and Social Affairs has indicated that in theory the Ministry would seek to protect any woman who claims abuse of her human rights. However, there is no documented precedent of women seeking protection from FGM within Togo. The Togolese Human Rights League states that non-governmental organizations (NGOs) may not effectively be able to protect women against FGM because it is considered "a family matter."

Moreover, if the practice of female circumcision continues in the Diaspora and people cling to certain traditional values in Europe, and the United States, we should recognize that deep rooted beliefs are hard to get rid of, and therefore multiply our efforts in raising consciousness about the health risks, including death, that are related to it. In this regard, different organizations including the U.S. Embassy's Democracy and Human Rights Fund (DHRF) and the World Health Organization, provided funds for research on the practice of female genital cutting in 1996 in Togo, and found that 12 percent, or one Togolese female in eight, has undergone this procedure. The quantitative study covered the entire country and the qualitative study concentrated in areas where the mild type of cutting/excision is practiced.[28] Let us wrap up the discussion on this sensitive topic of female circumcision, female genital cutting (FGC), body transformation, and subsequent psychological traumas with the following free verse:

---

[28]United States Department of State, Togo: Report on Female Genital Mutilation (FGM) or (Female Genital Cutting (FGC), 1 June 2001, available at http://www.unhcr.org/refworld/docid/46d5787d32.html [accessed 23 May 2010].

For Rama[29]

In memory of those little girls
Who underwent the "Bath"
Without being capable of fleeing
Or protesting
To save and protect their fruit

In memory of Ramota Aduni
Whose beauty was un-common!
Whose freshness was like passion fruit!
May your innocent soul rest in peace!
Like a young bird whose wings are plucked
You fell down, prey to that outrage!

O parents!
Protect us against that "Ritual"
That has become so casual

Never again,
Shall this be done to someone in our family!
Be it nipple, Jewel or navel,
Let us wage a war of peace
To save that body piece,
And say
Never again!

Never again should we let go of
A small piece of our body

---

[29]This poem was written in memory of a sibling who bled to death after being circumcised very young. Though the practice has stopped now, I have never recovered from that loss. Now, instead of doing it to very young children, the girls and young women were/are convinced to undergo this practice secretly, not only for respect at the family level but from the would-be husband's family level.

Never again should we torture
Our body by piercing it

Whole are Mind, body and soul
Let us protect that sanctuary!
Never again should we
Mutilate our body and let
That diamond or golden ring
Hang on it
For beauty
Or cupidity! (From "Reminiscence" by S. Boukari, 2007)

For fear of extrapolating further into thematic and paradigmatic discourses about female circumcision and its ramifications related to violence, abuse, and the treatment of these serious issues in the literary production of the new generation of African women writers such as Adichie, let us keep our attention focused on the first generation of pioneer writers mentioned in the beginning of the book and proceed with a look at the role of the medicine-man, or the traditional doctor in Igbo society. The *"Dibia,"* or traditional doctor, not only plays a pivotal role in the sustenance of the community members' physical health, but s/he is often the spiritual link between the humans and the traditional gods.

The Traditional Doctor or *"Dibia"* in Igbo Society

The existence of gifted people who are able to predict the future and/or prevent a mishap is found in traditional African societies. Unlike in the modern society whereby the medical profession has different specialized areas and physicians are there to help patients with a particular health problem, in Igbo society the *"dibia"* uses a holistic and wholesome approach to healing. He is there to help people live in harmony with their cosmic environment. He is a "jack of all trades." His primary role is to diagnose the causes of misbehavior, or anything people feel to be wrong with their inner or physical balance in the society. Most of the *dibia*s who are presented to readers are males, but there are also gifted women who perform the fortune telling who are not accorded the same visibility as men. The following paragraphs highlight a few characteristics of the *"dibia"* in traditional Igbo society.

An example of women playing the role of *dibia* is illustrated in Achebe's *Things Fall Apart* in which Chielo, the priestess of the oracle of the Hills and Caves, Agbala, came to Okonkwo's compound to claim his daughter Ezinma at night, and took her to the Oracle of the Hills and Caves. Though this woman is supposed to have some supernatural powers, she passes for an ordinary woman during the day. Therefore, her role in that arena is "invisible." Men are usually well-known to consult the oracle. As a matter of fact, we have had so far a male domination in the characterization of the *"Dibia"* in the writings of both men and women. The *Dibia* plays both the psychiatrist and herbalist roles. He is also known as the "medicine man." As such, the role played by the medicine men or *dibia* in Igbo traditional societies is very significant in the sense that they are the ones who foretell the future, explain the significance of some events and even prevent some mishaps by warning the persons concerned. In other words, a visit to the *dibia* in difficult or casual times is part of a normal life. The presence of the *dibia* is a recurrent element in a lot of post-colonial writings. Elechi Amadi's *The Concubine* and Flora Nwapa's *Efuru* will serve as examples. In *The Concubine*, Anyika, the wise medicine man of Omokachi, warned Ekwueme's parents that Ihuoma was the wife of the "Sea-King". The latter had caused Ihuoma's husband Emenike's death; he had blinded Madume and driven him to suicide; and he might harm Ekweme if he dared to marry Ihuoma. Such perfection as Ihuoma could only belong to the gods. But Ekwueme would insist on marrying Ihuoma. These aspects in Ihuoma's depiction are also noticeable in Efuru's character.

In Flora Nwapa's *Efuru*, the role of the *dibia* is also significant. When Efuru, after two years of marriage, found it difficult to become pregnant, she and her father went to consult the *Dibia* (Nwapa, pp. 24–25). There, she was told she was not barren but should perform sacrifices. What the *Dibia* forecast proved to be true. After a few weeks, Efuru became pregnant and later gave birth to Ogonim, a baby girl who would later die during her father Adizua's absence. After the baby's birth, Efuru decided to go back to the *Dibia* to give thanks and gratitude. She informed Adizua:

'It would be a good idea,' her husband said.
'But as you know you never go empty-handed to play the
   masquerade.'
'Yes, I know. We have to take along with us some presents.'
'What are you going to give to the *Dibia*?'
'We shall buy two heads of tobacco, kola-nuts and a fowl.
   Perhaps, we shall take some yams also.'
'These will do, when do we go?'
   On Eke day, the things were put in a basin and Efuru carried it. Her husband followed her with his walking-stick. Their mother looked after the baby. When they got to the gate, the *Dibia* cleared his throat. "The daughter of Nwashike Ogene; who is bringing you to my house today? And that's you, Adizua Ukachukwu. I saw you last when your father died. Come along and sit down, my children." Thus welcomed, Efuru and Adizua came in and sat down: "Njeri, my daughter, bring kola for us." The girl brought some kola. The old *Dibia* took it and proclaimed: "Nwashike Ogene' s daughter, to your health! Ogonim, to your health"! Efuru pinched her husband. "Ukachukwu's son to your health! "Our fathers have some kola. I have been a *Dibia* for more than thirty years. I have been upright." (*Efuru*, p. 34)

The *dibia* who knew everybody in the village also possessed all its secrets. He apparently recognized Efuru and her husband Adizua from a distance. Unlike in some African societies where matrilineal inheritance is practiced and the mother's name is added to her child's for recognition and praise, here the primacy of the father is remarkable in this Igbo community. Efuru and Adizua are identified through their fathers' names similar to the Western European culture in which patriarchal trends are dominant. The customary greetings, praise names, and wishes, not to mention threats to enemies, are part of the welcoming process.

> 'I have never caused anyone to die.'
> 'Ise.'
> 'I have never prepared poison to kill anybody.'
> 'That's how it happened,'Adizua and Efuru said.
> 'I inherited all my medicines from my father, who inherited
>   them from his father.'
> 'Ise,' they nodded.
> 'Our family is upright, and fear God. So, God see to it that our
>   enemies are crushed.'
> 'Ise.'[30]

The *Dibia*'s incantation reflects an aspect of inter-generational transmission of traditional knowledge that is handed down from ancestors to the younger generation. The current *Dibia* cannot perform or practice his skills without acknowledging, praising and giving credit to his ancestors. Lineage and the family heritage are strikingly important for the continuation of those medical practices, as a cycle. The simple fact of mentioning the trustworthiness of his family strengthens his social status as a powerful man, who despite those remarkable abilities is still not comparable to the supreme God. Notice here the humility and wisdom the *Dibia* needs to exhibit before proceeding with his blessings:

> 'Let Ogonim live long.'
> 'Ise.'

---

[30]Nwapa, Flora *Efuru*, Heinemann, UK, 34.

'Let Efuru have one baby, one baby until the house is full.'
'Ise.'
'Hear us, our fathers.'
'Ise.'

He broke the kola, and frowned with pain. "Our fathers forbid, God forbid. God won't agree to this." The old man said in one breath. "Why have I not seen this before? We have only two pieces of kola. It is not good sign my children. Njeri, bring another kola."Njeri brought another kola. The old man started again.

'Our father, here is kola'
'Ise'
'I am upright.'
'Ise'
'I have made people rich though I am poor myself. It is the will of God that it should be so. In our family we are good, but poor. God has willed that it should be so. Our work is to make others rich and remain poor.'[31]

A *Dibia* must display an exemplary life of integrity and respect. Here, invoking God in the work he does reflects his divine mission of healing and fortune telling which is a must and should not be commercialized. The result of this social service is for him to remain poor and gain a moral satisfaction rather than an accumulation of material wealth.

The *Dibia* broke the kola. Again, there were only two pieces:
"This is strange. My children come again on Eke day when the sun is here," and he indicated the place he meant. Efuru and Adizua understood the time he meant.

---

[31]Nwapa, Flora, 1966, *Efuru*, p. 34.

"We brought this to thank you, our father." Efuru said. "Last year my father and I came to see you, and now as you know I have a baby girl. 'Agundu' thank you."

'My wife and I have one voice,' our father. Thank you 'Agundu'. But we do not understand what is wrong now. We are blind though we have eyes to see. 'We are nothing at all.'

'Don't worry my children. Thank you for your presents. Go home and come back on Eke day. I shall tell you all then.' Efuru and her husband went home.

'Something will go wrong. I can't prevent it. But, I must be given time. I have seen it, but not clearly yet. Our fathers will help me. I shall sacrifice to them. I shall ask their aid,' the *Dibia* said slowly to himself as Efuru and Adizua were leaving his hut. On Nkwo day, a day to the appointed day, Efuru heard that the *Dibia* was dead. He died in his sleep.[32]

The above passage illustrates the traditional way of dealing with medicine-men and the importance of their role in society. Here again, you could notice the religiosity surrounding a *Dibia*'s consultation. The soliloquy is meant to illustrate the seriousness of the visit as well as the dramatic effect on the audience, here Efuru and Adizua. The reward that Efuru and her husband presented to the *Dibia* was much more of a symbolic act of respect than a payment to the *Dibia* for helping them to get a child. The language used in such a situation is not the normal conversational style people use. It is more of a cryptic language full of imperatives reflecting order and imploring the ancestors to fulfill their wishes. The *Dibia*'s breaking the kola into pieces and noticing something wrong that he cannot prevent is implicit of his own death and that of Efuru's baby, Ogonim. As a fortune-teller, the *Dibia* or medicine-man seldom asks for payment for his services. In this particular

---

[32]Nwapa, Flora, 1966, *Efuru*, pp. 34–5.

case, he would get a reward when the people he has helped are satisfied with the result they got.

Another example illustrating the traditional doctor's social role is seen when Efuru is back in her father's house and her second husband, Gilbert, wanted her to confess that she cheated on him. After Omirima and a *Dibia* accused her of adultery, Efuru consulted another *Dibia* to get explanations about her repetitive dreams, and was told that she was chosen as an honored worshipper of a river goddess, Uhamiri, also referred to as Idemili in Amadiume's *Male Daughters, Female Husbands*. But, do all *Dibia*s tell the truth? Based on the example above, one should realize that the credibility of *Dibia*s has faded with the introduction of money in traditional societies where everything can now be marketable. The *Dibia* who used to occupy a central and respectable place in traditional society has lost his/her place to the universal religious leaders of Christianity and Islam because of the massive conversion of natives to these new orders. The *Dibia* is now trading his gift in exchange for money or goods, so today there are fewer and fewer *Dibia*s who are trustworthy.[5]

The portrayal of the *Dibia* in men's and women's writings is more or less similar. Both genders portray the *Dibia*s' role in African society and their centrality in not only Igboland, but also in other indigenous communities around the world. Today, one should acknowledge the dilemma between drifting back to *Dibia* consultations in combination with modern technological therapeutic practices, and totally rejecting old archaic ways of healing to embrace the increasingly growing digitized and advanced ways of treatment in hospitals. Moving from the literary works and looking at societies around us, some instances could be found in other ethnic groups, such as the Bassar people in the northwestern part of Togo, where the medicine-man or woman is called "Oubo," or in the southern part, where s/he is referred to as "Bokono." Though the purpose of those healers is not to divert from good deeds, in addition to their ability to heal they are also well-known to possess supernatural powers that could harm in case of vengeance, or for the purpose of punishing an evil-minded person. In other words, the *"Dibia,"* "Oubo," "Bokono" or "Babalawo" (in Yoruba) serves as a society regulator in traditional African societies. One cannot end this section dealing with ritual practices without touching on the different forms of relationships, including the institution of marriage, which are prevalent in traditional African society. Taking a passage from Jean-Marie C. Apovo of Universite National du Benin, who worked on the anthropology of "Bo," the root of "Bokono," the name is given to someone who has the secret knowledge of using medicinal herbs and the ability to tell the future.

The authenticity of the African is found in his fervent practice of Bo. His thought, action, relations with others-his entire way of life-is based on the practice of Bo insofar as he wears Bo names. Bo is deeply rooted in his cultural values and comprises the background for all social organizations and thus acts as a social regulator. In Western anthropology there is a scientific mind; in African anthropology there is a Bo mentality that attempts to understand the world and then conquer it.[33]

The above ideas join those of others. In his book, *Religion, Ritual, and African tradition: African Foundations*, Ghanaian anthropologist E. Kofi Agorsah also states that the beginning of all societies relates to their environmental settings and human resources. Human beings, who have lived for several millions of years in a world of peril and uncertainty, are compelled to seek security, and the best way to achieve this is to control nature.

Relationships & Marriage: Polygamy versus Monogamy

To open the discussion on relationships and marriage in contemporary society, it would be interesting to offer a few questions as food for

---

[33]Jean-Marie C. Apovo "Anthropologie de Bo (Theorie et Pratique du gri-gris) IIAIAEIA, Philosophical Anthropology, (XXeme Congres Mondial de Philosophie) p. 1.

thought and discussion. What distinguishes monogamy from polygamy? How are these terms defined in a social context? What is the general perception of African marriage practices? What is your definition of marriage, co-habitation, and other forms of living with another person?

Taking a cue from authors Marilyn Ihinger-Tallman and Debra A. Henderson in *The Free Encyclopedia*, one would agree that relationships such as friendship, kinship, courtship, dating, and marriage are common in almost all societies nowadays. The difference between the practices is dependent on the place and culture. Thus, in African societies where customs vary drastically from one county to the other, there are nevertheless shared features in relationships and practices. Whereas nowadays one tends to trivialize relationships, and to trade our personal individual interests, traditional indigenous societies cherished the communal life of sharing rather than accumulating. Marriage ceremonies around the world are as varied as the couples who marry. They may be formal or informal, religious or secular, expensive or modestly priced. In all cases the ceremony symbolizes a couple's transition from single to married status and represents willingness on the part of the couple to become a family and begin a new generation.

Rituals or ceremonies that celebrate a newly achieved marital status are nearly universal. Why is that? The assumption of husband and wife roles, before or after the birth of a child, clearly marks the beginning of a new generation. The fulfillment of these roles—husband, wife, and parent—is fundamental to the continuity of a society. Therefore, both the larger social group and individual families have an investment in the institutions of mate selection, marriage, and parenthood. This investment is recognized and acknowledged with a variety of ceremonies, including engagement or betrothal rituals, marriage ceremonies, and christening or naming ceremonies. Using a comparative approach and looking at other parts of the world, such as rural communities in the Balkans, people from communities, villages, or kin groups that are antagonistic to one another sometimes intermarry. In these situations, the marriage ceremonies often allow for the safe expression of hostilities between the groups through wrestling matches and the ritualized exchange of insults.

In African societies in general, weddings are opportunities to bring families closer to one another regardless of past feuds or hostilities. A key component of marriage ceremonies is the symbolic expression of the new status of the bride and groom through an alteration of their physical appearance. Change in clothing style or hairstyle, as among Hopi women in Arizona, and the exchange and wearing of wedding rings or other types of jewelry such as ankle bracelets, are a few of the ways this custom is played out in different cultures. Marriage ceremonies are common across cultures for multiple reasons.

First, marriage is an important emotional and social transition for the bride and groom, and participation of family and friends in the process can be a major source of emotional and financial support for the newlyweds. Second, marriage usually marks a dramatic change in social status for newlyweds. In most societies, marriage signifies adulthood and potential parenthood. The couple is expected to establish a new home apart from their natal families or, in some societies, one spouse is expected to join the community or home of the other spouse's family (in most cases, the bride moves to the groom's community). The marriage ceremony emphasizes the importance of these new statuses and the behavioral expectations associated with them, both for the individuals and the community. Third, ceremonies are often paid for by families of one spouse, sometimes both, and this emphasizes to the couple their parents' investment in them and their parents' expectation that they will produce and raise the next generation in the family. Fourth, in some societies, much wealth is exchanged between families at marriage. This exchange may take the form of bride-price, where the groom's family makes a payment to the bride's family or kin group, or dowry, where the bride brings wealth to the marriage. This exchange may also take the form of an expectation of a large inheritance in the future. Take for instance, the situation of Efuru and Adizua in Flora Nwapa's *Efuru*. The young man was unable to provide the bride price for his in-laws and the couple was obliged to work and pay it when they could afford to do so in order to honor not only Nwashike Ogene, Efuru's father, but also to show the bride's worthiness and respectability in the community.

Though the institution of marriage has existed in all societies under various practices, the union of a man and a woman has often brought about controversy, depending on the society. The secret or official existence of another woman apart from the first one has led to the distinction between monogamy and polygamy, having one or several wives, regardless of religious belief. There is no topic as challenging and exciting to students than that of men marrying more than one wife. I remember how interested a student was just contemplating the idea of being able "to eat different kinds of food" and change partners as he wished. But beyond the rosy image that the idea of this practice might bring, one needs to be aware of the risks and challenges that go along with it, not to mention the conditions under which it is accepted and widespread in some parts of the world.

Relationships & Marriage: Polygamy a Way of Life?

Though polygamy, the practice of having several wives, has been widely practiced in Africa, one cannot easily conclude that it is the "African way of life," as some would like to think. Others brush the discussion off by simply stating it is "their culture," which would mean that they themselves are not concerned with such a practice. To avoid engaging in lengthy discussions going back to Biblical scriptures in reference to relationships between men and women, it would be simple to state that polygamy has always existed alongside monogamy. Though the socio-economic conditions in agrarian and nomadic societies led men to take many wives to generate labor through the children who would help in farming or herding, there have always been some families with a single woman leading the household regardless of the man's presence or whether she has many or fewer blood children. Apparently, in case of necessity, as when the wife was unable to bear children, was ill, or had been absent for a long time, men were justified to seek another companion in the majority of societies in the past. Contrary to this convenience created for men's needs and satisfaction, mainstream society has not provided women with the same privileges regarding relationships. Had women been given the same opportunity to take another man when their husbands were unavailable, the world would have been quite different.

Recent news coverage has highlighted the somewhat exploitative and psychologically damaging nature of the practice of polygamy/polygyny in today's modern society. Except for the alleged multiple marriages and uncommon nature of the fundamentalist Mormons' current life in the United States, especially in Utah, polygamy is illegal and mostly frowned upon in the United States and Europe. Rather than engage in judgment of values and fall into the same bias trap, let us try to uncover the roots of this age-old practice for a better understanding of its ramifications in our modern society. Is polygamy a way of life for Africans, as some would want us to believe? Is it just their culture?

The purpose of this discussion is to identify some socioeconomic reasons and cultural ethics surrounding the original institution of polygamy in Africa in juxtaposition with the modern practice and justifications in today's society. In today's modern society where marriage is sanctioned by law, polygamy is illegal in the majority of countries around the world. However, accessibility and availability of more than one wife seems to have developed regardless of the increasingly widespread health risks. Not until recently have some scary statistics been released as a wake-up call for modern societies about the risks involving HIV/AIDS. Long before the awareness of this disease, people had practiced polygamy, marriage with more than one wife, for many reasons. What would we say about relationships with multiple partners either in a legal marital situation and/or through having an affair, or having several marriages after divorcing one after the other? Where do you stand in the idea of sharing one partner in heterosexual and homosexual relationships?

In traditional agrarian societies, possessing multiple wives was a sign of economic wealth, a source of human resources, meaning a large family with many children who in turn provided free labor for farm work. In addition to that, social status and respectability came along with being a polygamist, because of the huge responsibility inherent in managing a big household. The bigger your family, the more respected you were, with all the privileges that were attributed to a highly-ranked person in the community. Not only would you need to be morally reliable in distributing resources equitably, you would be accountable for any emotional abuses in your family. Though traditional societies were based on a subsistence economy, they gradually lost that status with their interaction with Western European countries characterized by a monetary economic system. Thus, little by little, not only did natives lose their property, they got entangled in the new economic system, which led them progressively into consuming manufactured goods made in European countries.

The result of the economic transformation created less and less need for a large family with several wives and children to provide free labor for farming. In some regions, the use of fertilizers and lightweight agricultural equipment have replaced free labor/manpower and helped farmers produce more and more without relying on family. With modern education having become a universal tool for development, and technology increasingly improving people's living conditions, the economic need for polygamy is receding. Subsequently, the need for money for educational and daily life expenses, like sending the children to Western schools also grew, thus rendering polygamy an expensive luxury for men.

How was polygamy perceived and practiced in most African societies? Considering the importance and complexity of marriage as an institution, one should note that in *Efuru*, Nwapa displays the simplistic and positive view of polygamy as normal, considering that it is accepted and even wished as a crisis or conflict resolution strategy between the man and the woman. Here, reference to Efuru's difficulty in bearing a child is illustrative. She was ready to accept a co-wife and even went as far as to offer to search for another wife for Adizua, her first husband. After her first marriage failed with Adizua's desertion of the family, she resorted to a similar solution by offering to give Ogea, her maid, to Gilbert, her second husband. Though this might have been practiced in a social context that apparently condoned polygamy, it certainly was not that easy to arrange such unions. A tentative discussion in two classes totaling 83 students yielded an interesting reaction to the following questions: How many of you would be willing to consider another partner sharing your significant other, wife, husband, girl/boy/friend? How many of you would accept the "other" partner or would take the courage to go the extra mile, and initiate such a relationship? A simple survey in two of my classes yielded only one young man out of the 83,[6] who expressed the willingness to consider the possibility of taking another partner in case his wife would be unable to provide him with a child. Note here that although the current trends of relative liberalism draw some couples towards wife/husband, and whole family swapping, the thought of sharing your partner with someone else is still difficult to accept. Could we discuss relationships and the importance of children by neglecting a comparative approach to the institution of marriage in other places in the present day?

Moving from the fictive setting and thinking about concrete life experiences and contemporary situations, for example, in the United States marriage is a civil action licensed by each state, but most people use the occasion for a special ceremony to mark a couple's rite of passage from singlehood to marriage, from youth to adulthood. Most states require the presence of one or more witnesses and a legally certified individual to oversee the vows. However, the majority of couples (80 percent) are married by a member of the clergy (Knox and Schacht, 1991). This holy/legal union ensures the approval of their religious group as well as evincing the degree to which people abide by the laws that govern the state. The remaining 20 percent of couples, who forego a religious ceremony, are married by a judge or justice of the peace.

In most African nations, arranged marriages were historically the norm, and wedding ceremonies were sometimes as simple as the paying of a bride-price, also called dowry. While Western influences have resulted in men and women having more opportunity to select a spouse, in most traditional societies, parents and other adult relatives must approve the selection, if they don't make the selection themselves. Traditional rites and rituals are still an important component of many African marriage ceremonies. Different ceremonies and rituals are performed depending on the ethnic and kinship group.

During a Yoruba wedding ceremony in Nigeria, for example, the groom is presented with two different women in place of the bride-to-be. He signals his disapproval toward these women, and they are escorted from the room. A third woman, dressed in hand-loomed fabric and brass anklets, is then presented to him. This woman, the bride, is accepted by the groom. During the wedding ceremony the couple tastes ceremonial symbols of life. The bride and groom share honey to symbolize sweet love and happiness and peppercorn for the "heated times" and "growing pains" of family life ahead. The eldest woman at the wedding then uses gin, which symbolizes the ancestral spirits, to bless the couple, and other family members offer praise and affirmation of the marriage (Mordecai, 1999).

Today, the most common wedding celebrations in Togo combine a religious ceremony with a "civil marriage" performed at the City Hall, or the Courthouse where a state administrator formally declares the bride and the groom to be legally united and bound in commitment to each other. It is during this ceremony that the couple can declare whether they will adopt monogamy or polygamy according to the Togolese Civil Law and Family Code. Parallel to this lay wedding is the religious one, depending on whether the married couple is traditionalist, Christian or Muslim.

Several rites and rituals make up the wedding ceremony in the United States. However, it is up to the individual couple whether they want to incorporate some or all of these into their wedding. Generally, the more formal the wedding, the more traditional it is and the more often these customs are followed. These traditions include the following: a bridal shower in which the bride receives personal gifts or gifts to help establish a household; a party for the groom given by male friends, meant to be a last fling before he gives up his state of bachelorhood; an exchange of wedding rings; and a white bridal gown with a veil to cover the bride's face. Another tradition is for the bride to throw her garter to the single men present at the wedding party and her bouquet to the unmarried women. Throwing away the bouquet symbolizes the end of girlhood, and the woman who catches it is supposed to be the next to marry. Rice thrown upon the departing couple symbolizes fertility (Knox and Schacht 1991). However, environmentally-minded couples now provide birdseed as a substitute for rice because many birds apparently died from eating the celebratory rice left behind on the ground. In some parts of Africa, a symbolic doll is given to the couple as a fertility wish to have many children. A traditional wedding often ends with a reception or banquet for the wedding guests. Often, music and dancing accompany the feast, and an important ritual is the cutting of the wedding cake. It reenacts the custom of breaking bread and symbolizes the breaking of the bride's hymen to aid in first sexual intercourse and future childbirth (Chesser, 1980).

The vows expressed at weddings are variable. Most marriage vows include the promise of a commitment, including permanency and fidelity. However, there have always been couples who create their own vows to express their individual philosophy toward marriage. Christian ceremonies emphasize marriage as a divine sacrament and call attention to the tie between the couple and God. In these cases, the marriage itself is under the jurisdiction of God (Saxton 1993). People of different ethnic, racial, and religious groups in the United States, such as Jews, Poles, Italians, Latinos, and African Americans, sometimes develop ceremonies that feature elements from both U.S. culture and the couple's specific ancestral cultures. The average cost of a wedding in the United States in 2002 was approximately $19,000. This expenditure for a traditional wedding is often beyond the means of many young people and their families; therefore, many weddings take place in less formal clothing and are held in backyards, civic gardens, and parks. Nevertheless, some people choose pompous celebrations and can only do these by contracting huge loans they will spend a long time repaying.

Marriage ceremonies, many writers noted, range across cultures, from very elaborate ceremonies including the performance of religious rituals, dancing, music, feasting, oath taking, and gift exchange over several days, to the virtual absence of ceremonies in the relatively few societies where individuals announce their marriage by simply acting married—that is, usually by living together and telling others that they are now married. Marriage ceremonies, along with those marking birth, death, and achievement of adult status in some cultures, are the major rites of passage in cultures around the world. Religion plays a role in ceremonies in most cultures. Prayers, sacrifices, and donations are often made and rituals performed to gain supernatural blessings or to ward off evil forces. Here, one might reiterate earlier explanations in Flora Nwapa's *Efuru*, the performance of excision that Efuru went through before getting pregnant as a concrete example of the importance of ritual practices in African societies.

According to John S. Mbiti (1991), initiation ceremonies prepare young people for the most responsible phase of life. This is marriage and the raising of families. These initiation ceremonies found in many societies, are performed either for the rite of passage from childhood to adolescence, or to adulthood with different kinds of rituals and meanings. In places where male circumcision and clitoridectomy are practiced, they symbolically represent the flow of life through the shedding of blood from the organ of reproduction. This is a profound religious act by means of which the young people accept to become bearers of children and their communities give approval to that voluntary step. In many African societies, marriage is looked at as a sacred duty which every normal person must perform. By failing to do so, one is, in effect, stopping the flow of life through the individual, and hence diminishing mankind upon the earth. Anything that deliberately goes towards the destruction or obstruction of human life is regarded as wicked and evil. Therefore, anybody who under normal conditions refuses to get married is committing a major offence in the eyes of society, and society will in turn look down on him. Everything possible is done to prepare people for marriage and to make them think in terms of marriage.

Myths of the creation of man agree that human life started with husband and wife. It must also continue in the same way. According to African religion, marriage is the meeting point of the three layers of human life, the departed, the living and those to be born. The departed come into the picture because they are the roots upon which the living (human beings) stand. The living are the link between death and life. Those to be born are the buds in the loins of the living, and marriage makes it possible for them to germinate and sprout. If one deliberately refuses to get married it means, therefore, that one is cutting off the vital link between death and life, and destroying the buds which otherwise would sprout and grow on the human tree of life.[34]

The above segment reiterates the widely held cyclic concept of life and the world as being an interconnectedness of elements that are apparently different but are part of a whole entity, the cosmic order. This helps to understand why the process of childbirth is still important in African societies today. The primacy of children becomes that which conditions and shapes womanhood in most couples' lives and may as a result break the stability of harmonious but childless marriages. Here again comes into play the crucial role of African women writers who in their works have tried to lay bare those touchy issues, such as barrenness, domestic abuse, and polygamy, just to name a few. Those pioneers such as Flora Nwapa and Mariama Ba have illustrated not only the African women's predicaments but also the lingering challenges facing women in general. The meaning of marriage and the traditional cultural

---

[34]Mbiti, S. John, 1991, *Introduction to African Religion* Heinemann International Literature and Textbooks, Great Britain, p. 104.

values would hopefully help younger generations make sure their unions, or their relationships including marriage, succeed. How does one explain the collapse of traditional values? What role does modernity play in that process, and why should we care about the transformation in people's mentality?

Gender and cultural issues in Igbo society cannot be discussed without mentioning the importance of religion and the impact it has on people's daily lives. Though our previous analysis of Nwapa's book, *Efuru*, alluded to Igbo traditional gods and deities such as Amadioha/ Idemili and the "Lady of the Lake," further attention should be given to the Igbo philosophy of life and the interaction of humans with the supernatural. Thus, the following section will try to elucidate the socio-religious factor in Achebe's *Arrow of God* and Obinkaram Echewa's *The Land's Lord.*

Religion in African Literature & Implications for Today's Society

Obinkaram Echewa's Treatment of Religion in *The Land's Lord*—Toward Religious Relativism and Ecumenical Perspectives

While Chinua Achebe has gained fame for his literary creativity and is widely known as one of the pioneers of African literature with his trilogy of *Things Fall Apart, Arrow of God,* and *No Longer at Ease,* Obinkaram Echewa is a somewhat covert fire beneath a piece of cloth that needs to be unveiled for the profound and complex issues he tackles in *The Land's Lord, The Crippled Dancer,* and *I Saw the Sky Catch Fire.* The following section dealing with Religion in African literature tries to highlight Echewa's depiction of two religious priests: Old-Ahamba, a traditional Igbo religious leader, and Father Higler, a Christian missionary, and his native African servant, a new convert. It also provides a platform for discussing the evangelization process in Africa and the reception of the Western God in traditional Igbo settings. With the Igbo society that Obikaram Echewa has described being still firmly rooted in traditional religion one should understand the tragic predicament of the protagonist, Philip, who has chosen to transcend the norms of his community. Despite his noble origin and predestination as the acolyte of a traditional god, Philip decides to break with his social milieu and fully adopt Christianity, the new religion brought by Western missionaries in the late 1950's. Will Philip, in spite of his understandable trauma similar to that of the white priest Father Higler, get over his spiritual despair? Will the white missionary, Father Higler, achieve without any trouble his mission as a Christian representative? As the discussion raises the unspeakable philosophical questions about the role of each religion, it also argues about the need for a Higher Being to unveil the significance of human life and its relationship with the cosmos.

Apart from the belief in the Supreme God mentioned earlier, one of the most important of a number of deities in Igbo cosmology is Ala, also called Ani, the goddess of the Earth and arbiter of morality. Ala also controls the coming and the going of ancestors who look after the spiritual and material welfare of their descendants and are in turn sustained by them. A significant aspect of Igbo theology is the belief that at birth, each person acquires a *chi* or spiritual double that could equate to a guardian angel. Achebe has described the concept thus: Every person has an individual *chi*, who created him, its natural home in the region of the sun but it may be inducted to visit an earthly shrine, a person's fortunes in life are controlled more or less completely by his *chi*.[35]

According to C. L. Innes, it is this cosmology which, in Achebe's view, provides the source not only for Igbo individualism and independence but also for his tolerance and egalitarianism. It encouraged a society which held a fine balance between the material and the spiritual: at the root of which lies a belief in the fundamental worth and independence of every man and in his right to speak on matters of concern to him, and flowing from that, a rejection of any form of absolutism which might endanger those values. It is not surprising that the Igbo held discussion and consensus as the highest ideals of the political process. This made them argumentative and difficult to rule.[36]

It is difficult to separate our way of thinking from our way of living. Man, as a spiritual being, needs religion, or at least needs to believe in something beyond his visible being in order to be in harmony with the existing, though invisible, cosmic order. With the Igbo society that Echewa has described still firmly rooted in its religious traditions, one

---

[35]"Chi in Igbo Cosmology," MYCD, p. 98 quoted in C. L. Innes, 1992, p. 5.
[36]In Innes.

should understand the tragic predicament of the hero, Philip, who has chosen to transcend the norms of traditionalism, the belief and worship of ancestors and deities notwithstanding the Supreme God. Despite his noble family background, and his predestination as the acolyte of a traditional Igbo God, Philip decides to break with his social milieu and fully adopt Christianity, the new religion that Western missionaries brought into his community. Old-Ahamba was not only the village elder and leader, but the guardian of Igbo traditional values, who welcomed the Christian priest, Father Higler, according to the Igbo hospitality custom, and even allowed him to sit in their social and religious gatherings (note that many African societies consider strangers as children who need guidance or refugees who need protection). Will Philip, in spite of his understandable trauma similar to that of the white priest who deserted war to join the Christian missionaries abroad, get over his spiritual despair? Will Father Higler achieve without any trouble his evangelic mission as a Christian representative in a remote African village? What kind of relationship will both religious representatives develop? What perception of God do both religious priests, Old-Man Ahamba and Father Higler, have? What difference is there between Christianity and Igbo traditionalism? The following discussion seeks to explore and if possible, provide partial answers, to the questions above.

Obinkaram Echewa's fictional work, *The Land's Lord*, allows us not only to focus on the Igbo religious beliefs, and West European missionary experiences, but it will also help to extend our understanding of African and European concepts of God and elaborate specifically on two apparently different religions, Christianity and what is generally called "animism," "fetishism," or "paganism," which will henceforth be referred to as Traditionalism. Particular attention is given to elements which have a religious significance to traditionalists though they may be, at the same time, deemed meaningless to the Christians. Fundamental differences are highlighted through different aspects of the relationship between Old-Ahamba and Father Higler. The seeming closeness and the misunderstanding between representatives of two religious orders testify to Echewa's mastery of the literary art as he tackles issues of colonialism and the Christian evangelizing mission in Igboland. The irony is illustrated by the importance of religion for traditional Igbo people as well as by their belief in natural things, which simply stop being natural in their eyes, once they have been sanctified, meaning invested with a supernatural power. Here, we witness how the author's use of the concept of relativity dovetails into emphasizing the apparent antagonism/conflict/tension between the two entities, Christianity and traditionalism, as if both could not coexist.

Old-Ahamba & Father Higler: Antagonistic or Complementary Relationship?

It would be helpful to define some concepts for a better understanding of this study. The expression "traditional African" refers to the religious behavior of people who remained close to nature, within the continental historiography. The so-called universal religions, namely Christianity, Islam and Judaism, underline the Uniqueness, Omniscience and Omnipotence of One Supreme God, whereas the traditional African religious concept promotes the plurality of gods, and thrives on their power in both space and time. In other words, Christianity practices Monotheism, which is a belief in one God, as opposed to traditional African religion, whose polytheistic practices, the belief in and worship of several deities, have a pattern common to most indigenous societies, such as Native Americans, and Hindus in India. Trying to understand the complexity of the philosophical discourse between Old-Ahamba and Father Higler leads us into grappling with two apparently opposed world visions and general religious beliefs, the mainstream traditional African religious view, and the Western European one, where God is a supreme entity beyond human access. Based on Christian, Islamic, and Judaic religious Scriptures, the reward awaiting any believer is something unknown that would materialize only after death. The Catholics even erect another barrier between the simple church-goers and God through confession, during which the priest serves as an intermediary between God and the individual believer. This phenomenon is not noticeable in the traditional belief system which Echewa discusses in *The Land's Lord*. However, after the Christian convert Paul's death, and his wife Martha's mourning laments, a conversation takes place between Old-Man Ahamba and Father Higler. During their discussion, Old-Man Ahamba asks a crucial question regarding the utility of God: "But what use is a God, if you cannot expect anything of him?"

Old-Man Ahamba's query is an unanswered universal question of God's existence, and apparent indifference in regard to evil and people's sufferings in the world. Nevertheless, it bears a particular contextual meaning as Igbo people generally have the power of creating and interacting with their gods. In the last part of this essay, we will see how the author developed this idea further. In questioning the utility of a God, Old-Man Ahamba is also posing the puzzle within the meaning of our lives. Trying to reason, and understand the importance of our being, not only are we plunged from the beginning of our lives into a world that we neither sought nor created, we can hardly seize the meaning of our birth and death, the significance of our existence. Also, considering the fact that even contemporary scientific advancement has not yet been able to help us fully master the miracle of life, there seems to be another dimension, invisible and unattainable to us. In light of these, one may understand why Old-Ahamba, representative of the Igbo moral values based on old truths, finds it difficult to understand and explain death.

With regard to Old-Ahamba's question, it is logically clear in that when you worship, you are inclined to expect a reward in compensation for the devotion you have for the venerated being. Likewise in Christianity or Islam, believers expect a salvation in the afterlife, or what some people may call the the abode of the ancestors and realm of the gods. Here, we are inclined to say there are limitations on human comprehension of all events in the world. This is what appeals to our religious instinct, and draws some people to a total denial of God's existence. There are countless events which escape our comprehension, and as a result, there are metaphysical questions left unanswered. Many human beings struggle with themselves trying to understand mysteries, but only the "chosen," the experienced or the initiated few, understand certain fractions of the truth, while a large part still remains hidden.

In the context of *The Land's Lord*, the temptation is to say there are two groups of people, the traditional Igbo people that Old-Ahamba represents, and the Western Europeans that Father Higler stands for in that part of the African continent. Unlike Igbo beliefs and world vision which promote a possible interaction between the supernatural and the human, in to Western European or Eastern religious beliefs they separate and distance the supernatural from the human to the point of impossible communication between God and humans, a situation which ultimately leads to creating a distance and subsequent fear in the minds of the believers. That concept of fear is tightly linked to the ideas of good and evil, sin, judgment, retribution, reward and punishment, whereas in African traditionalism, there is no room for an imaginary salvation of the soul, fear of retribution or judgment day, an idea of hell or shaded gardens with recliners awaiting you after life. On the contrary, Islam and Christianity are based on the mere fear of a Supreme God who could only be reachable through the intermediary of the prophets, the Holy Spirit, or any of religious representations. In this light, Father Higler's response to his spiritual opponent Old-Ahamba is significant in that the essence and existence of God are shrouded in mystery: "A God that can be understood is no God," Father Higler states. But thinking about it further, he would argue paradoxically that the Christian God, his God, the Supreme is *everywhere*, meaning even in the remote African village where he came for his evangelic mission. A further comment on this observation reflects the irrationality of religion by definition, and particularly of the universal religious attitude that is self-denial and faith. The concrete example of the fatalistic attitude and belief in predestination is found in Christians and Muslims, just to name a few. There is a sort of resignation on the part of the Christian or Islamic followers to display a feeling of subordination with respect to God. Though the concept of a supreme God is also noticeable in most traditional African beliefs, the relationship existing between human beings and deities is more or less an interactive one, leaning towards that of master and servant. Moreover, there are times when that relationship becomes an egalitarian discourse, as when priesthood is involved.

When the individual has gained some supernatural powers that help him understand better the unknown and also communicate with the gods, there are times when there is a need to bargain and negotiate with the gods. This is the time the interaction between the gods and the people is similar to that of a customer and a supplier whose respective roles depend on one another. The gods have their distinct roles to play as well. The perception of Igbo gods is that they possess more dynamism; they can be considered living and terrestrial in the sense that they are involved in people's daily lives, inasmuch as their worshippers can even communicate with them. For instance, during occasional ceremonies, the gods and the dead ancestors are invited to participate in the village gatherings. Notice the significance of the triangular or circular phenomenon in the African world vision, a communication between the gods, the living human beings, and the dead ancestors. Furthermore, the cycle comes to its end when the unborn children are involved in the discourse process. This example reflects the cyclic concept of natural phenomena in the traditional African world vision where there is a kind of cosmic inter-linkage between things and a continuum in time and space. The past, the present and the future constitute a whole which cannot be separated or segmented. This is understandable when we look at the traditional African attitude towards God/the supernatural, generally as an active participant, in comparison to the Western European Christian beliefs. Sometimes, when the gods fail to perform their duties, or to do what they are supposed to do, they can be destroyed and replaced by other gods forthwith. These aspects are fully developed in the next section of my study, entitled "Originality of Traditionalism."

The fact that indigenous Africans have not undertaken evangelizing missions of conquest over other people reflects tolerance in the African religious attitude towards other religions and beliefs. In reference to history and trying to understand the concepts of relativism, freedom and the practice of tolerance through the acceptance of others, one could mention the significance of the Moorish invasion of Spain and Portugal in the eighth century. According to Dr. Jose Pemienta Bey's (2002) *Othello's Children in the New World*, the Moors, African descendants who invaded, and dominated Europe for several centuries, did not overlook or try to devalue the existence of Christianity. On the contrary, they respected the pre-existing religions and established Islam side by side with Christianity, knowing that both religions complemented each other in many ways. Their philosophy of life being a combination of Ancient Egyptian values, belief in MAAT, the practice of truth, justice and order, coupled with Islam, helps us to understand the practice of remnant values in contemporary African societies. We can then understand the natural goodwill and acceptance that African societies showed to European settlements, including their subsequent religious, economic, and political implantation.

With regard to *The Land's Lord*, the author's discussion presents the reasons why Christian missionaries are allowed to settle in the country. Strangers or foreigners are considered to be "refugees" who need protection and shelter. For some traditional African societies in general, and the Igbo in particular, refugees are sacred, and therefore accepting European missionaries was done out of good-heartedness and duty to their gods and their cultural values. This tolerance is obvious through Old-Ahamba's social behavior and his attitude towards the white priest, Father Higler; they are frequently invited to participate in the community public gatherings. This moral value is also well illustrated in the former's statements, such as: "we do not exclude; they have excluded themselves—wait, their white man is raising his hand to speak. Speak, white man!"[37]

---

[37]Echewa, Obinkaram, 1976, *The Land's Lord*, p. 55.

During this encounter, a drink was passed round for everybody to sip some out of the same container, and Father Higler declined the offer. By refusing to drink the sacred wine with his followers, the White man has offended the Igbo tradition, thus excluding himself from the blessing of the whole group as a full member participating in the final step of the ceremony which is regarded by Igbo natives as sacred. Perhaps his refusal is justified, but one could also think of embedded preconceived ideas of downplaying the importance of that ritual coming from a Christian angle, as the Igbo were not Christians. For instance, Father Higler has repeatedly referred to indigenous Igbo people as "faithless" or "non-believers," and the Christian adherents as the "faithful." Here is the irony, and the paradox in people's way of perceiving others' beliefs and innovations. Relativity is much apparent as Father Higler thinks that the Christian God he worships is the one and only true God, the one suitable for everybody to follow, and Old Ahamba feels the ambiguity of his coming to Igboland as the Igbo people also have their belief system, and have, apart from "Chuku" the Supreme, deities to protect them the same as Christians, Muslims and Jews. Although Donatus Nwoga, with due respect to him, was of the view that the Igbo did not believe in a supreme deity or the supreme God and his book entitled *The Supreme God as Stranger in Igbo Religious Thought*, testifies to that, the reality and references in the contemporary Igbo worldview and sociocultural practices apparently confirm the belief in a Higher being.

Unlike what should be expected of the so-called "heathen people," to be obedient and accept the new path through the "civilization" the church symbolizes, we witness the outrage and offense on the part of the Igbo, headed by their priest, Old Ahamba:

One true God?
Which God is true?
Our own gods are false, then?
The dare! He insults us. All of us!
The ground you are walking on,

Is it false, White man?
And these trees are they false?
The rains and the rivers, the yam in the farms!
Look about you, White Man, pinch yourself,
Is the pain false?
Show us the power of this true God![38]

Through these words of Old Man Ahamba, the narrator reveals the traditional people's perception of the Western God. In other words, we witness here the concreteness of the African belief regarding the supernatural, which is not remote but so close to the humans. The narrator goes as far as to ridicule the fundamental dogmatic Christian concepts based on the omnipresence of God stating that God is everywhere. Using arguments based on natural surroundings, Old-Man Ahamba expresses the strangeness of the Christian priest's idea of God, as follows:

He, this God of yours, was among us
Since time began, and we did not know?
I find that strange, White Man. Strange.
But life is full of strangeness. So all I can say is:
Let Him prove himself.
If he can absorb the thunderbolt of our Amadioha,
Or make more powerful ones,
Then, I say he is to be feared.[39]

The above comparison, a blatantly outrageous statement in the eyes of Christian or Muslim believers, reflects very well the complexity of religious beliefs, and perception in a cultural framework.

Although the existence of a supernatural being is recognized, in the minds of traditionalists there appears not be a scientific demonstration

---

[38]Echewa Obinkaram, *The Land's Lord*, p. 55.
[39]Ibid, p. 16.

or explanation for natural phenomena. Of course, in case there is no understanding of an event, people have the tendency to believe in a mysterious power rather than to try to discover the secret behind everything.

This pattern could be verified in ancient European civilizations, such as the Greco-Roman mythologies, as well as contemporary indigenous/traditional religions worldwide. Further, and in comparison to the ancient world, Old-Ahamba's question about one true God and the existence of the Supreme God everywhere could be paralleled to the conversation Moses had with the old shepherd, his father-in-law, who came to visit him with the wife and two children, when he left to join his Hebrew people back in Egypt before leading them to Israel, and ultimately obtaining the ten commandments for his people to live in a straight path.

In Echewa's *The Land's Lord*, what seems mysterious for the traditional priest, Old Man Ahamba, is obvious in the eyes of Father Higler. As much as the majority of natural phenomena can be scientifically explained and understood today, the use of rain, thunderbolt and the like to explain the existence of God might seem naive to some. For the indigenous people who still live close to the Land, or what is often called Mother Earth, or Nature, these beliefs are not only necessary for harmony between human beings and Nature, but are also vital for people's spiritual equilibrium to carry out their daily struggle for survival. These beliefs give an acceptable meaning to their existence on earth.

An important element to consider is the level of religiosity and the extent to which people rely on the supernatural for the solution of their daily problems. Would we call this superstition? A humble observation reveals that Africans have a more intensive religious life. On the one hand, there is little scientific development and people tend to go back to the past to find meanings for present day problems. In the traditionalist's mind, nothing happens by chance: everything is explainable, and linked to another parameter or dimension. On the other hand, scientific progress which allows Westerners to understand more and more the functioning and composition of natural phenomena also reduces and diminishes people's beliefs in the existence of God. Consequently, the polarization of beliefs about the existence of any Super Being is not uncommon in today's society, where people worship anything that is of interest to them. Regarding indigenous ancient beliefs, or even today's believer, we spontaneously tend to situate their values among the inevitable "survivals" of outdated traditions. We say to ourselves something like this: "They had religion (or cosmology); we have ethics." That, in effect, suffices for us to know how to lead our day-to-day lives. There is no need of religion in order to be honest or charitable. No need to believe in God in order to do our "duty." Even more, the struggle for secularism is rightly a priority. Briefly, one could point out that contemporary society offers a wide range of temptations, opportunities, and technological devices that drive people away from the normative concepts of God as the Holy Scriptures recommended in the Old Testament, the Qur'an, or the Talmud and Torah respectively in Christianity, Islam and Judaism.

Coming back to the dialogue between the two priests, and resulting from their virtually opposed religious stance, the writer seems to display a philosophical concept of relativity which, in a way, validates and negates both protagonists' viewpoints addressing African and Western European religious concepts. For instance, when Old Man Ahamba asked the White priest to let his God prove himself, this challenge could be considered as won in today's scientific and technological environment, inasmuch as in reality it is possible to absorb the thunderbolt by lightning-conductor. This encounter between both priests is important, as the call by Old-Ahamba for the Christian God to appear in battle is deeply Biblical. It reflects the close kinship between the descendants of Abraham's concept of God (and the spiritual/material landscape) and that of present day Africa. In a discussion with Dr. Amy Carr of Western Illinois University, she pointed out that the Psalmists are calling for God to prove "Himself" all the time, and also recalling when God *did* come down to do battle against the Egyptians in order to free the Hebrews from slavery (see 1 Samuel 8:1-22, and surrounding verses). Old-man

Ahamba's questions and calls have remained open for the sake of the writer's project, for some reason. Those open-ended questions could be interpreted as a weakness or ignorance in the priest's dialogue. One might also think that Echewa used this strategy to hold our attention, to reach his goal as a novelist who seeks to attract an audience and keep it focused through suspense. However, a critical approach to this strategic discourse might be a hint at the significance of our different beliefs which in essence comes from the same centrifugal pillar, the belief in the Supreme God, a Higher Being, or the Creator whose presence would explain all that exists. If one bears in mind objectivity in regard to the African conception of religion and the instances given so far, we should concur with the Nigerian writer, Wole Soyinka, (1976), who stated in *Myth, Literature and the African World*, that the African cast of mind has a cohesive understanding of irreducible truths. Creativity is governed by man's knowledge of the fundamental unchanging relationship between himself and society within the larger context of the universe.[40]

Another characteristic of Judeo-Christian behavior that needs to be mentioned is that of passivity in the face of daily events in hope that salvation would come regardless of one's sufferings. It should be understood here that the passivity mentioned should not be confused with the lack of dynamic attitude in Muslims and Christians promoting an active moral life and active efforts to transform the social order. According to Dr. Carr, this passivity of the Christian, Muslim or Jewish behavior rather refers to the belief in Calvin's predestination idea, which maintains that everything that happens was meant to be, which spawns a certain submissive and resigned work ethic. Going back to Echewa's book, and our literary approach, that sort of passivity is also given substance through Father Higler's answers to Philip's questions about religion:

---

[40]Wole Soyinka, 1979, *Myth, Literature and the African World*, Cambridge University Press, pp. 37–96.

We still hope. Like little children, we trust in God,
Our only refuge, God is the author of all justice.
We take what we are given and pray for more.
And hope that our pursuits in life, our faiths, prayer
And offerings have not been in vain.
And nothing is really up to us?[41]

Man is seen here to have no power in face of the Western God. As we
have learned from the Christian priest, "nothing is really up to us." So,
God is the One who decides everything and nothing happens without
His agreement, a fatalistic attitude towards life. In fact the ambivalent
and challenging position of Man as regards his creator is significantly
developed in several chapters in the Qur'an. Similar to the Christian
priest's response to his servant, the following Islamic scriptures expand
on the idea of God's omniscience, omnipotence and omnipresence, notwithstanding the denial and sometimes arrogant positions human beings
may take when they find themselves in other situations. The Qur'anic
verses below are more illustrative.

Does not Man see We created him from a drop of semen?
Even then, he becomes an open contender,
And applies comparisons to Us
Having forgotten his origin,
And says: "Who can put life into decayed bones?"
Say: "He who created you the first time.
He has knowledge of every creation,
Who gave you fire from a green tree
With which you ignite the flame."
How can He who created the heavens and the earth
Not be able to create others like them?
Why not? He is the real creator all-knowing.

---

[41] *The Land's Lord*, p. 112.

When He wills a thing, He has only to say:" Be" and it is.
So, all glory to Him who holds
All power over everything, to whom
You will go back in the end (Qur'an, Soura 36:77-83).

In the above Qur'anic verses related to creation and God's relationship with human beings, we notice a clear-cut expression of superiority and absolute authority of the Supreme God as opposed to the
traditional Igbo concept of God which turns around negotiation and
understanding of God's actions. In the Christian or Islamic scriptures,
God is placed high above the humans and has unequivocal comparison
to nothing in the world. Therefore, no possible negotiation is laid out,
based on the belief that human beings are created to worship and praise
God. Humans can only hope for salvation through their deeds and by
the grace of the Supreme God. Reference to the Supreme God leads us
into extrapolating a little to show how strikingly the concept of God's
supremacy is a universal belief regardless of religious affiliation. Contrary
to what might be perceived as non-existent in African traditional beliefs
based on common Christian or Islamic preaching, the traditionalists do
believe in the Supreme God that is placed high above all deities. Those
little gods or deities are attributed different functions by humans like a
labor division with delegates doing their master's work.

Taking a cue from Mircea Eliade's *The Sacred and the Profane* (1959),
and considering what he called "primitive" as opposed to "more civilized
peoples" religions, we can realize that his discussion of the "Sacredness
of Nature and Cosmic Religion" reflects features all religions share in
common. According to the writer in another work (1956), the world
stands displayed in such a manner that, in contemplating it, religious
man discovers the many modalities of the sacred, hence of being. Above
all, the world exists, it is there, and it has a structure; it is not a chaos but
a cosmos, hence it presents itself as creation, as work of the gods. The sky
directly, "naturally," reveals the infinite distance, the transcendence of the
deity. The earth too is transparent; it presents itself as universal mother

and nurse. The cosmic rhythms manifest order, harmony, permanence, and fecundity. The cosmos as a whole is an organism at once real, living, and sacred, for the sky, by its own mode of being, reveals transcendence, force, eternity. The philosopher/theologian pursues his explanation of the sacred and Supreme God existence with more examples from different social groups around the world; it exists absolutely because it is high, infinite, eternal, and powerful. Uwoluwu, the Supreme god of the Akposso in Togo, signifies what is high. Among the Selk'nam of Tierra del Fuego, God is called Dweller in the Sky, or He Who is in the Sky. Puluga, the Supreme Being of the Andaman Islanders, dwells in the sky; the thunder is his voice, wind his breath, the storm is the sign of his anger, for, with his lightning he punishes those who break his commandments. The Sky God of the Yoruba is named Olorun, literally Owner of the Sky. The Ainu know him as the Divine Chief of the Sky, the Sky God, the Divine Creator of the Worlds, but also as "Kamui," that is, Sky. The Chinese T'ien means the Sky and the God of the sky. The Babylonian Anu also expresses the idea of sky. The Indo-European supreme god, Dieus, denotes the celestial epiphany and the sacred (cf. Sanskrit *div*, to shine, day; *dyaus*, sky, day; Dyaus, Indian god of heaven). The Celestial god is not identified with the sky, for he is the same god who, creating the entire cosmos, created the sky, too. This is why he is called Creator, All-powerful, Lord, Chief, Father (by Christians) and the like.[42]

In traditionalism, God is lowered down to human's level, as much as there can be direct interaction between Him and His creations. We also see that God would not be solely responsible for his creations; humans have their roles to play in maintaining harmony and accomplishing specific missions in their earthly life. Briefly, we are faced with Man's powerlessness and helplessness, what may be regarded as passivity in face of God's will, as opposed to full activity and participation in the process of

---

[42]Mircea Eliade, 1956, *The Sacred & The Profane: The Nature of Religion: The Significance of Religious Myth, Symbolism and Ritual within life and Culture*, Harcourt Brace Jovanowich, New York, p. 116.

the traditional believer's life. This participation is done through religious ceremonies and rituals with explanations of or justification for an event apparently giving significance to the indigenous people's existence on earth. The use of deities or little gods as intermediaries between man and the Supreme God not only equates to the use of Saints in Christianity but it also explains dynamism in traditional believers' actions.

The next section focuses on Echewa's tactful treatment of religious beliefs and how he sheds light on the part Man plays in God's action. Such a statement highlights how the individual rejects the belief in predestination or resignation to become an active participant, an actor without whom God's existence, creations and human life would not be meaningful. However, it should be noted that the extent of man's participation depends on the entire cosmogony, where there is still a hierarchy dominated by the concept of Supreme God, considered to be above all, and whose mysteries are not accessible to human understanding. Aren't we joining to some extent universal beliefs of the Almighty God, here? Of course, yes. If there is an overlapping level of beliefs between the traditionalists and universal religions, where then does the difference lie? Why do people call others true believers and heathens? The ultimate point that could be made of this issue is related to the limits of Man's interactions which are situated within the boundaries of minor gods or deities. Therefore, the human ability to create and invest power in a Man-made God situates him at the center of his beliefs as well as validates his actions, which in turn give a relatively acceptable meaning to his life or being. We then understand the flexibility and the concrete functions existing in African traditional belief systems, which allow human beings to adopt and adapt their environmental sustainability with gods created to satisfy their needs.

Originality of African Traditional Religion: The Power to Create or Destroy Deities.

The particularity of traditional or indigenous religious practices lies in the purposes they are made to serve because the people worshiping the gods have the power to create them for different purposes. Hence, the plurality of Igbo gods is a reflection of the diverse circumstances and ritualistic performances existing in traditional Igbo society. Therefore, each god has a specific role to play in the harmony of the cosmic process. "What use is a god if He cannot be understood?" The functions of minor gods determine the behavior and conditions upon which human beings' relate with them. Such examples of minor gods are: Edo, Goddess of fruitful womanhood; Amadioha, God/Goddess of thunder and rainstorms; Agwu, small wooden idols which make trouble for you if you offend them, not big trouble but bundles of little mischief. You hurt your finger, fall and break your leg. They push you and your children into accidents; Mgbarala, the Land god. According to Igbo cosmology, "The Land god" rules over the Earth. Hence, we have the following passage to illustrate the role of each deity:

> Land is greater than all deities.
> Greater even than the sky-god, because
> When the sky cannot any longer hold its rains,
> It releases them to the Land to hold.
> And the Land is everywhere.
> We reincarnate from it.
> We are always standing on it, whether
> We are on top of a tree, on top of water.
> The rivers and the seas have the Land to hold them up.[43]

The irony lies in the plurality and ability of the diverse deities which Old-Ahamba defines clearly. As if to wrap up his instruction and put the white priest in his place, Ahamba adds sarcastically,

> Just know that there is no lack of god. We make them ourselves.
> In other villages there are other gods, just as it is where you come
> from. We create our gods to guide, rule and protect us.[44]

---

[43]Echewa Obinkaram, 1976, *The Land's Lord*, p. 134.

[44]Ibid., p. 130.

Following the traditional priest's sarcasm regarding the existence of myths and religious practices in any society that has ever existed in harmony with the universe, we cannot but realize the relevance of the traditional priest's logic, and conclude that the Christian priest's mission was difficult. The village people did not need to believe in another god coming from an unknown place, let alone embrace Him. The human power to transform the natural environment in a sanctuary reflects the impact of our mind and its influence on our physical, and consequently, our social behavior. Regarding Ahamba's statement, the Land is more important than the Sky-God that Christianity and other universal religions elevate as the supreme, higher in hierarchy. The reversal appears to be the logic in this Igbo society.

The African world vision is presented as a circular one, where there is a relationship between humans and the Land, which seems to be the source of everything. The cycle is illustrated through the belief in the interconnectedness between the living, the dead, and the unborn. Through reincarnation, the ancestors are brought back to life in the form of the newly-born. Similar to Native American indigenous world vision, and their belief in the sacred hoop along with the interrelatedness of humans and Nature, including its creatures, the Igbo world view is presented as a circular one, where there is a connection between human beings and the Land. In other words, the belief and reverence to Mother Earth seems common to Africans and Native Americans.

Looking at the interaction between deities and humans, there seems to be a relatively flexible rapport which makes it easy for human beings to reach a higher entity without endangering their status as spiritual beings. Hence the dilemma some traditional religious representatives may find themselves facing. Just as they can create deities to guide, rule and protect them, as Old-Ahamba said earlier, Igbo people can destroy their gods when the latter fail to do what they are expected or supposed to do. There is a role assigned to each of the traditional gods. Their relationship with people is clear to everybody in the community. When an event occurs, people know which god is involved, and react consequently by performing sacrificial ceremonies, if necessary, and in case they offended the latter. Conversely, when the god is declared wrong, he/she is punished according to the level of the deed, or sometimes even destroyed. This is illustrated significantly in Eze-Ulu's behavior in Achebe's *Arrow of God*. The latitude in humans' capabilities, and specifically, the power of destroying the gods, are well expressed in Wole Soyinka (1976). When gods die, that is, fall to pieces, the carver is summoned and a new god comes to life. The old is discarded, left to rot in the bush and be eaten by termites. The new is invested with the powers of the old, and may acquire new powers. As most of these deities are made of carved wood, they fall to pieces in the long run and have to be replaced by new sculptures. Let us note the importance of sacredness in this particular context. For instance, the simple piece of wood, which has been carved by an artist, would cease to be a simple object of decoration once it is invested with the powers of a deity. To the eyes of a traditional religious believer this piece of wood would play a magic role, whereas a profane individual would continue to look at and see that wood as a mere object, as long as its physical appearance or material substance has not been altered. Man's ability to create and destroy the deities is not comparable in universal religions.

As Father Higler pointed out earlier, the powerlessness humans have in face of life events, the use of the term passivity illustrates that Christians and Muslims do not have a dynamism that allows the destruction and creation of God. Though the saints and angels exist, the Supreme God is an entity that is omnipotent and omnipresent, not needing any creation. However, through African people's migrations to different places of the world, the very idea of God and its representations themselves shift in different contexts. For example, in Christianity, diverse versions such as Candomble, Santeria, Hemaya, and others sprang up throughout the African Diaspora as a response to the former African slaves' need to worship their gods while the practice of Christianity was imposed upon them by their owners. As a result, one contemporary trend is the replacement of a white Caucasian image of Jesus with a relatively darker one in Black churches, where they also sometimes have Black Virgin Mary icons rather than the white European ones.

At this point, one should emphasize the importance of symbolism and representation. For example, one could make an extension and point out the value of the Christian communal bread and wine as symbols of the flesh and blood of Jesus Christ. Therefore, the meaning we make of things and events would mostly depend on the symbolic representation we make of them in our mind. Hence, the power of the mind in focusing on, transforming simple things into complex ones or vice versa according to our will, and then reshaping our beliefs to command our behaviors in social life. But does this ability of the mind shed total light on the meaning of our presence on earth? Could our human intelligence understand how we evolved apart of the "drop of semen" mentioned earlier, and what our finitude would be like? Before European intrusion, and subsequent transformation of disenfranchised people's lives, what did indigenous people believe in when they needed some form of explanation in face of metaphysical questions in their daily struggle for survival?

Echewa delineates the relevance of such queries and provides tentative solutions through the characterization of "seers" or what other Igbo writers called "*dibia.*" These healers, who treat the physical and mental sickness of people, appear whenever there is need to understand or solve a problem in the plot of *The Land's Lord.* They are equivalents of Western psychics who foretell the future. When a seer told Old Ahamba that Amadioha, the god of thunder, was threatening to kill his first son, the old man reacted not only by performing a sacrifice, he also warned the god that if anything happened to his son he would burn down its hut, and bury it. Another instance is shown when Ahamba goes as far as challenging the deities' power and revealing what happened to gods he owned in the past. When speaking of his Agwu, he says:

> I have not repaired the roof of their hut for more than one year, so when it rains, it rains on them. And they know that I am not bluffing, because they are not the first set that I have owned. They are the third!

The first set, I threw out to the termites. The second, faced
even worse. In anger one day, I made them into a pile, took my
prick like this and pissed in their eyes . . .
        And then I burned them . . .

Here, the traditional priest has changed his Agwu, wooden idols,
deities, when he thought they had become obsolete and useless. This is a
normal reaction when a god fails to live up to his creator's expectations.
An important point is that despite the traditionalist's power to destroy or
to create the deities, there is no occasion on which the human is substi-
tuted for the gods in their protective role. It is needless to emphasize that
there is a limit to consider human involvement in the relationship with
even the minor gods. In their religious beliefs, many African indigenous
people are aware of the existence of the Supreme God, the Almighty Esso
in Them, Mawu in Ewe, Unimbote in Bassar, or Olodumare in Yoruba,
just to name a few. Referring to the notion of Supreme God, and based
on Nwoga's argument, Chukwu is one of the Igbo gods venerated as
Chukwabiama, and housed in Arochukwu. In dismissing the Igbo belief
in the Supreme God, the argument Nwoga is making is that the notion
of a supreme god is not the Igbo God, which by extension explains the
quid pro quo in the conversation the Christian and traditional priests,
Father Higler and Old Ahamba frequently have during their encounters.
Nevertheless, the key point to note is a limit beyond which traditional
worshipers may not push their gods, or God. It is only when African
people can no more understand their deities that they destroy and replace them with more efficient ones. Further, the destruction can only
be done to the shrines housing the physical or material representation of
the failed deities.

Using a comparative perspective, and considering universal or advertised religions, namely Christianity, Judaism and Islam, one realizes
the similarities in traditional indigenous beliefs and advertised religions.
The belief in the Supreme God is as much consistent across all these religions as the fundamental powers with which the Almighty is invested are

absolute, and incomparable to any other being in existence. So, taking into account the above ideas, and narrowing our judgment down to the mere belief system, we find that the difference between traditionalism and Christianity lies in the belief in and worship of minor terrestrial gods, as opposed to the belief in the unique God Westerners have. The Igbo, like many other Africans, believe in the Oneness of the Supreme God. However, they have minor gods to whom they can assign specific missions and even challenge at times when those small gods fail in their tasks. Conversely, the traditional believer's possibility of action over the deities observed in the African context is nonexistent in the Christian context. Mr. Brown and Akunna's conversation in Achebe's *Things Fall Apart* is a significant illustration of the religious incompatibility, when neither of them succeeded in converting or understanding the other despite the seemingly positive exchange of ideas and knowledge:

"You say that there is one Supreme God who made Heaven and Earth," said Akunna on one of Mr. Brown's visits. "We also believe in Him and call Him Chukwu. He made all the world, and the other gods."

"There are no other gods," said Mr. Brown. "Chukwu is the only God and all others are false. You carve a piece of wood-- like that one" (he pointed at the rafters from which Akunna's carved *Ikenga* hung), "and you call it a god. But it is still a piece of wood."

"Yes," said Akunna. "It is indeed a piece of wood. The tree from which it came is made by Chukwu, as indeed, all minor gods were. But He made them for His messengers so that we could approach Him through them. It is like yourself, you are the head of your church."

"No," protested Mr. Brown. "The head of my church is God Himself."

"I know," said Akunna, "but there must be a head in this world among men. Somebody, like your-self must be the head here."

"You should not think of him as a person," said Mr. Brown.
"It is because you do so that you imagine He must need helpers.
And the worst thing about it is that you give all the worship to
the false gods you have created."

"That is not so . . . We appear to pay greater attention to the
little gods but that is not so. We worry them more because we
are afraid to worry their Master. Our fathers knew Chukwu was
the Overlord and that is why many of them gave their children
the name Chukwuka—Chukwu is Supreme."

"You said one interesting thing," said Mr. Brown. "You are
afraid of Chukwu. In my religion Chukwu is a loving Father and
need not be feared by those who do his will."

"But we must fear Him when we are not doing His will,"
said Akunna. "And who is to tell His will? It is too great to be
known."

Akunna's remark is relevant as we are dealing with metaphysics and
abstraction where humans imagine the existence of another entity beyond their terrestrial and human power and understanding. How does
one know what the Supreme God wants? Similar to Akunna's religious
discussion in *Things Fall Apart*, the different encounters between the
Christian priest, Father Higler, and Old Man Ahamba carry the same
tension and apparent misunderstanding of one another in *The Land's
Lord*. While the Christian religious attitude emphasizes the belief in, and
the submission to the Supreme God, the traditional Igbo belief shows
a more stratified hierarchy and relative submission based on fear as well
as flexibility. That submission or obedience to one God is significant in
Christianity, as it is acute in Islam, where adherents do not allow the
possibility of the prophets being elevated to the level of God. For them,
there is no other God, apart from the Almighty, the Unique, the Supreme and Absolute God.

The most striking paradox is that, in the Muslim context, there still
is a possibility for direct communication between human beings and the

Supreme God, without the interference of a third party. Even the Imam, the leader of prayers, cannot interfere between the believer and God. Each individual will be judged according to his/her own deeds on the judgment day.

One salient remark is the reality of life and concrete perception of things in traditional indigenous understanding, which differs from the subjectivity of life and fatalistic attitude noticeable in universal religious concepts regardless of their dynamic promotion of social transformation on different levels. This point has been substantiated earlier. However, one could highlight it once more through Echewa's use of stream of consciousness technique to express the characters' emotions as well as paint a vivid picture.

One example is shown in Father Higler's ideas after his experience of the long walk through the sacred forest, while going to Paul's house. The latter was a Christian convert who had just died: Life here was immediate, earthly and real, and seemed to abhor abstraction like the Latin phrases of his breviary. As a contemplative, he has served an abstract God.

Another issue that needs to be addressed in this section is that of unity and the universality of an essential belief in a higher being. In reference to the concept of Supreme God and in relationship with some common features existing in both Western and traditional religious behaviors, we already pointed out that African religious concepts and traditional practices join Christian beliefs, despite the multiplicity of gods in the former. Therefore, we should not be surprised to notice a universal religious statement coming from the Igbo priest. Addressing the Christian Priest, Old-Man Ahamba tries to highlight the human connectedness to nature through the following: "The Land is everywhere. We come from it, we live on it, we return to it."

Christians as well as traditionalists believe in the same hypothesis about the essence and origin of human beings, who are said to come from the Earth, or Land. As some would say, the food we eat is grown on it and, the houses we stay in are built on it and we are in constant contact with it in our movement. When we die, we are buried in it; therefore, we return to the Land, as stated earlier on. It is important to notice here the subtlety of the writer who has tried, through the cosmic comprehension of a traditionalist, to convey obvious instances that reflect some common features both Western and African people share unknowingly. In spite of the apparent similarity between Western European and traditional African beliefs in the Supreme God, there is a huge gap between their world visions and the ways in which they deal with cultural issues, mainly human relationships. Belief in the Supreme God is far from sharing a collective or segmented world vision, making sense of the connection between human beings and their cosmic environment, and having inclusive perspectives in dealing with others.

Discussing thematically the Christian and traditional African concept of God, Echewa has tried to display the relative aspects of religion as a whole, and by so doing has shed light on the prejudicial and antagonistic positions we take, thus falling into the trap of discrimination due to stereotypes and misunderstanding. A good illustration of that is shown in the following:

> Father Higler—"He (God) needs no bringing anywhere. He was
> always here. Always will be"
> Old-Man Ahamba—"Even before you came he was here?"
> Father Higler—"Yes, even before I came. From all eternity, He
> has been among us"
> Old-Man Ahamba—"Then why did you come?"

A glance at the above dialogue leads into realizing that the author poses questions, the answers to which are destroyed by other questions. This is not only an original style that reflects the African dialogical pattern of call and answers, an ongoing discourse. It is also a strategy to help us understand the ambiguity, sometimes ambivalence, of religious concepts, as well as to demystify the reasons or justifications of Christian missions in Africa or elsewhere. So questioning the usefulness of the Christian evangelizing mission does nothing but negate the justification for Christian religious settlements in Igboland. In other words, the writer has tactfully invalidated the general Western contention of holding the absolute truth in sciences and humanities, and of "civilizing" indigenous people in Africa and other parts of the world. By imposing foreign cultural and religious values, and by so doing, altering their traditional beliefs and destroying that which helped sustain the autochthonous balanced social and spiritual life, religious missionaries have had such an enormous impact on the diverse people they have interacted with to the extent of not being able to to fully explore or uncover them. Here, the writer has demystified the Christian views on African natural/traditional religious practices, and shed light on the controversy existing in prejudice, stereotypical beliefs and reality.

The stereotypical labels, which are attributed to the indigenous people as "faithless" or 'heathens," are shattered to make way for understanding and appreciating non-Western ways, as simply different and nothing else. Moreover, in placing Christian stereotypical labels on others as "faithless", the writer sheds light on the ignorance surrounding the invaders' attitudes towards the villagers, the unknown and the fear of failure in their mission. An analysis of Father Highler's ideas reflects a general belief in an abstact Supreme God that should be feared and who apparently is disconnected from and distant in his relationships with human beings. Whereas the African religious concept is apparently based on the concrete and visible, or palpable manifestations of the supernatural, it is not as clearly marked in advertised religions such as Christianity, Islam and Judaism where the trend is rather geared towards the simple belief in the abstract, despite the different manifestations the believers may observe. This idea is highlighted when Old-Man Ahamba tells the White priest that the Christian God could do nothing for them, because they need a god that does something (concrete) for them.

Another aspect of the novel that needs attention is the relationship existing between the White priest, Father Higler, and Philip, his servant, a newly-converted Christian. The intention is not to focus unduly on this relationship, but to mention what both characters have in common. However, prior to drawing commonality and differences, an explanation should be given of Philip's revolt and subsequent downfall through a tabooed act against his clan and gods. Philip could have gone back to his folk after discovering that Christianity would not provide him with the spiritual satisfaction he was longing for. He could have combined Christianity and traditionalism, like some of his brothers. But why has he decided to end it all by hitting his own blow, as he said: by committing suicide?

The author has done this on purpose to achieve his artistic goal, that of conveying a message to the readers and informing them of the critical rupture in Igbo people's relatively harmonious lives before European colonization. The hero of *The Land's Lord* must disappear for the re-establishment of traditional cosmic order, or the normal transformation, and ultimate change of the village and its people. Philip's tragic ending is an appropriate event in the unfolding of the plot because he offended the traditional gods by breaking the "juju" shrines and denying completely his kinship and identity, thus betraying the community through his tabooed act, suicide. For the sake of the writer's vision, the hero must die for the triumph of *The Land's Lord*. Moreover, in such a rigid traditional society as Echewa describes, there is a limit to lopsidedness. Thus, Philip is ostracized and condemned by his people not because he joins Christianity, but mainly because he rejects his community in his decline of responsibility. This is illustrated through his uncle Nwala's discussion with the white priest: "No, I'm not against you or him or your church . . . but, duty . . . I am against a man who is blind and will not see what his duty is."

Here again, we realize how much the concept of duty is stressed in traditional African society. Sometimes duty exceeds the normal boundaries of individual personal desire, and people cling to it without looking at a situation objectively. Referring to Okonkwo's similar tragic ending in Chinua Achebe's *Things Fall Apart*, and scrutinizing Echewa's Philip in *The Land's Lord*, one cannot but realize how deeply some communities have been hurt by the coming of European missionaries. Nevertheless, the natives have struggled and managed to cling to the remnants of the religious and cultural values they have had for centuries. One instance of this is reflected in the primacy of moral values such as duty. Duty and self-sacrifice are moral values which bind people together and promote the supremacy of the group over individual personal desires. In sum, these two values provide a sense of belonging, a spiritual and social balance, and they shape the individuals' comfort zones and lives within the community. Otherwise, how can we explain the fact that in real life, people who embrace Christianity so often drift back to their traditional practices?

Making the argument in support of duty and tradition, *The Land's Lord* shows that Old-Ahamba has warned Father Higler about his churchgoers: "So, I say to you, white man, these people in your church now, they are like birds that have left their nests in a tree. They may fly all day long, but they must come back to the tree." Nwala, Philip's uncle, adds later on: "You see, a man cannot run away from the Land, even if he flies like a bird. They must come down to it." This comparison of man to a flying bird is very illustrative in explaining backsliding from Christianity.

In spite of the proliferation of Christian sects, traditional religion has never really been in danger of obliteration. The reason is that many of those who adopted Western religions often tend, after a time, to drift back to traditionalism to find psychological balance. In real life, a mixture of traditional practices and advertised religions, like Christianity, Islam, and the like, is not uncommon. In *Culture, Tradition and Society in the West African Novel* (1975), Emmanuel Obiechina contends that, no matter how attractive the new ideas and institutions, there are always built-in responses which pull those exposed to the lure of change back in the direction of the old ways, either because fear of the unknown is implicit in the encounter with the new, or more probably, because the old has been found to answer the needs of people in the particular environment. Even those who remain Christians generally combine both the old and the new, by performing Christian and traditional rituals at their convenience. For instance, during seasonal or annual festivals, they can be seen practicing sacrifices to their ancestors and juju shrines. During marriage ceremonies or the naming of a newborn, they can also undergo ritualistic performances to avoid any possible mishap, thus combining both religions at their convenience. Although the majority of Muslim converts have apparently lost their "Africanity" by sheltering themselves under the umbrella of Islamic practices, the dualistic trend of sacrificing and honoring the ancestors has been part of mainstream African social life. Perhaps one should think of a model ecumenistic society where people have lived side by side without any trouble until recently, when the monetary economic drive led people into social unrest in different parts of the African Continent, and elsewhere around the world.

At the beginning of *The Land's Lord*, one notices a master-servant relationship which exists between the white priest, Father Higler, and Philip, the Igbo native who left his family to join the Christian mission. The master-servant hierarchical relationship is illustrated through the conversations between Father Higler and Philip. Father Higler is the one who speaks very often, and Philip often says nothing but "Yes Fada." This pattern of submissiveness and domination coupled with the servant's respect and obedience replicates that of the slave owner and the slave. How do we explain this complex relationship between the White priest and the Igbo Christian convert? There seems to be a closeness which goes beyond ordinary priest and congregation members.

Philip and Father Higler share some common features, for in their respective social environments, they are misfits. Father Higler, a deserter in World War II, became a priest. He shares the same moral predicament as his servant, Philip, who was chosen by his folk to be the acolyte of a farm god and who also fled to avoid being initiated in the traditional ritual. Father Higler seems to understand his servant and tries to sympathize with him, but Philip is reluctant to share his sense of failure and keeps his agonies tightly clasped to his chest. The narrator tells more about what the white priest feels for his servant in Chapter Eleven: empathy, fellow feeling and comradeship.

Father Higler now feels drawn even closer to Philip, for here in the middle of the darkest Africa was a man whose life coincided with his own, in the present, and in the future through their association as servant and master, and whose past also was a replica of his. Philip was no longer a faithful servant, but a brother. They were survivors of similar past hazards, co-expectant of similar futures; he had found his twin, his dark reflection. For, in the secret heart of the taciturn servant was trapped an echo of his own life cowardice, desertion under fire, abandonment of love. Father Higler had this to say when discussing with Philip: "'I am sorry, I just wanted to tell you that I am very much like you." Father Higler and Philip have fear as common feature and have joined Christianity as a refuge where they might find solutions to their problems and relief for their mental anxiety.

The Symbolic Value of Building the Church: The Role of the Christian Cross & the Traditional "Ofo" in *The Land's Lord*

The sacred is the foundation of the world because it fixes the limits of Man as a simple being and establishes the order of the world. Through the erection of shrines or the building of sanctuaries, let us say any holy place, the sacred is made present and communication with the gods is assured. Any site chosen for the building of a religious meeting place becomes sacred after its sacralization through religious rituals for traditionalists, or any advertised religion such as Christianity or Islam. Father Higler, who has come to advertise and to make Igbo people know the Western God, needs concrete things to materialize his presence. Thus, just like Mr. Brown, who decided to build a church and a school to attract Umuofia people in *Things Fall Apart*, for the Christian priest in *The Land's Lord*, the church will crown all his efforts and symbolize in the eyes of the world and throughout history not only Christianity, the Western religion, but civilization.

The church will be erected as a justification of Father Higler's godly evangelizing mission. Throughout the novel, through foreshadowing, the author leads us step by step, from the outset of the story to a progressive building of the church with many suggestions in different chapters. To substantiate the point, here is an example: "We're all going to get along now, and build a big parish here? And spread the word of God, huh? Very well—very well! Starting right tomorrow huh? No time to waste."

In *The Land's Lord*, the gradual building of a parish, which will be finished in an indefinite period of time, is revealing of the European agenda in not only their religious imposition but also, the long-term enculturation African people will undergo, and thereafter be acculturated without too much effort. In fact, this mention of the church is a realistic example of the concrete material things that African countries inherited from colonization.

When the Europeans left, the buildings became historical monuments and administrative offices. One should not dwell on this physical Western legacy, considering the importance of the cultural bequeathal inherited through education and the languages African countries are still using for communication with one another within and outside the continent. Keeping in mind the subject of our study, the importance of symbolism, and the essential role rituals play in the religious context, one should not overlook the similarity existing between the daily use of simple objects such as the stick, stone, water, or cross during religious ceremonies.

With respect to the role religion plays in people's lives, as the basis of each belief, there is a hierophant, a symbolic object that is supposed to possess some supernatural power to protect man. Thus, the Christian cross is known to have a magic power of protection and to play the role of intermediary between man and the supreme God. With Christianity and other monotheistic religions, there are conventional sacred items such as the cross and the holy book that are meaningful to the believer. But with traditional religions practiced in an environment such as Igboland where there is a plurality of deities, one is expected to notice different dimensions of symbolic things. Since the traditional people make their gods themselves according to the roles the latter are assigned to play, one might be tempted to think that the worshipers' faith is not as strong as that of the Christians. But the irony of the situation is in the actual religious life of those traditional people. When taking into account the situation throughout *The Land's Lord*, the jujus and the Ofo play a symbolic role of protection similar to that of the Christian cross and the like.

Going back to some different aspects traced to the Western concept of faithful and faithless people mentioned earlier in this essay, and taking into account Christian behaviors as regards traditionalism and other religions, the concept of faithful and faithless people is not verified. Therefore, negative attitudes and behaviors based on religious affiliation should be classified mostly in the stereotypical labeling and boxing of others in an exclusionary category. This reminds us of the symbolic names given to newborn children in *The Land's Lord*. For instance, on page 121: "Onyemachi," that is, "who knows what God is thinking?" Who knows the best religion, if we may so say? So, when Father Higler asserts in *The Land's Lord* that some beliefs are superior to others and the holy cross couldn't be compared to the African/Igbo jujus, one can say that the opposite is likely verified in the context of the traditional setting at stake. The jujus and Ofo staff do play a similar role of protection for Igbo people as does the Christian cross to Christian believers. Because the present study is based on the socio-cultural impact, and the role played by the symbolic objects in traditional people's lives, one came to the conclusion that there should not be any judgment of value in regard to socio-cultural matters, and especially, religious beliefs and practices. One might only speak of difference of forms between the cross and the Ofo staff, but their symbolic role is comparable and quite similar in both traditional religion and in Christianity, Islam and Judaism. Hence, an argument of a religious relativism and an ecumenical trend in our contemporary beliefs for a future social stability would be necessary at this point.

In partial conclusion to this discussion about Father Highler, a Christian priest, and Old Ahamba, a traditional priest, one notes that although possessing major differences in their conception of God and their ritualistic practices, both priests share a fundamental universal truth, the belief in a superior being, an entity beyond humans. Echewa has made this clear in his subtle development of the philosophical concept of relativity coupled with faith, where the following lines are best illustrative of my point: "The faithful and the faithless were indiscriminately condemned to wayward suffering and haphazard death. No signs, no halves, marked the true believers. Nothing exempted them from the common lot."[45] Concrete instances of the "common lot" are natural disasters like earthquakes, tsunamis, wildfires, and mudslides that unpredictably occur in different parts of the world.

The final point made in the above lines opens a range of queries that could lead into a new book. One crucial issue is that of limitations, the inability to protect people regardless of race, ethnicity, sexuality, gender, or religious creed in the face of evil, natural disasters, and the like. If we are to undergo the same sufferings, how should we consider the differences existing between religious beliefs? Why should we feel some are superior or better than others, if nothing exempts us from the common lot as regards death? Not only do we have no absolute answers or scientific explanation to the above questions now, but here again, we have an illustration of Echewa's talent in dealing with religious syncretism and a complex issue that most African writers have failed to address for a long time, including those in the metaphysical and philosophical arena. He has used an objective perspective to present the hidden religious antagonism that has been a source of many socio-cultural and spiritual imbalances both at the individual and group levels, from the colonial era through the present. Such psychological traumas and religious conflicts are running through contemporary African and other indigenous societies, where

---

[45] *The Land's Lord* , p. 16.

individuals find themselves caught between two worlds—religious/ secular, traditional/modern, local/western, native/imported cultures— just like Philip in *The Land's Lord*. Some people drift back to tradition- alism to find answers to their daily struggle for survival, or to questions that Christianity failed to answer. Not only do we have a demystification of Christianity as one of the best religions, but we also come across a Christian priest who has gone through an incredible experience of tra- ditional Igbo "baptism." Father Higler has been initiated into a different world vision and a new perception and conception of God through his evangelic mission in Africa.

The crucial element which shows that Ahamba took the lead in reli- gious matters is the ironic re-baptism of Father Higler. He who initially came to convert Igbo people to Christianity and show them the right path seems to have been the one who got converted to the Igbo reality. After he was pulled out by fishermen, Ahamba led Father Highler by the hand to the water's edge and told him to kneel, as is often done for a Christian baptism ceremony. Then, taking him by the scruff of the neck, he immersed his head three times in the dirty foot waters of the river. The philosophy that is revealed through Old Ahamba's behavior is described by Echewa as the secret which makes us human and keeps the gods divine to us. Few men find the truth and survive it. It is a dangerous secret. The trick is to take as much truth as we can and go on living. The relevance of this statement lies in the idea that we need to believe in some supernatural power to be in harmony with ourselves, no matter the path we choose. Should we by extension say that the creation of God is a pure imaginative production of Man, because there are mysteries we try to understand in vain? Considering this tentative discussion, where would we draw the line between Christians and traditionalists?

At the end of this section, and based on the complexity surrounding religious discussions and religion as a fundamental pillar of the over- arching political trends, one cannot help but think of the symbolic similarity between Old-Ahamba, an African traditional/religious leader, and Father Higler, a European missionary, and of the news broadcasts about Pope Benedict XVI's visit to Turkey, and particularly about his joining the collective prayer in the Blue Mosque next to Istanbul's Mufti Mustafa Cagrici, the Muslim religious leader, and the Orthodox Christian leader, Patriarch Bartholomew, in Istanbul. Another significant contemporary religious marker is the Saudi king Abd'Allah's visit to Rome and his exchange of gifts with the Pope.[46] Pope John Paul II, Benedict's predecessor, made the first papal visit to a mosque during a trip to Damascus in 2001.[47]

Are these mutual travels symbols of a kind of reparation or forgiveness? Do they have a sociopolitical bearing or do they symbolize a simple ecumenical friendship that the mainstream population fails to grasp? Though the Madrid "El Mundo" called the Pope's visit to the Blue Mosque as "a scandal," according to CBC News the Pope's visit to Turkey-his first trip to a Muslim country since becoming leader of the world's 1.1 billion Roman Catholics in 2005—was hailed as an attempt to heal the divide between the Christian and Muslim worlds.[48] In any case these endeavors foster at least a semblance of understanding between different religious leaders allowing an ecumenical trend to the benefit of all, should we be tolerant and accepting of each other.

Curiously and coincidently, this reunion of the Christian and Muslim leaders has been made after the Pope's outrageous speech classifying Islam and its Prophet as fostering violence, just as Father Higler qualified Igbo traditional beliefs as being pagan, heathen. Unlike Old-Ahamba, who immersed the Christian priest in the dirty water several times as a sign of initiation, the Turkish Imam did not have a similar natural environment. The mosque represents the sacred place just like a church building or Jewish temple. Not only does Pope Benedict's visit to and prayer in the Blue Mosque in Afghanistan symbolize the

---

[46]Pope's Visit to the Blue Mosque, Retrieved 10/25/2010.

[47]Al Gezeera, Retrieved, 02/09/2011.

[48]Pope Visits Blue Mosque in Istanbul, CBC News, November 30, 2006, wwwcbc.ca/world/. . ./bartholemew.html. Retrieved 11/24/2010.

willingness to acknowledge Islam, but the imitation of the ritualistic posture, standing up facing Eastward towards Mecca could be equated to the immersion of Father Higler's head in the river by Old Ahamba.

The Christian priest Father Higler's experiential discoveries in traditional Igboland, and the Pope's initiations in the Blue Mosque, are testaments of their acknowledgment of other religious beliefs regardless of how their practices differ from Christianity. It would be very interesting to know whether King Abd'Allah attended a Christian mass. Contrary to the focus of one radio commentator, who downplayed the event and took pleasure in describing the metal in which the gifts were made, "one being in gold and the other from the Pope remaining to be verified," the symbolic value of the endeavor is what should matter in this turbulent era. The lesson one should draw from both priests' experiences is tolerance and acceptance of our differences for a better and colorful world. To borrow poet Alice Walker's image of a garden, just imagine a beautiful garden with beautiful flowers, and think about how the world would have been if we valued each other as unique and beautiful people bringing our differences and contributions to our different geographical and professional locations. If religious Ecumenism could be a way out of a chaotic and conflict-filled situation full of tension, we might want to try it and see its outcome.

Beyond the thematic discussions in the above article, one needs to look at the motivation of crusades and Christian evangelizing missions in launching "civilizing operations," or of contemporary democratization missions launched on so-called "terrorist" countries. Reference must be made to Old-Ahamba's discussion with the White missionary who stipulates that "God was everywhere." The traditional priest responds, "If God was everywhere, then, why did you come?" thus questioning the usefulness of the Christian evangelizing/civilizing mission in Africa, and by the same token elsewhere around the world. One can draw a parallel with the situation in which, despite the absence of a direct threat to the nation, we hold a belief in fighting a righteous war and hope to build a democratic country afterwards.

A few queries worth considering for further research and discussion might be helpful at this point. Is the aforementioned religious misunderstanding that led to the destruction of the protagonists, Okonkwo in Chinua Achebe's *Things Fall Apart*, Ezeulu in *Arrow of God*, and Philip in Obinkaram Echewa's *The Land's Lord*, not a reflection of cultural conflict? In other words, could we help thinking of ignorance coupled with arrogance on the part of the invader? Why would such a paradox exist in our ethical behaviors? Instead of the former blatant evangelizing missions through Christianity that often prepared the terrain for the colonizing administrative settlements and economic exploitation of colonies, aren't we experiencing a new form of evangelization, colonization, or crusade through the pervasive concepts of democratization and globalization that lead us to attack and destroy whomever we want, wherever we want and however we want? Finally, what is the future of societies whose socio-political structures and religious practices do not follow the Western world vision? As much as literature creates fiction apparently far from reality, the similarity between our real lives and fiction has a thin and blurred line. Perhaps looking at the literary elements and techniques Echewa used to render his message would help understand the author's genius. The following picturesque, cinematographic description of the German priest's puzzle in this remote African village is so vivid, and reveals his misunderstanding and loss amongst the Igbo people:

> *Libera nos, Domine!*
> He walked as if he had to get somewhere at an appointed time. His legs kicked noisily into the large folds of his soutane. And then he stopped. The mission was ahead. The village was behind. He looked in one direction and then the other, uncertain which way salvation lay. He opened his breviary as if the answer could be found there.
>
> Do me justice, Oh God, and fight my fight against a faithless people. For you, Oh God are my strength: why do you keep me so far away; why must I go about in mourning with the enemy oppressing me?

He snapped the book shut and walked forward again. God had not chosen to answer.

"All Gods are a little mad," Old Ahamba had often remarked to him, his strong teeth bearing heavily on a cola nut.

"If you have a mind to serve them properly, you should be a little drunk yourself."

Were they also a little deaf?

'Fada Nwambee' his parishioners had called him when they first saw him. 'The Orphan Priest.' He had looked like an orphan to them, underfed and ill-used. Ill-used by circumstances, Undernourished by God's grace.

He shrugged and continued walking feeling a little of the confidence of his priestly call. His voluminous soutane gave him bulk. His large flowing beard conferred substance.[49]

The irony here is to see how the Igbo villagers perceived Father Higler at his arrival and how the challenges he has to go through to attend Paul's funeral influenced his vision of the place and its people. To him, they turn into faithless people; moreover, he ceases to see them as partners but rather they become "the enemy." If Father Higler was unable to partake in the hard times his "Christian brothers" were going through, how could he possibly teach them the basics of his religion? Where are compassion, tolerance, and understanding? Should belief in a different entity transform you into an enemy?

Though Echewa's novel, *The Land's Lord*, appears more as utopian rather than a realistic depiction of what has actually happened in African history, the triumph of the traditional God over Christianity has fulfilled the writer's creative goal. The tragic death of the protagonist illustrates the psychological traumas and spiritual death of the natives who turned away from their African traditions to embrace Western ways

---

[49]Echewa, Obinkaram, 1976, *The Land's Lord* Heinemann Educational Books, pp. 1–2.

and beliefs. On the other hand, the ambivalent success and triumph of traditionalism over Christianity is also delineated through the character of Old-Ahamba, the Igbo priest. In other words, the nullification of Father Higler's evangelic mission of Christianity as the best religion is shown through the paradoxical image of Father Higler, the evangelizer, being initiated by immersion in dirty rather than clean water, as if going through a rebirth. Here the subtle irony of the situation is foreshadowed and implied as if the Christian priest's adventure in Igboland led him to the "Lord's Land" where all beliefs are equal, no religion is superior or inferior. In closing this chapter, perhaps an objective view of religious conflicts and their tight interconnectedness with the sociopolitical could lead us to think critically when dealing with religious issues. Until human beings learn to understand the foundations of our various religious practices and understand their relationship, that we all are more alike than different, we still have a long way to go.

PART FOUR

Character Depictions

The Prototypical Perfect Character Creation: Efuru

Efuru is the story of a heroine whose fate is not understandable to her neighbors. She is a beautiful and good-hearted creature who cannot marry because a river goddess Uhamiri has chosen her as her worshipper. The story begins in the pre-colonial times through the colonial era, and extends into postcolonial or modern times. Efuru is a young woman at the crossroads of her personal fulfillment. She is a woman in a transitional position who is trying to fulfill the obligations of her traditional pre-colonial society, and who does not hesitate to resort to the new Western means when necessary.

Our objective is to see how the story of the main character, Efuru, reflects the lives of other young women in Africa. Her generosity is acknowledged among her people, who are grateful, but who cannot share the tragedy of her destiny. All her love affairs fail in spite of her tremendous efforts to cope with different situations, such as paying her dowry and taking care of her first husband's household. An aspect of Efuru's characteristics that can be traced in modern women is related to work. Most young West African women are known to be industrious and to have aptitudes for trade activities. Some might say there cannot be a perfect character, but situating our judgment at Efuru's behavioral level, Nwapa has created the perfect young woman that the mainstream would wish to have, a beautiful, caring and economically independent young woman. Nevertheless, are these qualities enough, in a society which holds on to rigorous gender roles regarding production and reproduction? What limitations does the protagonist have, considering the importance of children in Igbo society, and the loss of her only child?

According to Amadiume, in the mythical ideology of Igbo people the beautiful woman was the one whose self-confidence usually made her reject numerous suitors, only to end up choosing a demon or monster in the disguise of a wealthy man. It was stressed that a woman's beauty was not only physical, but must also be seen in her mind, good character and hard work. Thus, in contrast to the bad woman was the good woman who usually was a good daughter, wife and mother. She looked after her children. She usually helped her husband financially through her own efforts. If her husband was unable to provide money for food, she was able to support the household through farming, marketing and trading. Industriousness, which is one of the main characteristics of a "good woman," was inculcated in a woman in her father's house, and was often rewarded in married life. (Amadiume, p.94)

In reference to Nwapa's Efuru, not only is she physically attractive, she also satisfies other qualities expected from a good woman—except for the temporary reproductive inability. Based on the Dibia's prognostics, Efuru was not barren; she had experienced motherhood in her first marriage with Adizua and lost the child during her husband's absence. Notice that in African society, in general, having a child is so significant that it determined a married woman's real womanhood as a child bearer and the degree of her social status. The reproductive role of a woman as bearer and perpetuator of the human species is part of the traditional gender role and social expectations. Not only does a woman have to be beautiful, attractive, and submissive in Igbo society, she should also be able to bear children. Not having a child is perceived as a debilitating and serious disability that could lead to divorce. The case is vividly rendered by Flora Nwapa's depiction of Efuru whose early marriage torments are well illustrated after her baby, Ogonim's birth.

> Is this happening to me, or someone I know?
> Is that baby mine or somebody else's?
> Is it really true that I have had a baby?
> That I am a woman after all?
> Perhaps I am dreaming.
> I shall soon wake up and discover that
> It is not real. (Nwapa, 1966, p. 31)

As a good woman, Efuru has at a certain point of her married life, fulfilled all the gender roles that her society expects from her as a woman. But this happiness felt when one achieves a kind of self-actualization does not last for Efuru. Her life is later darkened by the desertion of her husband and the death of her daughter. One of Amadiume's stated qualities of a good woman that clearly fits Efuru's situation is that of industriousness, caring for the family in the event the husband fails to do so. Efuru is the head of household of her first marriage. Amadiume points out that the roles of men and women, which are sharply defined nowadays, were not originally divided in the Igbo society, so that we notice only a slight modification in the roles of the sexes. Thus the egalitarian division of labor that was rooted in the traditional Igbo society before the introduction of the Western patriarchal concept of man as breadwinner is expressed with an exaggeration in *Efuru*. Nwapa is purposely making her heroine take over completely a supposedly male role as a breadwinner. This characterization is to illustrate the invisibility of most women's responsibilities in their homes. Clearly, this was a change in the mentality of traditional people because it undermined the position of women who were equal or sometimes even superior to men. Therefore, privation, or sacrifice, means that the woman has to shoulder a large part of the burden of providing for the family, a role that in the traditional social milieu would be performed by the man. On some occasions, the woman becomes the sole breadwinner. But Efuru's examples are far more significant in that in her first marriage, Adizua, her first husband, makes virtually no financial contributions to the household. Taking on these family responsibilities contributes unmistakably to Efuru's empowerment, financially and socially. Since the social status of people in either society is based on criteria such as wealth, responsibility and respectfulness, it is no wonder Efuru is called a "great woman." The more money she makes out of her crayfish trade, the more powerful she becomes. Consequently, her husband's manhood seems to have been taken from him in his failure to provide for the home. The society's critical attitude is illustrated through the multiple inferences Ajanupu often makes when attacking her younger sister Ossai, Efuru's mother-in-law. Ajanupu symbolically represents the keeper of traditional values based on integrity, honesty, respect, selflessness and resilience. She has not only taken over her sister's role as a mother-in-law by protecting Efuru and helping her when need be, she also plays the role of the other-mother in the absence of Efuru's mother, through nurturing. The flip side of all these positive characteristics and of the brilliant image of Ajanupu is a dark side the reader can hardly perceive. As much as we see the involvement of Ajanupu in Efuru's life, the former's personal family life is kept secret from the reader. Nwapa has done a good job creating that suspense, which holds the reader's attention as well as it keeps us wondering and guessing about the actual relationship with men, and the kind of life Ajanupu might have in her household.

Flora Nwapa's Ajanupu: Traditional or Postmodern Activist?

Reiterating some of Afigbo's ideas on Igbo cosmology, Ifi Amadiume says in her *Male Daughers, Female Husbands* that in every society, men and women are expected to behave in certain specific manners and are in turn talked of or judged according to their social status as fathers, mothers, or wives. Amadiume's work is a detailed study of the Igbo society, with concrete examples and full explanations of the cultural, political and economic structures. In the Igbo society what was stressed about men was their duty to provide for and protect their families. Unlike the men's situation, the women were stereotyped as bad or good women. Further sections will focus on the different types of women depicted in Nwapa's characterization of Efuru, the main protagonist and other secondary subjects such as Ajanupu and Ossai. The latter is Adizua's mother, Efuru's mother-in-law and Ajanupu's younger sister. Let us look at a few Igbo cultural practices, which can also be seen in other African societies. Though some male writers like Achebe have depicted male characters as social failures, at times their treatment of these characters does not reflect a similar critical social attitude compared to women's perspective.

With the exception of Achebe's (1958) portrayal in *Things Fall Apart*, and Obinkaram Echewa's depiction of Philip in *The Land's Lord*, there was no stereotyping of men who failed to achieve their duties as men.

The characterization of Okonkwo's father, Unoka, was one of the rarest depictions, which proved necessary for the unfolding of the plot. Unoka was lazy, crippled with debts, enjoyed playing his flute and drinking, and was finally known as an "Agbala" meaning emasculated, less than a man, a man lacking masculine characteristics and morally weak, and metaphorically fragile like a woman. This character creation on the part of the author provides explanations for the recurrent theme of fear which undergirds Okonkwo's life. Okonkwo grew up fearing laziness and humiliation. This obsession was the ultimate stimulus that led him to commit tabooed actions by beating his wife during the Week of Peace, killing Ikemefuna, his stepson, despite the warnings, and finally committing suicide, which to date is regarded as the most outrageous crime in Igbo life.

Another point which is worth making is the place of women in mainstream social attitudes towards women. Women's social failure was looked upon more severely by society. Therefore, the following discussion will focus on conflicting characteristics in two types of women. When dealing with Nwapa's character depictions, it is important to point out recurrent themes of duality and ambivalence existing in everything, according to the Igbo and some universal beliefs. The expression "Ajo nwanyi," or "bad woman," immediately brought to mind the picture of a woman whose behavior contrasted with that of the term "Ezigbo nwanyi," meaning "good woman." Bad women were those who failed in their wifely and maternal duties and feelings. Such a woman was bad-tempered. As Ifi Amadiume says, "her mind burned her like pepper." She was always scolding and at odds with her neighbors. She gossiped and quarreled a lot with people. In other words, a bad woman was someone who enjoyed wrong-doing and her aim was always to break up some relationships. These characteristics listed above are illustrated through Ajanupu, Ossai's sister. Some concrete examples of a bad woman's behavior are significantly highlighted in the context of Igbo beliefs. A look at the aforementioned secondary characters, Ossai and particularly Ajanupu, unveils a rather complex depiction of a character worth scrutinizing. This raises the question of whether Ajanupu was really a bad woman or something much more uncommon.

According to Romanus Egudu, in "Flora Nwapa's Ajanupu: The Legacy from Tradition to Feminism" (2000), Ajanupu is generally acknowledged by critics as a very important character. Adewale Maja-Pierce (15) describes her as "the most important character after Efuru," and as "a bitchy, unsentimental and exacting woman." Another critic, Chimalum Nwankwo (48), characterizes her as "fiery." Even Eustace Palmer (5), who in an early review of the novel finds little that is commendable, makes an exception of Ajanupu by saying that Nwapa "has created a perfect feminine character—Ajanupu—the bitchy but good natured aunt of Efuru's first husband . . . She is . . . a triumph." I personally would back Maja-Peace in characterizing Ajanupu as the second most important character after the heroine, Efuru. Had Flora Nwapa disregarded the depiction of Ajanupu, her portrayal of the traditional African woman would have been incomplete in a traditional setting where there is hardly room for hypocrisy, and where women mingle and interact with one another openly.

Egudu maintains that in revealing her "bitchy" and "fiery" characteristics, Ajanupu projects at first the image of a mean, profiteering, and nosy person in that she uses Ogea, Efuru's maid, to help her in washing up and sweeping the floor and still rebukes her as a child of no use. When Efuru fails in recovering her money from a debtor, Ajanupu goes to collect it for her. The debtor, who pleads not having money to pay, ends up giving Ajanupu the last pound that she possesses in addition to a piece of cloth to guarantee her payment of what she owes Efuru. Contrary to this situation in which she refuses to understand Nwabuzo's situation, Ajanupu refuses to pay her own debt until she quarrels with her creditor and attracts many people around. Beating children is an aspect of a bad woman. This is seen when Ajanupu sends Ogea to the stream and the child breaks the water pot on her way back home. Ogea places her hands on her head and yells, refusing to go back home because of the punishment she might receive. But Ajanupu follows her to the stream after waiting in vain. "Foolish girl, have this, and this" (*Efuru*, p. 43). She gives Ogea two strokes of the whip. Ajanupu is the symbolic keeper of the traditional women's roles. She is known to be tough and helpful at the same time. She is sometimes seen to accomplish Efuru's role in nursing the baby and seeing to the young maid Ogea's informal education:

> Somebody fetched some water for Ajanupu and she began to prepare some food. Her eldest daughter who was about fourteen was in school. The little ones were too small to be of much use. So Ajanupu did all the cooking with Ogonim on her back. She finished cooking and gave Ogonim some to eat. After eating, she fell asleep. Ogea came back when Ajanupu was pounding the fufu and hid at the back of the house. When she saw that Ogonim was asleep and Ajanupu was about to eat, she appeared.
>
> "Have you finished running you fool? Now go to the kitchen and wash up."
>
> Ogea went to the kitchen and began to wash up. Ajanupu came to the kitchen. "The mortar is not properly washed. And wash the whole length of the pestle. When you finish, sweep the floor. And be quick about it."
>
> When Ogea finished, she began to sweep the floor. "Bend down properly, you are a girl and will one day marry. Bend down and sweep like a woman." Ajanupu commanded.
>
> When she finished sweeping, she began to eat. "You don't sit like that when you are eating. Put your legs together and sit like a woman."
>
> Ogea did as she was told and continued eating. She ate some fish in the soup and Ajanupu came along again. "You eat your fish last. I wonder what Efuru has been teaching you. I must tell her to handle you better. Children eat their fish last. You will steal at this rate. Efuru will have to bring you here for a few weeks."

When Ajanupu saw Efuru in the evening she told her about
Ogea. "You are spoiling Ogea. You just leave her to do what
she likes. Remember she is a girl and she will marry one day. If
you do not bring her up well, nobody will marry her." (Nwapa,
1966, pp. 44–45)

Is Ajanupu a typical traditional Igbo woman or a transitional character that leans towards postmodernism? The dual, not to say multi-
faceted, aspects in Ajanupu's character depiction are much evident in
the punishment she administers to the young maid and in the accurate
informal education she lavishes freely on Ogea, notwithstanding her
blaming Efuru for not teaching appropriate female gender roles to her
maid. Here again, the traditional gender roles of a girl destined for marriage and homemaking are apparent in Ajanupu's words. As young girls
learn very early not only how to keep a house, but also how to take care
of a baby, by the time they are ready for marriage there is nothing left
that needs to be learned. But has Efuru trained her young maid to fulfill
the societal expectations of a young girl? The following section speaks for
itself when Efuru answers Ajanupu's question:

"She can boil yam for Ogonim. That's all she can do," Efuru
answered.
"You mean she doesn't know how to pound fufu?"
"No, she does not pound fufu, I do that myself."
"A girl of her age should know how to cook everything. You are
to blame."
"I am busy, Ajanupu. Our trade is bad. People don't pay their
debts, and so when I return from the market I go to collect
these debts and have no time for anything else."[50]

---

[50]Ibid, pp. 44–5.

As a watchdog and guardian of traditional gender roles and societal expectations of a woman, Ajanupu warns Efuru for neglecting an aspect of Ogea's education, that of a good homemaker who knows how to cook. We see the importance of providing a young girl with all the necessary tools for her future survival not only as a woman, but as a good wife. Being a maid should not limit Ogea's role to only taking care of the baby. She should be taught everything a woman should know in order to operate in that social environment.

Child abuse and battering coupled with gossiping are yet other characteristics of Ajanupu. She is the one who knows everything that is going on. For example, during Efuru's pregnancy, Ajanupu was the one who informed Efuru about her husband Adizua's affair with another woman. Ajanupu has a sort of opposite or dualistic behavioral trait. Compared to her sister Ossai, who is laid back and a fatalistic type, Ajanupu is a hot-tempered person.

> Ossai had always been a good younger sister. She was not impudent as younger sisters sometimes are. She did not have that fighting spirit which Ajanupu possessed in abundance. So when her misfortune came, instead of fighting against it, as Ajanupu would have done, she succumbed to it. She surrendered everything to fate. Ajanupu would have interfered with fate. She would have played her own tune and invited fate to dance to it. Not Ossai. When Ajanupu and her mother wanted her to do something after her husband had left her, she did nothing. She merely folded her hands and waited for her truant husband to come back to her." (*Efuru*, p. 79)

We have two totally different character depictions here. On the one hand, Ossai is a calm and passive woman who does not question her life situation. On the other hand, Ajanupu, an apparently hot-tempered and quarrelsome woman having all the attributes of a bad woman, is the opposite of her younger sister. Although Ajanupu has apparently taken over Efuru's role in training Ogea to become a good and hard-working young girl who would make a future wife, her behavior toward the child is never frowned upon or her intentions questioned. This is a concrete reflection of traditional informal education which expects every community member to get involved in children's education re-gardless of whether they are relatives or blood offspring. Hence, the African proverb which has become universal and used even in political campaigns: "It takes a village to raise a child." But there is a peculiarity in the character of Ajanupu that needs to be mentioned, apart from her apparently boisterous behavior. It is her possession of extra gifts and skills, including her sense of morality and philosophy of life in general. For example, she positions herself vis-a-vis her sister's situation and ac-cuses her of having a share of responsibility for Adizua's behavior toward his wife, Efuru. Putting aside her bitchy behavior, Ajanupu has some commendable gifts and qualities. She tells the truth and on many occa-sions she is called upon to assist in childbirth. For instance, when Efuru gives birth to Ogonim, Ajanupu assists in the delivery. She is called once again when Efuru gets sick. Despite her hot temper, Ajanupu is a multidimensional character, playing the role of midwife and medi-cine-woman at the same time. Nevertheless, she resorts to the modern doctor when necessary, and knows when she has reached her limits. She takes Efuru to the hospital when she is sick. She is even seen to possess the power of fortune-telling because many things that she predicts end up happening in the future. For example, she predicted that Efuru will leave Adizua, and it happens.

Another particular character trait of Ajanupu's that should not be overlooked is her virtue. She is always there as a watchdog to call on her younger sister, Ossai, and remind her of her responsibilities. Ossai is not dynamic enough to struggle for her own life and thus, not able to teach her son how to be a man. Ajanupu is the character who reports the vil-lage people's surprise and negative attitudes toward Efuru and Adizua's union. For example, in the following segment, she reproaches her sister's passive attitude:

Didn't my mother and I tell you to leave that wretched husband of yours? . . . You remained in your husband's house and put yourself out from the world. You wanted to be called a good wife, good wife when you were eating sand, and put yourself out from the world. You wanted to be called a good wife, good wife when you were eating nails. That was the kind of goodness that appealed to you. How could you be suffering for a person who did not appreciate your suffering, the person who despised you? It was not virtue it was plain stupidity. You merely wanted to suffer for the fun of it, as if there was any virtue in suffering for a worthless man. (Nwapa, 1966, pp. 79–80)

Here, the narrator is using the character of Ajanupu to speak her mind and raise questions regarding humane and equal gender relationships. In the depiction of Ossai, the reader could hear the writer's Voice. Through both sisters' opposite attitudes towards their life conditions, we have an example of women's complete submissiveness and obedience to the customs as well as to their husbands. On the one hand, being in Ossai's position is not far from being enslaved to the tyranny of a slave-owner. The desire to be called a good wife leads some women to a total denial of themselves as human beings with sensitivities, and their loyalty to their husbands is so blind that it costs them a lot of suffering. The author is probably against a subordinate relationship and uses Ajanupu to refute this alienating situation of her sister's and move to Adizua's particular case as a good-for-nothing.

Now, your son, instead of settling down with Efuru and working hard to rebuild the family, which your husband left in a mess, did exactly what his father did. This time your son ran away with a woman who had left her husband. . . . You are the cause of your child's bad ways.
You never scolded him because he was an only child.
You failed to make him responsible.

You failed to make him stand on his own.
So that he leans on these rich women not
Because he loves them, but because they
Are rich (*Efuru*, p. 80).

She goes on further to say:

But I tell you, there is a limit to human endurance. She is not
meant to suffer, she will leave your son if nothing is done and
done quickly. You can't even see it. You have eyes but don't see.
I tell you, she will leave you. This is where it has been written.
(Nwapa, 1966, p. 81)

As she says this, she draws a line on the mud wall. This act shows the
expression of unchallenged truth.

Acknowledging her gift as a midwife, Ajanupu does not hesitate to
resort to the modern doctor when necessary. For example, during Efuru's sickness, she takes her to the hospital to be treated by the Western
medical methods. The significance of this detail is symbolically illustrative of the changing habits in traditional people's lives. This change can
partly be interpreted by the dual nature of Ajanupu's depiction as a step-
ping-stone for the continuity of Igbo people's lives. Her ideas reflect an
ambivalent personality. Being Ossai's sister she finds herself in a critical
situation caught in between her personal opinion about Efuru and her
nephew Adizua's unusual marriage, and the villagers' comments. How
long can she hold her anger and patience? She finally bursts out one day:

Let me tell you the truth for it is when you are angry that you say
the truth. I was one of those people who wondered what Efuru
saw in that son of yours. I did not say anything then. I was up in
arms against those who criticized the marriage because Adizua
was my sister's son and not because he was a good match for
Efuru. (Nwapa, 1966, p. 80)

Other aspects noticed in Ajanupu's character reflect her self-reliance and dignity, especially when talking to her younger sister, Ossai. Her outspokenness and self-reliance coupled with self-sufficiency are remarkable throughout the novel, and the use of imagery and proverbs in her verbal expression is also a testament of her rhetorical abilities. Through Ajanupu's portrayal, the writer expresses her voice, a womanist cry for justice and a call for women to stand up for themselves, rather than putting themselves in a victimized position, which does nothing but perpetuate men's domination at the same time that it belittles and deprives women of their basic rights as full human beings. The ultimate instance, which testifies to the call for other voiceless women's consciousness-raising and self-determination, is Ajanupu's statement that "there is no problem in this world that cannot be solved." This last point reveals Ajanupu's positivist view of the world as an evolving entity which is subject to change and the human intellectual ability to adapt to the different environmental influences within time and space. Based on the aforementioned, there is every reason to be optimistic about daily life challenges or struggle. Ajanupu transcends the norm in all areas and stands in juxtaposition to her sister. She is the type of woman who would not wait resignedly when her man is gone, and who would return the blow when struck by a man. This is proved when Efuru's second husband Gilbert slaps her during Efuru's sickness and falsely accuses her of adultery. Ajanupu's role is similar to that of a mentor, or a protector, of Efuru in this particular case. She would not hesitate in protecting other women in a male dominant situation who face domestic violence or any kind of abuse. Her forced intrusion into Efuru's marital life exemplifies this, as she confronts Eneberi (Gilbert) with the likelihood of his mother's interfering with his marriage with Efuru and warns him in the following manner:

But Eneberi, have you told your mother about Efuru? You know that I do not look at people when I talk to them, Eneberi, if I don't say it to you, I won't say it to anybody. Your mother is difficult to please. She is going to give Efuru trouble. I am sorry to say it, but it is true. You are going to help Efuru in seeing that your mother does not interfere too much in your affairs since you and your mother are going to live in the same compound. . . . Efuru, I know you can live with the devil himself. You are going to follow your mother-in-law with sense. With sense, I say. You are not a child, so I trust you will be in control of everything. When your mother-in-law talks harshly to you, do not answer back. (Nwapa, p. 134)

PART FIVE

African Women's Voice: Critical & Comparative Perspectives

Flora Nwapa: A Woman Writer in a Male-Dominated Literary World

In trying to compare the main characters' plights and relate them to each other, I would like to show how two male writers, writing more or less in the same era, portray quite opposite representations of African womanhood. First published in England in 1958, *Things Fall Apart* is Chinua Achebe's first and most famous novel. It is considered a classic of modern African writing. It deals with the predicament of a "strong" man whose life is dominated by fear and anger. This novel is a social document dramatizing traditional Igbo life in its early encounters with colonialism and Christianity at the turn of the nineteenth century. It was written to show "the traumatic effects of our first confrontation with Europe." But the novel also lays emphasis on the old African way of life by pointing out how Okonkwo, the respected warrior of Umuofia, a self-made man, is prevented by his own blind pride and selfishness from acquiring the honorific traditional "four titles." In that novel we are taken to a time when superstitions and human determination were prominent. In the exhortation of the past values, Chinua Achebe has only shown the supremacy of the male voice through his characters such as Okonkwo. In other words, the author presents the past both through the experience of male characters and also with a male perspective. We notice the striking absence or invisibility of women in the power structure despite the predominant place that the priestess of Agbala, Chielo, occupies in the socio-religious arena.

In *Things Fall Apart*, however, we learn almost everything about the diverse ways of living in the traditional Igbo society where superstitions are the main guides for people's lives. In *Efuru*, similarly, we are taken to an age of forthrightness, tremendous voluntary actions and the acceptance of fate. The existence of the myth of the Lady of the Lake in the Igbo tradition endows the abundant inspiration of Efuru's story with deep religious symbolism. "The Lady of the Lake" is a traditional goddess who is believed to reside in the lake, river or sea, depending on the Igbo village.

In Achebe's first novel, we do not have a clear-cut idea of the roles played by the women. The male-biased attitude is reflected in the dialogue between Uchendu, one of the older men in the society, and his nephew, where the position of the woman is ambiguous. On the one hand, she is presented as subordinate to the men in her society, and on the other hand her society idealizes her as a figure of supreme motherhood. This ambiguity is illustrated through the following from chapter fourteen: "we all know that a man is the head of the family and his wives do his bidding. A child belongs to its father and his family and not to his mother and her family. A man belongs to his fatherland and not to his motherland. And yet we say: 'Nneka-mother is supreme', why is that?" (*TFA*, p. 135) The old man answered his own question by explaining that the mother's supremacy comes from the fact that she plays the role of protector. She is the one who comforts the child in trouble, and her homeland, not the father's, is the traditional refuge for any family member who encounters serious problems in adulthood.

Referring to the above quote, and analyzing Uchendu's question and answer, we can say that Achebe has presented a twofold situation, an idealized image of womanhood and the subordinate role of the woman in Igbo society. Moreover, he has presented a mythic concept of supreme motherhood and the limited status of the woman who is required to do her husband's bidding in her daily life. This aspect joins to some extent Amadiume's description of general beliefs about women in Igbo societies and the stereotyping of a bad or good woman. The bad woman is seen as the one who does not submit to her husband or does not do his bidding. Despite the deference for women as a source of protection, the form of descent and family inheritance are far from being matrilineal, referring to the quotes in Achebe.

To further our analysis, we understand that it is a clear illustration of a male conception of things and a patriarchal world. Since Achebe himself is a man, this is not surprising. After being educated in the Western school and inheriting unconsciously from Western concepts of patriarchy and the domesticity of women, Achebe has often given small roles to women in his novels. Amadiume poited out that male bias is reflected in the use of some terms rather than the appropriate traditional ones. In her book, *Male Daughters, Female Husbands*, she noted change in the gender of the Goddess Idemili into the "God of Water," a male deity. Though this use might be an unconscious language use a similar tendency is not only noticed in Achebe's novels but also in part of the work of another Igbo male writer, Obinkaram Echewa's *The Land's Lord*. One should point out that all deities do not play the same roles in different places. There are national, regional, village, and even clan gods in Igbo religious beliefs. The only female character in the entire novel, "Ogushi," is depicted as alienated and insane. When Ogushi is discussed, we learn she has committed a tabooed act with Philip, her stepfather.

Nowhere in these novels do we have female characters expressing their thoughts about a problem, or playing honorable and respected roles. In other words, women are not portrayed in serious issues, which require their intellectual expression. Everything seems to be done in such a way that their voices are silenced. Were male writers much more interested in other salient concerns at that time, or were women purposely neglected?

Flora Nwapa seems to have understood the importance of women's participation in a male-dominated literary arena. This understanding is expressed through her characters' choices, and through the women's perspectives covered in her novels, *Efuru* and *Idu*. In contrast to the male-centered works previously discussed, Nwapa depicts complex female characters whose roles challenge the social constructs of their time. In her novel *Efuru*, the heroine Efuru is the opposite of what patriarchal society expects from a woman in her youth. According to her family status, she is supposed to find a man who can present her with a dowry, and officially ask her for marriage. Further, she is expected to marry into a "known family," meaning a respectable family lineage in her community. In small communities where everybody knows each other, the social background is crucial, as the partner you are choosing needs approval from both your family and your partner's to guarantee solid and successful marriages and family relationships. But Efuru will not follow the steps of her elders; she chooses her own way.

The gender bias noticeable in Achebe's *Things Fall Apart* and Echewa's *The Land's Lord* is not apparent in the work of another Igbo male writer, Elechi Amadi's novel *The Concubine*, published the same year as *Efuru*, in 1966. These two novels deal with the same traditional setting and virtually with the same kind of heroine except that Amadi's Ihuoma has children. Both *Efuru* and *The Concubine* have heroes who are characterized as semi-goddesses, for they are larger-than-life figures. Efuru and Ihuoma seem to be the incarnation of the perfect feminine depiction. Yet in both female characters, happiness as is perceived by human beings is not for them. Ihuoma is the wife of Emenike, a good-hearted tribesman. Very respected in her society, Ihuoma is courted by many men. Among them is Madume, who is deeply disappointed when he cannot marry her. At last, he forces a fight with Ihuoma's husband Emenike, who ends up dying from his injuries. Madume is described as "big-eyed" for his behavior that metaphorically reflects his greed. Based on the African superstitious beliefs, which find an explanation for any occurrence in human life in relationship with the supernatural, the interference of the gods in the re-establishment of the cosmic order leads Madume to commit suicide (the most awful act of abomination in the African way of life) after being blinded by a spitting cobra. Madume's body, like Okonkwo's in *Things Fall Apart*, is cast away in the forest as an apparently cursed thing. After Emenike's death, no one is able to seduce Ihuoma except the eligible bachelor of Omokachi, Ekweme. With Ekweme near her, she experiences an inner peace and security that has eluded her for a long time. She encourages Ekweme to stroll with her on many occasions through the village and does much to dispel his feelings of shame and humiliation over past events. He is amazed at her boldness. The comparative characterization of Ihuoma as similar to Efuru is illustrated through their unusual personalities.

Nandakumar emphasized this in her study, "Another Image of African Womanhood": "Here was an Ihuoma he had never known, a new Ihuoma-confident, self-respecting yet approachable, sweet but sensible. Ekweme's respect for her grew daily until he came near to worshipping her."[51] Ihuoma's boldness was unusual in the traditional society; walking around with a man in the street was ordinarily offensive to elderly villagers. Yet Ihuoma does it without criticism. This detail symbolizes the progressive change in young people's behavior, which now has a Western characteristic. In *The Concubine*, Amadi has depicted a character whose fate prevents her from marrying despite her personal qualities as a woman, just like the character of Efuru that Nwapa describes in her novel. Amadi deserves some credit for trying this portrayal discussing women's issues. However, his representation is to some extent typical of mainstream African writings of the immediate post-independence era. Besides the victimization aspect, which draws Amadi's heroine close to Nwapa's Efuru, the female character that Amadi portrays is a woman of bad luck to men. The title *The Concubine* is significantly edifying for its bad connotation.

Put in the context of African women writers, Nwapa's *Efuru* paved the way for a serious study of African women's different experiences by dealing with the traditional rural woman who is trying to attain self-actualization in a village. Her second novel, *Idu*, which again takes its heroine's name for a title, is to some extent a development of the first protagonist, Efuru's, characterization. "What we are all praying for, is children. What else do we want if we have children?" These two sentences from *Idu* contain the basic theme of children being the source of happiness for a woman. Unlike Efuru's story set in a totally traditional area, Idu's story takes place in a small town where the life of the individual is more or less woven into that of the community as a whole. Many themes such as barrenness, resourcefulness and trade are carried

---

[51]Nandakumar, Prema," Another Image of African Womanhood" in *African Quarterly*, An Appreciation of Elechi Amadi's *The Concubine*.

on in the second novel. For a long time, it appears as though Idu is unable to reproduce, and her husband Adiewere even takes a second wife. Finally, Idu gives birth to a boy, Ijoma, but it is not until four years later that Idu becomes pregnant for the second time. Before the second child is born, however, Adiewere dies. Idu refuses to weep, as required in the custom:

> Idu laughed a dry laugh. "Mother, I will not weep. That is not what we agreed. Adiewere and I planned things together.
>
> We did not plan that. We did not plan that he would leave me today and go to the land of the dead. Who will I live with?
>
> Who will be my husband, the father of my only son? Who will talk to me at night? What are you telling me? Asking me to weep? Mother, thank you for your advice, I will not weep. I am going with my husband. Both of us will go there, to the land of the dead. So, Adiewere, my husband, wait for me after you have crossed the stream. I am coming to meet you there and we shall continue our lives there.[52]

Like Ramatoulaye, in the Senegalese Francophone writer Mariama Ba's *So Long A Letter*, Idu transcends all traditional conventions by refusing to marry her husband's brother, preferring to follow her husband into the next world. Here, Idu's reaction in refusing to marry her brother-in-law is similar to Ramatoulaye's refusal to marry Modou's brother after the former passed away. At the brink of lunacy through her laughter, we realize the amazement Idu displays at the death of her beloved husband. The ultimate end of her life is ineluctable. Idu's death reflects that unlike the general primacy of children over anything else, children are not the only things she wants in life. She needs love, and someone who shares her ideas, not only children and wealth, to be happy.

---

[52]Nwapa , Flora, 1970, *Idu*, Heinemann Educational Books, p. 210.

Comparative Approach: Nwapa & Other West African Women Writers

This section will explore the ways in which Flora Nwapa's work is more or less related to that of Buchi Emecheta, another Igbo female writer who began to write in the 1970s, and was published a decade after Nwapa. Younger than her predecessor, Buchi Emecheta has thoroughly dealt with the predicaments of African women in general, and principally, the different genderized social constructs that the post-colonial era brought about in Nigeria. Emecheta's *Second Class Citizen*, published in 1974, is a genuine depiction of an African woman at the crossroads of civilizations. The main character is depicted as torn between the traditional African culture and the modern European ways of living.

Second Class Citizen is the writer's fictionalized autobiography. It tells the story of Adah, a young Nigerian whose dream of Britain is disillusioned by her husband's patriarchal and sexist attitudes. The story starts in Nigeria with Adah's struggle to acquire education in her hometown. When she follows her student husband to Britain, she is struck by the frustrating and humiliating treatment that black immigrants undergo there and discovers that London is not the "Kingdom of Heaven" she was brought up to believe. Unlike Flora Nwapa's fictive character creation in *Efuru*, Buchi Emecheta's Adah in *Second Class Citizen* is a real-life character creation. The educated African woman's portrayal in a subordinated and helpless situation is recurrent in Emecheta's writings. An extreme illustration of it is remarkable in *The Joys of Motherhood* in the following: "God, when will you create a woman who will be fulfilled in herself, a full human being, not anybody's appendage?" This cry is a kind of utterance bemoaning the fate of all humankind, especially some women's aspirations for liberation from a patriarchal domination and objectification. In novels such as *Second Class Citizen* and *The Joys of Motherhood*, she expresses some common predicaments of women, such as being always overshadowed by men, as well as the societal tendency to confine women in general, and particularly African women, to their traditional roles of wives and mothers.

According to Eustace Palmer (1968) in *"The Feminine Point of View: A Study of Buchi Emecheta's The Joys of Motherhood"*, the African novel has until recently been remarkable for the absence of what might be called the feminine point of view. This has been partly due to the scarcity of female African novelists. Those few voices, like Flora Nwapa, who attempted to present portraits of African womanhood from a female point of view, were, to say the least, muted. However, today Palmer's argument can easily be rendered obsolete with the increasing number of African women writers of the younger generation. A concrete example is reflected in the large number of South African women writers from the official end of the Apartheid regime and the democratic election in the year 2000. Today the trend is shifting toward a relatively important representation of the female voice in the African literary canon. In the twenty-first century, there has been an increasingly large number of women of African origin writing mostly in Southern Africa and the African Diaspora.

Palmer pursued that before the rise of the aforementioned pioneering women writers such as Ama Ata Aidoo, Flora Nwapa, and others, the representation of women in the African novel has been virtually entirely left to male voices. Women were muted in different ways. On the one hand, the small number of women writers' voices could not be heard because the few women critics, like Lilyan Kesteloot, Molly Mahood and later Omolara Ogundipe-Leslie, with some reservation, had the same attitude as men. They, in their critiques, turned a blind eye to women in African literature. The problem is that in most male novelists' work, interest in African womanhood took a secondary place as compared to other socio-political concerns in the post-independence period. Male novelists such as Achebe and Amadi, who portrayed African women largely in the traditional milieu, generally communicated a picture of a male-dominated and male-oriented society with a Eurocentric view of women's roles. Achebe and Kenyan writer Ngugi wa'Thiongo (James) have portrayed women who complacently continue to fulfill the traditional roles expected of them by their society, and to accept the superiority of the men. Even Buchi Emecheta presents a traditional society in which the roles of men and women are very sharply defined in *The Joys of Motherhood*: "You are to give her children and food, she is to cook and bear the children and look after you and them . . . A woman may be ugly and grow old, but a man is never ugly and never old. He matures with age and is dignified" (Emecheta, p. 22). Here, we see the universal division of traditional gender roles, and the idea of ugliness, including decay, associated with women and not with men. Why would men grow and mature rather than becoming perishable just like women? This is given evidence in some instances in Achebe's *Things Fall Apart*, where we clearly have a male-dominated society. But does the writer really favor a total subjugation of women to the advantage of patriarchy, or does he decry the blind egocentricity of some men which leads to the virtual invisibility of women? When we refer to many African males' works, we notice that women come and go with their traditional roles—homemaking, preparing food, going to the market with baskets, fetching water or kola, being scolded or even beaten—before they disappear behind the huts of their compound (Palmer, 1983, pp. 38–55).

The argument is that, whereas Achebe and other Nigerian writers have projected many facets of the African male, Flora Nwapa, Elechi Amadi and Ama Ata Aidoo have elevated African womanhood to a pedestal. Thus, Efuru and Ihuoma emerge as hardworking, openhearted women who are capable of infinite love as well as great self-sacrifice. The combined attributes do nothing but elevate the protagonists to a higher level or an idealized and perfect world. Some questions come to mind: Is there some relationship between Flora Nwapa and other women writers in the sub-region? To what extent does her writing contribute to African women's writings as an angular stone, symbol of the African woman's voice? After trying a comparative approach between Nwapa's work and that of some Igbo writers from the same ethnic background, male and female, let us see if there are any extensions to make in regard to other women writers in other parts of West Africa. After considering Buchi Emecheta as another Nigerian woman writer, let us move to a different place, Ghana.

The post-independence era of the 1960s, as mentioned earlier, was marked by lack of women writers. Apart from Bessie Head in South

Africa, the first ones to appear were Ama Ata Aidoo (1965) in Ghana and Flora Nwapa (1966) in Nigeria. Though the writers came from different countries in West Africa, they apparently have both created a new type of heroine who transcends the traditional female portrayal that men used to paint. With new ideas, the aforementioned heroine challenges the constricting roles which have been traditionally reserved for women, and seeks something more than marriage and children in the quest for fulfillment. She has a "voice" characterized by a sort of self-awareness and self-worth, as opposed to operating behind the scenes or being overshadowed by male dominance. There seems to have been a sort of dialogue between the two writers. Flora Nwapa's *Efuru* and Ama Ata Aidoo's *Anowa* present heroines who reject the accepted norms and try an experience by themselves with something new. They are part of a new breed of women. Marriage being the focal center in a woman's traditional role, it is through their conception and arrangement of their own marriages that Efuru and Anowa declare their intention to rebel against the old tradition. Unlike Ihuoma in *The Concubine*, who married a respectable man, Nwapa's Efuru blatantly overturns the societal rules right from the beginning of the novel by ignoring the usual procedures for an Igbo traditional marriage. She does this by simply packing her things and going to live with the man she chooses. This act is a kind of blow to his family and to the conservative social milieu:

> They saw each other fairly often and after a fortnight's courting she agreed to marry him. But the man had no money for the dowry. He had just a few pounds for the farm and could not part with that. When the woman saw that he was unable to pay anything, she told him not to bother about the dowry. They were going to proclaim themselves married and that was that— Efuru was her name. She was a remarkable woman. It was not only, that she came from a distinguished family, and she was distinguished herself. Her husband was not known and people wondered why she married him. (*Efuru*, pp. 12–13)

Efuru's next step is to reject the occupation of farming, regarded exclusively as a feminine preserve. Not only does the heroine break the traditional rule of marriage by packing her clothes and joining her lover without dowry and ceremony, she also refuses to perform the traditional women's roles fully. Efuru's action reflects her not behaving according to the pre-established social rules that required women to work side by side with men on the farm including performing the domestic duties. Efuru's attitude is explained in relation to her husband and society in Amadiume's *Male Daughters, Female Husbands.* In the commentaries of other people we learn that "she refused to go to the farm. Instead of farming, she is trading. She said she was not cut out for farm work. And I don't blame her. She is so beautiful. You would think that the Woman of the Lake is her mother. Her mother died five years ago, she too was a very beautiful woman." In *Efuru,* the eponymous Efuru not only chooses to make big money by trading but she sometimes directs the life of her husband. "If you like" she said to her husband, "go to the farm. I am not cut out for farm work. I am going to trade." Here we have a self-acknowledgement that reveals the strong personality of Efuru as a deviant and unusual character. She is capable of making her own decisions regardless of the social constructs and pressures that had already designed for her a life as a farmer. Although trade might be considered to some extent as an acceptable role for women, not all women could choose not to go to the farm and to devote themselves to the market only, especially early in their marriages.

When Adizua has failed at farm work, which is shameful in most Igbo communities, he comes complaining to his wife. Efuru treats him almost like a child. "In that case, I would like you to leave. But you have to wait until the harvest and after that you can come to town. Both of us can trade together" she advised him. Efuru is not showing dominance over her husband; instead, she takes care of him and expresses her great affection for him. She gives Adizua money to trade together in crayfish. "They were the first to discover the trade that year. The place where they bought the crayfish was three days' journey on the Great River . . . Four trips gave Efuru and her husband a huge profit."

The whole relationship between Efuru and her husband is a device
the author uses to create an atmosphere of crisis. Considering the post-
colonial period when patriarchy overshadowed and totally subdued
women through the expropriation of their political and economic power,
the depiction of such a character denotes courage. The fact that Efuru
was the decision-maker at the beginning of her marriage was unusual.
She decided policies between herself and Adizua. When she refused to
work in the farm she did not suggest another alternative. She also organized the trade, and when one line of strategy failed, she proposed another. This aspect shows that Efuru was ahead of her community women
in terms of intellectual capacity and business aptitude. "We won't go
again," she told her husband. "Yes, we won't go again. But what are we
going to do?" "We are going to look for another trade. These women
spoil trade so easily. When they see you making profit in one trade, they
leave the trade they know . . . and join yours. And, of course in no time
it is no longer profitable. So, we shall look for another thing to do." Perhaps an explanation for Efuru's depiction as a powerful young woman
who apparently knows what she wants and where her interests are would
be helpful at this point. The writer's own immediate culture and regional
traditions might have impacted the choice of the heroine as Flora Nwapa
comes from a place where women are known to take on masculine roles.

It was well known that Adizua was not good at trading. It is Efuru
who is the brain behind the business, and her husband knows this as
well. Efuru is the one who manages the money and takes care of the
expenses. For a while, all is well for Efuru and Adizua, but gradually,
without her knowing what was happening, power and control slipped
out of Efuru's hands. Adizua deserted Efuru without warning. If we try
to explain this, what has happened is that in a society as male-dominated
as in Africa, even the weakest man, just by virtue of being a man, can
claim the same traditional submission from his wife. Since there is no
hint in Nwapa's novel that explains Adizua's desertion, we might assume
that he got tired of living under the supremacy of Efuru even though
she was good to him. Another interpretation is that Adizua might be

ashamed of being taken care of by his wife. The ultimate superstitious explanation might be found in the supernatural powers of the "Lady of the Lake," who instead of killing Efuru's husband as in Ihuoma's case, might have directed him to another woman. One might ask what drives men away from good women. Don't we have parallel cases to that of Efuru and Adizua close to us? In the same manner as Efuru, Anowa, in Ama Ata Aidoo's *Anowa*, challenges her parents' authority in her choice of a marriage partner. The similarity between these two heroines is remarkable. The parallel development of their marriages and lives is of equal interest. As Juliet Okonkwo put it so well:

> Both Efuru and Anowa are good, generous, lovable, hard-working women. Their good will towards their husbands knows no bound. They are ready to sacrifice everything they have for the comfort and prosperity of their husbands, provided they are allowed the liberty of self-expression and initiative. In one thing, however, they stand at cross-purposes with their husbands. Anowa's mother puts it succinctly thus: "A good woman does not have a brain or a mouth."[53]

Looking at the last part of the quote related to the good woman not having a brain or mouth, one is tempted to think of women simply as objects. Since the difference between things and human beings is intelligence, as opined by Anowa's mother, a woman should not be vocal in expressing her ideas. If these words came from a man there would be a different interpretation. But the reality is that the relevance of this resigned position is accepted, maintained and perpetuated by women themselves. As Juliet Onkonkwo noted, the liberty of self-expression and initiative that Anowa and Efuru are longing for is hampered by negative beliefs that a woman's place is subordinate to a man's. While Efuru's

---

[53]Okonkwo Juliet, 1975, "The Talented Women in African Literature" *Africa Quarterly15*, Nos. 1–2, p. 33.

beauty is in everybody's mouth, Anowa is referred to as "a dainty little pot well baked and polished to set in a noble man's corner." Efuru and Anowa both have, and insist on exercising, what men hate the most: too much zeal, and authority. They reject the clearly defined roles of men and women in a patriarchal African society as portrayed in Achebe's *Things Fall Apart*, and attempt to take over men's roles, in contrast to societal expectations of male and female roles. Usually this type of character who does not follow the norm in a traditional environment is considered to some extent unfit for the harmony of the group. As Juliet Okonkwo put it, "Not only do both women Efuru and Anowa fail, they are also destroyed in the process. Moreover, they reject the clearly defined roles of men and women in an African society."

According to the writer, they (female characters) attempt to substitute the humanization of men and women. Regarding the life experiences of both Nwapa's Efuru and Aidoo's Anowa, the author's argument might refer to their frustration as wives but not as full human beings. Could we really maintain that Efuru has failed? Of course, she has failed to satisfy her society's expectations as a wife, a mother, and a farmer. Nonetheless, she has maintained her independence and financial power to accomplish social work through charity or philanthropy. Does the writer want to suggest that in a largely traditional African setting, an intelligent and ambitious woman is doomed to failure in marriage? Maybe, considering the importance of collective action and the group supremacy in traditional indigenous societies, non-conformist characters have a hard time fitting in. One would support the critic's opinion though some reference to literary works written about heroes or heroines who challenge conventional roles shows that such marginal characters are often destroyed at the end of the plot. They have to die, be killed, commit suicide, or become lunatic because it is inconceivable for authors to let such characters lead happy and successful lives. Not until the mid 1960s do we have a different literary genre in which rebellious characters are left to live at the end of the plot. However, Nwapa's heroine, Efuru, whose story is set in the pre-colonial era, is left to lead a spiritual life of tranquility contrary to the conventional destruction she might have undergone in other situations.[54] One would argue that not having a successful marriage does not necessarily equate to failing and being destroyed in the process. The peaceful position in which Efuru is lying at the end of the novel illustrates how she has accepted and taken her life in her own hands without blaming it on someone or herself. After her disappointing marriage, she is back in her father's house and proceeds with her philanthropy in the community, including being now dedicated to the "Lady of the Lake" as a worshipper.

Since there are women who choose, despite society's criticism, to live their lives outside marital spheres, not having a happy or successful marriage does not necessarily equal a life of frustration for all women. The example of Efuru's situation is significantly illustrative for the reader and society to learn how to accept exceptional or nonconformist characters, prototypes of the rebel. The tranquility she has at the end of the plot reflects the peace of mind she has after her failed marriage experiences. Nwapa's portrayal of her heroine, Efuru, shows the opposite of frustration or failure. On the contrary, the delineation of a character as behaviorally perfect as Efuru can only lead one to perceive her sacredness and closeness to the realm of the gods. Her identification with Uhamiri's happiness, and apparent physical and mental equilibrium, illustrate a logical ending to the novel. The novel, which starts with Efuru's marriage, ends with a poetic interrogation about her future as a worshiper of the Sea goddess or the "Lady of the Lake." In the present day, Efuru could have led a peaceful life as a single woman or chosen a friend with whom to share common interests, regardless of gender.

Efuru slept soundly that night. She dreamed of the woman of the lake, her beauty, her long hair and her riches. She has lived for ages at the bottom of the lake. She was as old as the lake

---

[54]Ibid, Okonkwo, Juliet, 1975, I. "The Talented Women in African Literature" *Africa Quarterly*, 15, Nos. 1–2 (April–Sept) pp. 36–47.

itself. She was happy. She was wealthy. She was beautiful. She
gave women beauty but she had no child. She had never experienced the joy of motherhood. Why did the women worship her?
(Nwapa, 1966, p. 221)

The concept of duality is a recurrent theme in the treatment of Nwapa's characters, and the messages of her writing. The living world is intri-
cately intertwined with the spiritual, and subsequently with the gods. A
comment upon the above passage seems necessary. Looking at the idea
of motherhood, and the question mark that the narrator put at the end,
we are led to uncover a paradoxical situation in the people's behavior and
the uncertainty of Flora Nwapa's opinion about motherhood. To interpret the traditional Igbo people's conception of a "woman," motherhood
is the characteristic of a "real" woman. The ambivalent and paradoxical
question would be, why do people worship a goddess who had never
experienced the "joy" of motherhood, if there is joy only in the act of
reproducing and caring for a child? Through trading and marketing,
Efuru starts accumulating wealth, which increases as she associates with
and worships Uhamiri. Since Igbo people have a lot of deities, Uhamiri
is a minor goddess in relation to Idemili, described as the "central goddess." Still, there is a similarity in the influences either goddess has on
her worshipers. The village *dibia*, Agora, calls Efuru "a great woman,"
chosen as she is to be a worshiper of Uhamiri.[55]

It is a great honor. She is going to protect you and shower
riches on you. But you must keep her laws. Look around
this town, nearby all the stoic buildings you find are built by
women who one time or another, have been worshipers of
Uhamiri . . . Uhamiri is a great woman. If you are to worship

---

[55]Uhamiri is the Sea Goddess who is often referred to as Idemili in certain areas of
Igboland and other parts of Africa as Mammy Water or better a mermaid in the Western
culture as mythology and visual aids present to the public.

her, you must keep her taboos . . . Above all you will keep
yourself holy.[56]

Efuru has achieved full material success and is highly ranked in her
society, but her financial wealth, seen from the villagers' viewpoint, is
not sufficient to provide her with happiness in her earthly social milieu.
The importance of children as related to the married woman's value is
reflected in the novel. Omirima, the gossip, puts it clearly when talking
to Amede, Efuru's second mother-in-law: "your daughter-in-law is good
but she is childless." In Igbo society it was a curse not to have children,
so Efuru's people do not just take it as one of the numerous incidents of
life. It is regarded as a failure because she is unable to leave behind her
any progeny; she is not able to accomplish her main role as a woman.
Dualities run throughout Nwapa's novel where opposed issues are displayed: good and bad, motherhood and barrenness, male and female,
human and god, earthly and spiritual. Though there seems to be a distinction between these oppositional situations, the lesson we learn from
both Amadiume and Nwapa is that ambivalence exists between the two
oppositional forces.

On considering Amadiume's argument about wealth for women and
title-taking in relation to first daughters, barren women, rich widows,
wives of rich men and successful wives, Efuru could be called a female
husband and deserve the honorific title of "Ekwe" woman. Though Efuru
has not taken a title in Nwapa's novel, the fact that she is better able to
take over a flexible gender role, in other words to perform the male functions in a household, than are most women is clearly significant. The
role she plays in her social environment displaces her two husbands and
places her on a pedestal as she takes over the expected male role as bread-
winner, instead of being content solely with homemaking and farming
as are the majority of women her age. But as a fictive character of the

---

[56]Nwapa, *Efuru*, p. 153.

purest kind, Nwapa's Efuru is presented above the ordinary social status of titles. She is a dual creature; not only does she have flexible gender options but she is also worshipped in her society by ordinary people.

The intricate sociological and political structures and the women's place in the Nnobi social milieu need to be mentioned at this point. The empowerment of women was illustrated by the taking of the "Ekwe" title, and this possession was associated with the goddess, Idemili. As Amadiume put it, there was a direct link between the accumulation of wives, the acquisition of wealth and the exercise of power . . . the title system was open to men and women. Moreover taking the "Ekwe" title was involuntary, it reflected in the woman's industrious behavior. It is also apparent that, if Ekwe is coming to you, it shows you the sign and throws in money for you." Efuru plays the role of a "female husband," according to Amadiume's book and definition of flexible gender roles mentioned earlier. For instance, she keeps Ogea, her maid, in exchange for money that she gives to the girl's parents. Efuru was getting ready to celebrate the wedding of her maid Ogea to her second husband, Eneberi, when she got sick. Efuru, realizing she was no longer able to have children, decided to give her own maid to her husband as a second wife. Thus Ogea could have become Efuru's co-wife.

Efuru's financial power allows her to face many responsibilities, such as paying her own dowry, and helping other people in her village. She got Ogea, a young maid, by providing her parents with money to pay a debt and survive the bad season. She sent Ogea's father and an old woman to the famous hospital in Onisha, and paid for all the expenses. One night in her father's compound Efuru met with the old lady, who mentioned she had a problem with her leg. Efuru proposed to take her to the hospital.

> "That leg of yours. So it still hurts you."
> "My daughter, it is still there, it will kill me. I have said it this leg will kill me. Why it has not killed me all these years is as a mystery to me."

"Sorry, if you like I can take you to the hospital. The doctor will
look at it and he can do something for you."
"Is it true? If you do that, my daughter, God will bless you."
"We shall see what we can do for you when the doctor comes to
town. I am going. Let day break."[57]

In these multiple actions that Efuru undertakes we see similar behavioral attributes related to many themes mentioned by Amadiume in
Male Daughters, Female Husbands. As Amadiume put it:

> In Nnobi society, there was a direct link between the accumula-
> tion of wives, the acquisition of wealth and the exercise of power
> and authority. The ultimate indication of wealth and power, the
> title system, was open to men and women. There were other
> means of becoming rich through control over the labor of others
> by way of polygamy marriage, either between man and woman
> and woman to woman. The Nnobi flexible gender system made
> either possible.[58]

Characteristics such as power acquisition through title or wife-
taking, mentioned in Amadiume's book, are not apparent in Nwapa's
novel. Though the description made of Efuru does not show that she has
taken wives, the Nnobi flexible gender system that allows women to take
honorific titles, and to have other people work for them, cannot apply
to this particular case. The kind of marriage that allows the woman to
deny the conventional norms and take over the husband's role in family
provision is the one we are dealing with. In other words, we have a flexible gender roles system, where boundaries are not rigid as compared to
other social structures, such as the Western European concept of gender

---

[57]Nwapa, *Efuru*, p. 123.
[58]Ifi Amadiume, 1987, *Male Daughters, Female Husbands*, p. 42.

where there is a clear-cut line between what men should do and what women should do. Briefly, we have breadwinning versus homemaking, and the extreme version is noticed in today's feminists' position, where they are accused of stereotypes and labels of not only male-bashing but also of overthrowing the "phallocratic kingdom." Evidently, male attitude is comparable in other places of the world, especially in developing countries where educated men have duplicated Eurocentric trends, notwithstanding a combination of extreme patriarchal behaviors regardless of a progressive transformation of society and an increasing number of well-educated women.

Nwapa's depiction of Efuru's character shows that through her trade, Efuru has been able to free herself from the patriarchal domination, as she has acquired financial independence and wealth. But her predicament as an earthly woman cannot find total solution and fulfillment for the societal expectations from her as a normal woman. The economic power that Efuru acquires enables her to take on roles which were originally for men and even to replace her husband in providing for the family, especially by taking over Adizua's male role as the bread-winner and caring for her mother-in-law. Here is where Amadiume's explanation of the concept of "female husband" and "flexible gender role" comes into play to shed light on some African beliefs and traditional practices which allow versatility in gender roles.

After analyzing Nwapa's *Efuru*, mostly set in the pre-colonial period, one cannot argue that the author has chosen to present only one aspect of African women's lives: the traditional rural life in a transitional process. She has laid the ground for the study of other aspects of African women's experiences as a result of British implantation in Nigeria. Her second novel, *Idu*, is the exploration of another type of woman, the trade businesswoman, who is married with children. Here, the focus will be on the challenges of contemporary life and the changing values of traditional beliefs that prioritized children over anything else. In this novel, the protagonist is projected as valorizing love and the relationship with her husband over all. This is much reflected in today's life, where people tend to cling less and less to their marriages because of children. The divorce rate is less dependent on the woman's inability to reproduce than on other material, or behavioral reasons.

Nwapa's Eponym Depiction in *Efuru* versus Mariama Ba's Portrayal of Ramatoulaye and Aissatou in *So Long a Letter*

Unlike Nwapa's novel *Efuru*, which portrays the situation of a purely traditional female character, caught between her desires of personal fulfillment and the obligations of her social milieu in the pre-colonial era, Mariama Ba's *So Long a Letter* (1989) presents another face of the African woman. It paints the educated woman with all the challenges that she has to face dealing with modern visions of women and the deep-rooted cultural constraints of her society.

So Long a Letter is the story of two Western-educated women, Aissatou and Ramatoulaye. Both women are actively involved in the process of their country's social change after independence in the 1960s. After choosing their lovers and marrying in the modern way, rather than accepting men of their parents' choice, both women are confronted with the second marriage of their husbands. The reaction of the two women will differ at this stage of their lives. While Aissatou rejects the polygamous situation and leaves her husband Mawdo, a doctor, for a successful professional career as an interpreter in New York, Ramatoulaye, the author's narrator, chooses to stay with her husband, Modou. Hoping that he will at least follow the traditional Islamic rules and practice of equal attention and sharing of the husband in a polygamous family, Ramatoulaye is prepared to endure the situation. The appalling outcome is that Modou deserts Ramatoulaye and her children in favor of the new wife, Binetou. Although Ramatoulaye accepts the polygamous tradition, her husband does not play by the Islamic family code of conduct, by giving equal attention to both wives. The new wife is showered with all the luxuries. Meanwhile, Ramatoulaye discovers why her husband wanted to have an independent account:

Now I understand the terrible significance of Modou's abandon-ment of our joint bank account. He wanted to be financially independent so as to have enough elbow room." She goes on. And then, having withdrawn Binetou from school, he paid her a monthly allowance of fifty thousand francs just like a salary due to her. The young girl who was gifted wanted to continue her studies, to sit for her baccalaureat. So as to establish his rule, Modou wickedly determined to remove her from the critical and unsparing world of the young. He therefore gave in to all the conditions of the grasping Lady Mother-in-Law, and even signed a paper committing him-self to paying the said amount.[59]

When Modou suddenly dies of a heart attack, Ramatoulaye rejects all the polygamous suitors, such as Tamsir, Modou's brother, and Daouda, a former suitor, who wish to take Modou's place. Ramatoulaye rejects both because she does not want to become another burden, or to submit to other men's caprices. She prefers to devote her life and energy to her children who need her for their education. Despite the daily professional occupation that the educated woman faces, she has to take care of the household and be at the disposal of family members. The virtually per-manent presence of sisters and brothers-in-law is a situation that women have to cope with. The woman is expected to welcome everybody at any time, and make all visitors comfortable with a shrewd diplomacy in order to satisfy them, so as to guarantee her popularity as a good woman. Diplomacy also helps assure marriage. But has this saved Ramatoulaye's marriage? Ramatoulaye describes the situation with her sisters-in-law: "I knew how to smile at them all, and consented to wasting useful time in futile chatter. My sisters-in-law believed me to be spared the drudgery of housework."

---

[59]Mariama Ba, 1989, *So Long a Letter,* Translated from French *Une Si Longue Letter* by Modupe Body Thomas, Heinemann, p. 10.

With your two housemaids! They would say with emphasis. Try explaining to them that a workingwoman is no less responsible for her home. Try explaining to them that nothing is done if you do not step in, that you have to see to everything, do everything all over again: cleaning up, cooking, ironing. There are the children to be washed, the husband to be looked after. The working woman has a dual task of which both halves, equally arduous, must be reconciled . . . Some of my sisters-in-law did not envy my way of living at all. They saw me dashing around the house after a hard day at school. They appreciated their comfort, their peace of mind, their moments of leisure, and allowed themselves to be looked after by their husbands who were crushed under their duties. Others, limited in their way of thinking, envied my comfort and purchasing power. They would go into raptures over the many gadgets in my house: gas-cooker, vegetable grater, sugar tongs. They forgot the source of this easy life; first up in the morning, last to go to bed, always working.[60]

A brief comment on Ba's narrative would reiterate the predicaments and obstacles African women still have to face in their diverse social environments. This is reminiscent of the interview Flora Nwapa had, at a conference on the Black Woman Writer and the Diaspora (East Lansing, Michigan, 28 October 1985), with Adeola James. When asked about how she managed to find time to sit down to write, considering the demands of African life such as family, extended family and societal expectations, she answered, "a Nigerian woman faces far too many problems in today's society. She goes to the university to get qualified, when she finishes, she gets a job. Then she gets married. Within a short while, she starts having children. Then she has to look after her children and her husband, and she also has a job to do. The extended family comes

---

[60]Ibid, p. 20.

in. She might be expected to send her younger brothers and sisters to school. How does she do all these things?"[61]

In light of these various social constraints, the painting Nwapa does of her character, Efuru, is illustrative in the sense that she combines all these responsibilities and assumes them without giving up on one. Similarly, Mariama Ba's characters seem to expand on her senior sister, Nwapa's, comment. The depiction Mariama Ba makes of her characters, Ramatoulaye and Aissatou, in *So Long a Letter* gives us a poignant story of educated African women caught in between the compelling choice of satisfying their dream as activist emancipated women with Western ideologies, and the weight of tradition. As the narrator put it, "Being the first pioneers of the promotion of African women, there were very few of us. Men would call us scatter-brained. Others labeled us devils. But many wanted to possess us. How many dreams did we nourish hopelessly, that could have been fulfilled as lasting happiness, and that we abandoned to embrace others, those that have burst miserably like soap bubbles, leaving us empty handed." (Mariama Ba, 1980, pp. 14–5)

The feminist urge those first educated African women had was/is often smothered by the oppressing tradition dominated by gerontocracy, patriarchy and polygamy. The majority of intellectual women have to negotiate marital lives that they did not want to experience because of the innumerable and complex problems, such as injustice, rancour and jealousy, that polygamy brings to the family. Gerontocracy, being the rule of the elders, is an important factor, which weighs in the perpetuation of gender discrimination and the practice of some archaic and obsolete customs. The traditional obligations are so overwhelming that the survival of an individual requires conformity and at times, a compromise within the group. Neither of these two attitudes spares the individual who has to subjugate her/his own satisfaction to the advantage

---

[61]James, Adeola, 1991, In their Own Words: African Woman Writers Talk, *Studies in African Literature*, Heinemann, Portsmouth, NH, 111 (Interview with Flora Nwapa, first African woman writer).

of the group. Further, contemporary women can easily identify with some features common to African society which are not very different in other cultures. Regardless of race and geographical location, women face similar gender obligations as homemakers in addition to working outside of the home today.

Though the trend is changing and some men are shifting to more egalitarian responsibilities by sharing labor, such as doing the dishes, cleaning, shopping, staying home and caring for the kids, the burden still weighs heavily on women's shoulders. This trend in big cities and Western societies is rarely noticeable in the majority of African countries, where the men have become masters for women to attend to regardless of their daily professional occupation and other responsibilities. The family and in-laws' pressure on the married couple often prevents the willing men from helping with the household chores. An external factor that also favors men's reluctance to share work at home is the cheap labor. It is often easier to hire a maid and a cook to help with the housework rather than get the partner to do what is now considered women's work, thus perpetuating the traditional division of labor in modern days.

Most traditional women have difficulty in refusing to conform. So the first rebels are easily distinguished and usually considered lunatics in the society. Traditional deviant characters have often been depicted to match the transitional and unstable historical period of the 1960s. Those depictions were created by men rather than by women. The stereotypical labeling of men who help with household chores is still vividly alive in today's African society, where women who find themselves in that fortunate position are known to be "sitting on their men," or to have used a magic love potion to tame and subdue their husbands to their will. In Benin and Togo, the common expression is "gbo-temi," which ironically means "listen to me," and by extension, "do what I want" in Yoruba. The belief is so ingrained in rural areas that it is often embarrassing for women to accept help when they need it, so as to avoid being criticized openly, or covertly labeled. In the midst of that, how does the educated woman find her way out of a complex social structure at the crossroads of two different civilizations, the modern Western ideologies of emancipation and the traditional customs which are deeply rooted in conservatism? As E. Obiechina (1975) puts it, the identification of the individual with the group of which he forms part, and with its social and cultural outlook, is the very essence of traditionalism. It finds expression in the individual's acquiescence in the beliefs and customs of the group and his sharing with the rest of the group a feeling of social unity. His individual self-interest is always subordinated to the overall interest of the group.[62]

A point to make here is that the ambivalent situation involves the concept of choice that is a common ground to both traditional and modern women who can either conform, as they obediently comply with the norms and abide by the status quo, or disobey, by rebelling. For instance, in *So Long a Letter*, Aissatou's divorce from her husband, Mawdu, is significant. Her decision to go back to school for a higher degree in order to improve her children's lives should be viewed as one of the most interesting aspects of emancipation tools in today's education, especially, considering the campaign for nontraditional programs that encourage adults or parents to go back to school. Ramatoulaye's refusal to marry after Modou's death is another element which goes against traditional rules requiring that she marry her husband's brother. The choice the two protagonists make is symbolic of sacrifice, self-definition and responsibility. Similar to other women from different parts of the world, educated African women find themselves in situations where they have to make tough decisions in their lives when confronted with various social constraints, including marital conflicts and emotional abuses, just to name this aspect. In such a challenging situation Mariama Ba has some insightful remarks:

To overcome distress when it sits upon one demands strong will. When one thinks with each passing second one's life is

---

[62]Obiechina Emmanual, 1975, "Culture Contact and Culture Conflict" in *Tradition and Society in the West African Novel*, Cambridge, pp. 39–59.

shortened, one must profit intensely from this second; it is the sum of all the lost or harvested seconds that makes for a wasted or successful life. Brace one-self to check despair and get it into proportion! A nervous breakdown waits around the corner for anyone who lets himself wallow in bitterness. Little by little it takes over your whole being.[63]

The French philosopher Jean Paul Sartre (1946) comes to mind when discussing the concept of choice. In his argument, it is not possible to dissociate choice from responsibility. According to him, Man is responsible for what he is. When we say that man is responsible for himself, we do not mean that he is responsible only for his own individuality, but that he is responsible for all men. Though the responsibility that is mentioned is partly referring to the role of a writer as a member of a particular group of people, in the context of our discussion, the responsibility a mother has is extended to taking care of her children and seeking their welfare. In light of this, the responsibility the woman has toward herself and her social environment will be dealt with further in our discussion.

Another parallel can be made with regard to the concept of choice. Similar to the situation in Mariama Ba's *So Long a Letter*, where Aissatou and Ramatoulaye have chosen to conduct their own destinies and be responsible for their children, Nwapa's *Efuru* has chosen to go back to her father's courtyard. She decides to devote herself to a spiritual life by worshipping the Lady of the Lake, and helping her community. Efuru probably no longer wants to live under a man's roof with all the humiliations that it involves. The case is verified in real life where some women, after deceptions in their relationships, drift back to a single or social life revolving around community-based and philanthropic actions. Other women, who are still longing for company, sometimes do not hesitate to

---

[63]Ba, Mariama, 1980, *So Long A Letter*, p. 41.

get into same-sex relationships to fulfill their romantic lives. Of course, if love is the giving and sharing of happiness and other emotional feelings, should the partner's gender matter? This is left to the reader to choose where s/he stands regarding sexual preferences and sexual orientation. Despite the pervasiveness of these practices in our communities today, the subjects of heterosexuality and homosexuality continue to be silenced, sexuality being perceived as a private and shameful domain of discussion. Not surprisingly, some relationships and marriages dissolve without people's knowing the real cause of their failure.

Another aspect that deserves scrutiny is related to the socio-economic role that Efuru's characterization plays in the African context. An analysis of African women, and especially of Igbo women, reveals a concept of gender roles which is opposed to the Eurocentric view. The fact that in West Africa women contribute to the well-being of their families, and themselves, is a testimony that all women are not confined to the domestic sphere. To some extent, Karen Sacks's point in *Engels, Revisited* (1974) is relevant when she says that the increased participation of women in social production increases women's status relative to men. The blurred boundaries between the domestic and the public spheres are striking in West African women's lives. This is confirmed in Niara Sudarkasa's explanation below:

> Women in West Africa do not work to get away from their domestic situation; they work because it is considered an integral part of their domestic responsibilities . . . West African women do not draw the sharp distinction made in America, between "domestic duties" and work outside home. Females regard employment, and money-making occupations, as necessary components of their roles as wives, mothers, sisters, and daughters. (Sudarkasa, 1981, p. 56)

Here we notice that there are no boundaries in the division of labor. The traditional conception of work before colonization, as stated earlier, was something diametrically opposed to the Western Eurocentric concepts of women's and men's work. In the Igbo tradition, and in numerous other African cultures, women have been expected to contribute equally to the well-being of the family, even after colonialism. According to Amadiume, the gender ideology governing economic production was that of female industriousness. "Idi uchu," perseverance and industriousness, and "ite uba," the pot of prosperity, were two gifts women were said to have inherited from the goddess, Idemili. The culture prescribing industriousness is derived from the goddess Idemili—the central religious deity. It is not rare even today to hear people refer to these concepts, for they have survived even after colonization.

Efuru's industriousness and kind-heartedness towards people, in relationship to her womanhood, reflects what Amadiume has described about the "Ekwe" women. Efuru's wealth did not come from agricultural production or large livestock, as did most women's, but from trade. Trade is an activity that is given importance in Flora Nwapa's novels, and especially in *Idu*, her second novel, published in 1970, four years after *Efuru*. For example, here is a dialogue between Nwasobi and Uzoechi talking about Ogbenyanu, Ishiodu's wife: "Does she know how to trade? No, she does not know how to trade. That is why we say that she has no sense. A woman who does not know how to trade in our town is not a woman. She is not a woman at all." (*Idu*, p. 29)

This reality is noticeable in contemporary African societies. Trade is an important activity that is valued and even influences people's attitudes in everyday life. In most West African societies, although preference is apparently for boys because they perpetuate their family name, young women are much more profitable for the dowry and the financial support they may bring to their families through trade. The majority of West African women are informal workers if they are not in official jobs or professions. A woman who has no profession should know at least how to trade. Moreover, commercial activities are such a broad phenomenon that even women working in the administration often augment official work with trade to make ends meet, or to increase their incomes. Here, one notices how diametrically-opposed this perception is to that of the female gender role as perceived in Western societies, where women were idealized as "homemakers" until it became necessary for them to leave their homes to work in the absence of their husbands, the regular breadwinners, who may have gone to war. In the African perception, activity, and particularly trade, equate to and determine womanhood and worthiness, and do not limit a woman to her homemaking and reproductive abilities.

Thus, we would agree with Flora Nwapa when she focuses on this aspect of women's occupations in social life. We are no longer in a subsistence agricultural era nor are poor countries developing steadily in a flourishing industrial era. Developing countries are rather in a mixed economy of exchange dealing with trade: the buying and selling of commodities in order to make profit. If we take the concrete example of most West African countries, and investigate the activities of the market women, we soon realize that the economy is in women's hands. Through trade, women acquire their financial independence, and as such are the ones who generally support the household by providing the family with food and clothing.

Throughout history, there is no better example of women whose roles normally extend beyond the domestic spheres than the market women and retail traders of West Africa. For market women on the West African Coast from Nigeria, Benin, Togo, Ghana and Cote-D'Ivoire, work outside the home has always been one of the fundamental characteristics of their lives. West African women, without exaggeration, were brought to the Americas during the slave trade because of their endurance and resourcefulness.

In the United Nations publication, *Women: Looking Beyond 2000* (1995), Ama Ata Aidoo's article, "African Women: Then and Now," reinforces the notion that for African women, work is a reality, a responsibility, and an obligation. Talking about the biological inheritance, that African women handed down to their children, Aidoo notes:

For most African women, work is a reality, a responsibility and an obligation. They have drummed it into us from infancy. We could never have fought for "the right to work"—a major departure from a concern of early Western feminists. In West Africa, for example, virtually no family tolerates a woman who does not work. So today, there may not be too many homes in that sub-region, including traditionally Islamic areas, where growing girls would be encouraged to think they need not to have ambitions because one day they would grow up to marry and be looked after by some man. (Aidoo, p. 91)

What Aidoo hints at here is that the notion of "work" outside the home, as opposed to "domestic work," is not something new to African women, who were used to working outside the home since the beginning of ancient African civilization. As a result, Nwapa has dealt with an aspect of work that does not even spare pregnant women in the traditional setting. This brings us to stipulate what old African mothers would say, that pregnancy should not be viewed as an illness. It should be considered a normal biological transformation of productive women, who in a way are given that gift of bringing a child to life. For instance, in Nwapa's *Idu*, the conversation between two village women highlights that, and presents work as having no boundaries. A pregnant woman who might be seen in bed during daytime is labeled as lazy:

> "Nwashobi, the sun was up, and was fast reaching its heights. And a young woman full of life was lying down because she was pregnant."
> "That's what we are seeing in this world nowadays. In our days, you could take your pregnancy to Okporodun, far."
> "And back in the same day" continues Uzoechi. "What pregnancy will keep me from looking for food to feed my children? The day I gave birth to my last child, though my body was no longer young, I went to fetch firewood in the

morning. . . . "I came back and cooked. Then I went to the stream to prepare cassava. By the time I had finished in the stream, my waist was not mine, but that did not prevent me from doing other work. I washed my clothes and those of my children and my husband. I was hanging them to dry when the labor came. I finished hanging them, went inside, and asked one of my children to call my sister Uzuaku for me. By the time she came, I had my baby. So, when I saw that girl lying down, I could not bear it. So, I told her my mind." "When she was lying there, who cooked for her husband?" asked Nwashobi." "Men of today are queer. You mean her husband cooked!" "Cooked, I say. He split the firewood, he fetched the water, and he cooked and took some to his wife to eat." "How did she manage to eat that?" "Ask her, lazy girl." "If her mother-in-law were alive, and saw such a thing, she would say that, she would say that mothers-in-law are all the same. Who will see such a thing and not say something?" "Nwashobi, let me go, one will never finish talking of things of this world." (Nwapa, *Idu*, 1970, pp. 196–7)

The multiple women's roles as reproductive beings are vividly painted through the narrative of pregnancy. The village women have so internalized the social constructs and accepted their domestic role as homemakers that they finally deny themselves of the help of a male partner. Should there be any shame in eating the food one's husband cooked, and especially when the woman is carrying a baby that both of them contributed to conceive? But the problem is that in some societies the gender division of labor is so well drawn that male and female spheres do not overlap or intersect. When men are not supposed to cook, women are expected to do this regardless of their physical situation. Though these social constructs of gender are progressively changing in today's modern societies in which there tends to be a relative understanding of equal division of labor, with stay-at-home dads and/or working mothers, traditional gender role expectations are still well-engrained in mainstream American, European or African societies.

Using the dialogical style, by making the characters talk in *Idu*, Nwapa wants to portray obsolete concepts used to justify and perpetuate patriarchy. The irony is the unconscious role women play in maintaining the status quo, in keeping women in a totally submissive and subservient position. Even today, there are still people, and especially women, who would object to the man's presence in the kitchen, thinking that it is reserved only for women. Should we think of a kind of protection of female spheres or should we rather understand a detrimental behavior that does nothing but strengthen patriarchal privileges while keeping women in a relatively inferior position, socially, politically, and economically? The paradoxical women's position regarding critical issues such as women's rights and the practice of polygamy is what has helped the patriarchal perpetuation of its treatment of issues concerning women. As a result, the present inequality and disparities in pay are strengthened because of the inability of women of all walks of life to stand up for their human rights and against gender discrimination and social injustices.

One cannot discuss gender, culture and specifically the impact of religion in Igbo people's lives, and the realistic characterization in West African writers' literary production without thinking of the tremendous influence the British and French brought through Christianity, on the one hand. On the other hand, the Arab invasion of the Northern part of Africa also had its outcome, with not only the Arabic culture from the Middle East, but also Islam, as the religion of conquest, just as the Christian missionaries brought their evangelization agenda to Nigeria and elsewhere in West Africa. Moving northward in the Maghreb and with an exploration of pioneer Moroccan woman writer Leila Abouzeid's life and work, we have a concrete example and a viable sample of the confluence of French colonial heritage and the traditional Arab-Islamic culture within which women have to negotiate their daily lives. Be advised that the following piece is provided as an informational entry, the purpose of which is to introduce this rather covert Moroccan writer, as compared to such giants as Egyptian Nawal El-Saadawi.

Leila Abouzeid: Pioneer Moroccan Woman Writer in Arabic Background

To fully understand the import of Leila Abouzeid's character delineations, it would be helpful to delve into the historical and geographical contexts that helped shape the author's creativity. Thus, this overview will first of all situate the writer in history and geography to allow a better understanding of the writer and her work in the North African literary canon.

Contextualizing North African literature in his course description, Mustapha Fall's comment about the advent of Islam in the Maghreb might be helpful to our study of the Moroccan writer, Leila Abouzeid. According to oral tradition, Islam first came to Africa with Muslim refugees fleeing persecution in the Arab Peninsula. This was followed by a military invasion, some seven years after the death of the Prophet Muhammad (PBH), in 632 under the command of Arab General Amir, Ibn al-Asi. It quickly spread in the West, from Alexandria in the Northern part of Africa, known as Maghreb today, except for Egypt, Nubia and Ethiopia, where Christianity had a relative dominance then. In the early centuries of its existence, Islam had tremendous influence over African people and nations. Many reforming movements and dynastic clashes were succeeding each other and people found spiritual refuge and economic relief in joining Islam. In that particular period, Islam became a driving force behind political, economic and social promotion. In sub-Saharan Africa, Islamic rulers expanded from the north to the south. In the last quarter of the 11th century, Islam dominated the Mediterranean region.

Geographically, the Atlas Mountains divide the country into two distinctive parts. The Northwest stretches into the plains and fertile agricultural areas where the Arabs settled into cities such as Fez, Rabat, Sale, and Tetouan, all constituting centers of nationalistic movement. These included the industrial city of Casablanca where the armed resistance took birth. The other part is made up of the Mountains and the Sahara Desert, poor, arid areas inhabited for the most part by Berber Nomads. From the 16th to the 19th centuries, much of the Maghreb was under the Ottoman Empire, and by the 1880s, Islam was firmly rooted in one third of the African continent. Though Morocco was never under Ottoman rule, it did succumb to Spanish and French imperialism and domination later in the 19th century.

The historical introduction Elizabeth Warnock Farnea provides in Leila Abouzeid's acclaimed novella, *Year of the Elephant*, is full of information that contextualizes North African literary development and specifically, Moroccan writers. The French, aware that Morocco had more fertile land than its neighbors, Algeria and Tunisia, appropriated the regions which could be exploited for economic gain. Farnea explains that the French implemented the classical colonization strategy of "divide and conquer" to overpower the Moroccan population. They stressed the Arab-Berber duality, constructing a Manichean world of "good Berbers" and "bad Arabs," thus developing policies that favored Berbers over Arabs. At one point, the attempted removal of Berber areas from the jurisdiction of the Sultan Makzen's government through the Berber Dahir (Decree of May 16, 1930), brought about the opposite result. Instead of separating the Berbers from the Sultan, their spiritual and political leader under Islam, the decree rallied all the Moroccan people under the Sultan's authority.

Alison Baker's book, *Voices of Resistance: Oral Histories of Moroccan Women* (1998), provides an insightful collection of women's contributions to Moroccan independence. Since Morocco got its independence from the French in 1956, it has been more than two generations, and only people over 50 years old have an actual memory of the colonial period. Yet little has been written about Morocco's Nationalistic movement under the French Protectorate. An explanation might be found in the value given to written records rather than the oral tradition mostly used by women. Though the few history scholars who have focused on armed resistance occasionally used some oral histories, the majority of Moroccan people considered written records to be more reliable and more important as source material for reference. The French, having taken advantage of the geographical conditions to divide Morocco into two distinctive entities, created unavoidable political, social and economic reverberations throughout history. To maintain the status quo and perpetuate their hegemonic agenda, the French encouraged Native educated elites to implement the "politics of modernity," which was nothing but empty words, as the outcome was acculturation, a lack of humanistic and democratic trends and a blind rejection of traditional values. As a result, women's writings were tacitly or intentionally excluded in the mainstream informational canon.

Under the French Protectorate, Government positions and schooling were reserved for only a handful of Moroccans, the sons of traditional elite or bourgeois families. In other words, only wealthy people could afford to send their children to school as well as maintain large households, where polygamy was practiced. Thus, two factors were geared towards excluding women from the educational process. Abouzeid touches on the French educational system by referring to Salah Dine Hammoud's (1982) information stating that "for a few thousand youngsters who were enrolled in school in 1955, 80% of their school time was spent either studying French or using it as a medium of learning rudiments of Arithmetic, natural science and geography. During the remaining few hours (about 11) in their school week, they were taught the Koran and some basic precepts of Islam as well as some classical Arabic poetry reading and grammar."

As Elizabeth Warnock Farnea added in her introduction to Leila Abouzeid's first book, *Year of the Elephant*, "the new Moroccan government was faced with a population largely illiterate and untrained, despite years of French educational missions. Although the French asserted that many Moroccans were being educated to assume responsibilities in a modern, changing world, the statistics tell a different story" (Abouzeid, 1989: xix).

Family, Education, Gender Perceptions and Islamic/Feminist Activism

Leila Abouzeid was born in 1950 into a middle class family in El Ksiba, a Middle Atlas village. Her father was among the first educated elite to serve as an interpreter in the French administration. She was six years old when Morocco gained its independence from French colonial rule in 1956. Like elsewhere around the world, independence from the European hegemony and colonial rule was not gained peacefully. The violence and dehumanizing treatment of the Moroccan people that the French colonizers used led to a mass consciousness-raising, which helped the nationalistic sentiment to spread all over the country. Abouzeid captures this difficult time of resistance in the narrative of her family life, her father's imprisonment, and the challenges of her going to the Western school in *Year of the Elephant* (1989). While her father was being jailed for political activism in the nationalistic movement, and her mother had to juggle between family constraints and fulfilling her husband's basic needs in jail, Leila was sent to school in the midst of this family ordeal. Thus, against external pressures and traditional gender role expectations, which discouraged sending girls to the Western school, Leila attended what is called the primary or elementary school, and later enrolled in the Moroccan Lycee, an equivalent of the American High School, where Arabic and French constituted a major part of the curriculum. As a tri-lingual, she went to Mohamed V University in Rabat and the London School of Journalism and became a journalist, writing for local Arabic magazines and newspapers while serving as press assistant to the Ministries of Information and Equipment, including the Prime Minister's office. She directed a popular talk show on the national radio, and was an anchorwoman for the new Moroccan television channel. This strategic position probably helped her to experience and to better assess Moroccan social life, as well as the patriarchal dominance coupled with men's macho behavior, which had been indirectly strengthened by the colonial culture.

Working in different environments and interacting with all levels of administrative and mainstream population, she understood not only the urgent need for women's liberation, but also the need for the liberation of her country from its entrapment between Arab-Islamic tradition and the French culture based on the politics of assimilation, which required mimicking the French and at the same time remaining in a traditional setting. Thus, for most North Africans, going to the Western school meant learning the British, French, German, Italian, Spanish or Portuguese languages and cultural values, including Christianity. These involuntary socio-contextual conditions put most colonized people at a multi-linguistic crossroads where they had to communicate in several different languages. Abouzeid also studied at the University of Texas in Austin. A former Fellow of the World Press Institute at St. Paul in Minnesota, Abouzeid left the Press in 1992 to dedicate herself to writing fiction. She is currently translating the *Autobiography of Malcolm X* into Arabic. She lives in Rabat where she is in high demand as a guest speaker and commentator on both radio and television. Her work has now been translated into English, German, Dutch, and Urdu.

One cannot talk about Leila Abouzeid's life and work without referring to gender perceptions and Islamic feminist activism, which despite its contextual differences was in turn influenced by Western European women's history. Hence, a glance at the Western feminist consciousness and its indirect impact on educated Moroccan women's nationalistic awakening and participation in the country's independence from colonial rule might be helpful. As a Francophone woman writer in North Africa (Maghreb), Leila Abouzeid's writing has been influenced by French education and culture, like Mariama Ba in Senegal, West Africa. The parallel is found in the similar patriarchal rules of Islam, Christianity, and traditional secular practices, which combined to keep women at the lowest level of the social ladder despite arguments to the contrary from religious scriptures and common sense in favor of human rights, social justice and equity in gender distribution of wealth and privileges.

One way of explaining Moroccan educated women's self-awareness in general, and the impact of Islamic feminism on the women's struggle for Moroccan independence, is to look at the revolutionary feminist movement occurring in Europe in the aftermath of World War II, and its reverberation in America with the Civil Rights movement in the 1960s, followed by the feminist movement in the 1970s. Despite the Women's Declaration of Independence in 1848, which demanded equality between men and women and women's right to vote in the United States, the Equal Rights Amendment has not been ratified. In that light, French feminist Simone de Beauvoir's *The Second Sex* (1949—interviewed in 1976), Betty Friedan's *The Feminine Mystique* (1963), Adrienne Rich's *Of Woman Born: Motherhood as Experience and Institution* (1976), and others all address the traditional female gender roles, the subjugation, annihilation and smothering of the female voice in Western society based on Christian religious values and ruthless patriarchal domination. Though the first book launched, to some extent, the feminist movement in France, the women who were involved in the fight for Moroccan independence were too young to be influenced by it. What was happening in terms of gender discrimination in the colonies was not that different from the West. The European colonization of Northern Africa and the declaration of a French Protectorate of the territory did nothing but strengthen the patriarchal trends already implemented through the misunderstanding/misinterpretation of the Qur'an and Islamic laws. With the difference of enforced seclusion, which is physical control of women, thus restricting their movement and activities in the outside world, some Western abusive behaviors and expectations towards women were/are comparable to the women's conditions in other places of the world today.

Additional elements that help to give a better grasp of Leila Abouzeid's work are the gender perceptions and women's educational participation in the Western schools. General information from the *Middle East and North Africa Encyclopedia* stipulates that informal training and upbringing are as important to their overall education as any formal schooling they receive. Gender roles are conveyed, modeled, and reinforced in ways that interact with schooling to shape students' expectations, desires and performance, thus exerting a profound influence on the future of women and girls. The informal educational structures and opportunities have variably and simultaneously served as sources of empowerment and of control. This is exemplified in the practice of arranged marriages and in family members' decisions over girls' lives, despite the changing times and Islamic scriptures requiring fairness, equality and justice in deeds. The complexities of gender perceptions in North African countries and the position of women have gradually shifted because of external influences, namely colonization, modernization, and now globalization, despite the tremendous impact of tradition based on Islam. Hence, any woman's activism would logically be rooted in the Islamic religion, which allows us to qualify it as Islamic woman's activism or more precisely, Islamic feminism. A thorough definition and understanding of the expression becomes necessary for the untrained reader to grasp the meaning of and the implementation of Islamic feminism in the literary production of North African women. To take a definition from Margot Badran's talk, "*Islamic Feminism: what is in a name?*" in which she argues that Islamic feminism is, on the whole, more radical than secular feminism,

> "Islamic feminism is a feminist discourse and practice articulated within an Islamic paradigm. Islamic feminism, which derives its understanding and mandate from the Qur'an, seeks rights and justice for women, and for men, in the totality of their existence. Islamic feminism is highly contested and firmly embraced. There has been much misunderstanding, misrepresentation, and mischief concerning Islamic feminism. This new feminism has given rise simultaneously to hopes and to fears."

According to Badran in Al-Haram, when feminists plead for changes in the Muslim Personal Status Code, one would concur that they obviously advanced Islamic arguments:

> Islamic feminism advocates women's rights, gender equality, and social justice using Islamic discourse as its paramount discourse, though not necessarily its only one aspect, . . . The basic methodologies of this Islamic feminism are the classic Islamic methodologies of independent investigations of religious sources

Ijtihad and an interpretation of The Qur'an, *Tafsir*. Used along with these methodologies are the methods and tools of linguistics, history, literary criticism, sociology, anthropology etc. In approaching the Qur'an not only do women bring to their readings their personal experience and questions as women. They interpret it through their own lenses, thus realizing how much the previous classical and post-classical interpretations were male-centered, and influenced by the patriarchal social environment in which they lived. (El-Ahram, 17–23 January, 2002)

The author goes on to add that the new gender hermeneutics renders compelling confirmation of gender equality in the Qur'an that was lost sight of as male interpreters constructed a corpus of *tafsir* promoting more or less a doctrine of male superiority reflecting the mindset of the prevailing patriarchal cultures. One should point out a similar trend of feminist readings of the Bible or the Torah (The Jewish Holy Book) which triggered not only a feminist interpretation but also a rewriting of the scriptures to balance the male bias with that of women. There are many ayaat (verses) of the Qur'an that apparently declare male/female equality. For instance, Al –Hujurat: "Oh humankind. We have created you from a single pair of a male and a female and made you into tribes and nations that you may know each other [not that you may despise one another]. The most honored of you in the sight of God is the most righteous of you [the one practicing the most taqua]." Ontologically, all human beings are equal; they are only distinguished based on their rightful practice or implementation of the fundamental Qur'anic principle of justice. Hence, there is no contradiction between being a feminist and being a Muslim, once we perceive feminism as an awareness of constraints placed upon women because of gender . . . and efforts to construct and implement a more equitable gender system.[64]

---

[64]Ibid: Badran in Al Ahram 2002, A lecture given and published in the Egyptian Weekly Newspaper, January 17–23.

Bolstered with a relatively modest definition of Islamic feminism, perhaps a critical approach to the writer and her work might help at this point. To what extent does Badran's argument apply or weigh in contemporary Muslim women's writing in general and in Moroccan women's writings in particular? Can we read Leila Abouzeid's work without reference to Islamic feminism, the female point of view, or voice? The answer to this last rhetorical question is no, because the portrayals and focus of her stories put female characters at the center rather than marginalizing them as they would often be in real life, or in traditional male writings. Does Leila Abouzeid advocate for women's equal rights, justice and empowerment rooted in Islamic values? Should we take into account the role of the writer in general, and that of the woman writer, living in an oppressive male-dominated society which holds its mandate from religious scriptures of the Qur'an, in particular? If that is the case, we would be attentive to African women writers who have something to say about it. Nigerian feminist Omolara Ogundipe-Leslie defines the feminist perspective of the woman writer as having two main responsibilities in society. First, "the woman writer has to tell about being a woman. Second, she has to describe reality from a woman's view, a woman's perspective as opposed to what men have done so far" (1995: 66). Two decades earlier, Anais Nin (1973:291) made a similar point in *A Woman's Wit*, namely that "the woman artist has to create something different from man. . . . She has to sever herself from the myth man creates, from being created by him, she has to struggle with her own cycles, storms, terrors which man does not understand." The following paragraphs will touch on a few salient aspects of Leila Abouzeid's work to help us elucidate the literary genre and the character delineation as well as the main issues she raises in her writing.

One cannot talk about Moroccan women and their feminist movement without mentioning Malika El-Fassi, born into the El-Fassi family in Fez. She constituted the first generation of the Moroccan women's movement, providing a model and mentor for the generations that followed. What made this other Moroccan woman's story unique for her time in the late 1920s and early 1930s, is that she was the first girl to be sent to school, when no other Muslim girls had that opportunity, thus opening a window of opportunities to other Muslim families to send their female children to the established colonial school.

Description of the Author's Work

Year of the Elephant: A Moroccan Woman's Journey Toward Independence

This English version of the novel was published by the University of Texas at Austin in 1989. The title of the novella refers to the Sourah "Al-Fil" in the Qur'an, Chapter 105, "the Elephant" referring to a historical event in Makka (the birthplace of Prophet Mohammad—PBH), where a fierce battle occurred in 571 A.D. Abraha, the Christian Viceroy, marched against the city with elephants and a large army with the intent of destroying the Ka'bah, but failed. The Sourah contains a parabolic account of that battle. Similar to the Christian attempt to overthrow the Muslim symbolic holy city, the French occupation of Morocco in the nineteenth century encountered social unrest and created a nationalistic sentiment and an intense movement which culminated in the country's independence in 1956.

The novel begins with the divorce of the protagonist Zahra and her frustration at having been treated unfairly by her husband, whom she feels rejected her without any protocol or remorse. From the story's outset we hear her complain: "I come back to my hometown, feeling shattered and helpless. He had simply sat down and said, "Your papers will be sent to you along with whatever the law provides." My papers? How worthless a woman is if she can be returned with a receipt like some store bought object! How utterly worthless! . . . Those few seconds destroyed the whole foundation of my being, annihilated everything I trusted." (Abouzeid, p. 1)

Zahra confirms further how deeply hurt she is by her husband's decision and words. Faced with her new reality, that of a divorced woman in a society where single-hood is frowned upon and religious law binds women to a state of powerlessness and apparent servitude, Zahra has to realize her social conditions as a woman with no rights whatsoever and entrapped by social, cultural and religious constraints. Referring to Abdullah Yusuf Ali's translation of *The Holy Qur'an: The Meaning of the Qur'an with Notes* (1996:542), scriptures in Sourah, Al-Talaq, Chapter 65 (Divorce) verses 1, 2, 4, and 6, are clear about the provisions and treatment of women in instances of divorce:

"When ye divorce women, divorce them at their prescribed periods . . . and turn them not out of their houses, nor shall they themselves leave except in case they are guilty of some open lewdness. Those are limits set by Allah and any who transgresses the limits of Allah does verily wrong his (own) soul . . .[65]

What traditional Moroccan law provides to a divorced woman is economic support for one hundred days, or three months and ten days, the standard time allowed for her to adjust and possibly find another suitor to take care of her. The three months also allow for time to discover whether the woman was pregnant at the time of the divorce, and require that she be taken in until she gives birth. Zahra's situation is unlike what today's youngsters would expect of a woman, based on Western standards of living and behavior; she is a traditional woman who normally should have been appreciated for being conservative and not mimicking the Western European ways deemed modern, as they are different and imposed by the colonizer's culture. She has to find a place to live, a way to make a living and a reason to live. Zahra not only has to face divorce, but she has nobody to turn to and the only inheritance she can claim is a room in her parents' house. Being victimized by multiple jeopardies: illiteracy, poverty, and being divorced without an emotional support or a

---

[65]Abdullah Yusuf Ali, (*English Translation of the Holy Qur'an*), Meaning of the Qur'an with Notes, 1996, p. 542.

shoulder to lean on, her previous life has not trained her to take the bull by the horns. She cannot join other women in running small trading businesses in the marketplace, as one would often see in most African countries. She finds herself helpless, hopeless, and worthless, not only as a woman but as a human being.

Though the Holy Qur'an provides answers and solutions to virtually all human, philosophical, and social questions and problems, Zahra's humiliation prevents her from accepting the provisions provided in case of divorce. She questions those laws that she presumes are being written down to the advantage of men although dealing with women. Cast out and divorced by her husband, she finds herself in a strange new world. Both obstacles and support systems change as she actively participates in the struggle for Moroccan independence.

It should be noted that before her somewhat arranged wedding, Zahra was an active advocate and militant of the Native resistance against French colonization and for Moroccan independence. She fought beside men, including her husband, who has grown corrupt and worse than the colonizers. Walking back to her parents' house, she remembers having helped to burn a French man's store during the nationalist movement. She recalls her contribution to helping free the country, including how she smuggled Faqih, a member of the nationalist movement, to the Spanish side of the country: "Missions came to me one after the other, missions carried out alone. If my grandmother had returned from the dead and seen me setting shops ablaze, delivering guns and smuggling men across borders, she would have died a second death. Had all that even been in my own imagination, let alone my grandparents? May God have Mercy on them! They prepared me for a different life, but fate made a mockery of their plans" (1989;38).

The depiction Abouzeid makes of Zahra projects her as an agent of Moroccan history through her multiple involvements in socio-political events during the years of resistance. Her story reflects the undeniable evidence that there is always another side to mainstream socio-historical narrative in all discourses. The impact of religion and of the Arabic tradition of secluding women, not to mention expecting them to be homemakers, probably prevents Zahra's openness to the outside world, once married. Zahra finds herself in a dilemma where not behaving as a modern woman damages her relations with her husband, while being divorced seems to have taken her whole humanity away. Zahra is repudiated not because she cannot bear children, but because she fails to incorporate the French social behavior that has become the standard norm of refined culture and civilization.

Her lack of French education becomes a weapon her brother-in-law uses not only to humiliate Zahra but to open her eyes to the needs and expectations of modern days. Refusing to be someone's appendage, Zahra rejects the offer of her brother and sister-in-law to provide her a temporary shelter after staying a whole year without going out. This rebellious reaction will lead the protagonist to develop survival strategies based on hard work, friendship, and religious faith. Religious faith or spirituality being the guiding element in human life, the protagonist's spiritual and emotional balance is strengthened, which helps her to reach a profound consciousness of her condition as an underprivileged woman, as well as serving as a stimulus for her to seek personal remedies. Zahra's desire for change in life and economic self-sufficiency is symbolic of her maturity as a responsible woman, and of her personal growth, which contradicts her confusion and loss of identity after being repudiated, as if a woman's value resides only in her marriage or relationship with a man.

In this novella, Abouzeid delineates female characters who, on the one hand, reflect common Moroccan social life and issues, including family life, marriage, divorce, unemployment, self-awareness and personal growth through personal experience. On the other hand, their political involvement, resignation and wisdom lead to their disillusionment with ideological aspirations and open activism. Such content and themes are well illustrated through her short stories, "A House in the Woods," "A Vacation," "The Discontented," "Divorce," "Silence," "Dinner in the Black Market," and "The Stranger."

The theme of independence and freedom from the yoke of male subjugation and objectification serves to show the women's plight and the need for change in traditional as well as in modern laws, which have been and continue to be detrimental to women. Not only does Zahra's husband end up cheating on her for her supposed barrenness, he becomes physically abusive. Zahra recalls an instance: "At the bedroom door, he turned around and slapped me. Holding my face with one hand, I pointed at him with the other and shouted with all my strength as if addressing an imaginary crowd. 'And we are waiting for reform to come from the likes of these! You are more dangerous than the colonizers!'" (1983:55). Taking a cue from Salah Mouhklis's article, "History of Hopes Postponed: Women's Identity and Postcolonial State" in *Year of the Elephant: A Moroccan Woman's Journey toward Independence*, might be helpful at this point. Here, reference to how the transformation of activists for independence into opportunistic politicians occurs is an eye opener for understanding colonial rulers' strategy of using local people against their own people and to their advantage. Considering the two different situations, on the one hand Zahra's experience with an acute sense of identity and determination, and on the other, the aunt's docility, objectification, misunderstanding, mis-education, and subsequent form of alienation in *The Director and Other Stories from Morocco*, Nawal El Saadawi's remark is edifying:

Even in the modern sector the colonial powers made sure only to encourage a modernization that served their needs and that therefore remained limited in both content and forms. In other words, just as was the case in economic and political fields, cultural modernization was exploitative in nature, elitist and deformed. It was aimed at achieving a form of acculturation, an alienation from society, and at transforming the urban elites, intellectuals and educated strata into willing or unwilling instruments of colonial and later neo-colonial exploitation. (El-Saadawi, 2003:75)

The independence which the main character, Zahra, gains at the end of her experiential journey, through the acceptance of a cleaning job in the French cultural center, serves as a metaphor for the whole country's independence from the colonizers' humiliating and brutal invasion of the country and their violent treatment of nationalist men (imprisonment, exile), women and children (shootings and killing of people after the city water was shut down during the resistance). This last aspect is in evidence in the second book, *Return to Childhood: the Memoir of a Moroccan Woman*, which Abouzeid published in 1998, through the Center for Middle Eastern Studies at the University of Texas at Austin. This feminist novel is a literary statement in a modern realist style. Many novels by women of the Middle East that have been translated reflect Western views, values, and education. By contrast, *Return to Childhood* is uniquely Moroccan and emerges from North African Islamic culture itself. Its subtle juxtaposition of past and present, of immediate thought and triggered instant memories reflects the heroine's interior conflict between tradition and modern demands. In this moving fictional treatment of a Muslim woman's life, the weaving of a personal and family crisis impels the heroine to reexamine traditional cultural attitudes toward women. This ambiguous position of the work might explain the dual denomination of novel and memoir.

Return to Childhood: the Memoir of a Moroccan Woman

In this novel, Abouzeid paints the tapestry of her deeply personal journey through family conflicts ignited by the country's civil unrest during Morocco's struggle for independence from French colonial rule. In this second book, *Return to Childhood*, the author does not hesitate to lead the reader into the most secretive practices by revealing her clan's taboos while legitimizing autobiography as an imported literary genre, which was not considered a valuable literary production until recently. This memoir recounting her family's struggle during the pre-independence era provides a forum where the women's contribution in the resistance against French domination could be acknowledged. The contradictions and ambiguities of the colonial experience are illustrated in the common patterns of political upheavals worldwide. Women often play a critical role in militant resistance and frequently end up bearing the brunt of the opposition. Becoming invisible, as a result of not reaping the economic and political gains of their struggle, they are expected to return to their traditional roles as homemakers once the fighting and social unrest is over. These very women who fought side by side with men are in for disappointment and disillusionment. Margaret Rauch put it clearly in *Culture and Imperialism* (2000) that,

> "Women played a significant role in the Nationalist movement. The sisters, wives, and other female family members of the men involved in the struggle for independence carried weapons concealed inside ordinary objects, like loaves of bread and fish in their shopping baskets. They delivered messages and documents and distributed leaflets and money. Women from all milieus, urban and rural, were recruited to help [. . .] The phase immediately following independence, in which women were excluded from the political scene was experienced as a great disappointment by many of the activists" (65).

Disappointed by the result that the end of colonization brought to the nation, including corruption and the collapse of her life through a failed marriage, the symbolic survival Zahra finds is a spiritual one. Her relationship with the Sheikh is symbolic as the latter represents the religious leadership that sustains the spiritual stability of Muslims. Her divorce is like adding insult to injury considering that her abusive and unfaithful husband has all the privileges. He has not only been rewarded with a teaching job after the struggle for independence, but he has the power to reject her like an unwanted and used commodity whenever he wants, without being accountable to anyone. Is Zahra's situation to be solely blamed on the French colonization? Of course, not. As the traditional Arab culture is highly patriarchal and the actual Qur'anic scriptures are misunderstood and interpreted to favor men, one would gather that the protagonist's, and by extension, the Moroccan women's predicaments are a combination of internal and external factors intersecting to produce an oppressive and alienating social environment. As Moukhlis quoted McClintock (1992) in "The Angel of Progress: Pitfalls of the term 'Post-colonialism'" in the following:

> The blame for women's continuing plight cannot be laid only at the door of colonization, or footnoted, and forgotten as a passing 'neo-colonial' dilemma. The continuing weight of male economic self-interest and the varied undertows of patriarchal Christianity, Confucianism, and Islamic fundamentalism continue to legitimize women's barred access to the corridors of political and economic power. Their persistent educational disadvantage reflects the bad infinity of the domestic double-day, unequal childcare, gendered malnutrition, sexual violence, genital mutilation, and domestic battery. (Moukhlis, 2000, p. 76)

A flashback to the female character depictions in *Year of the Elephant* and *Return to Childhood* reflects that the writer intentionally chooses her protagonists to serve her agenda. What makes Abouzeid's writings unique is not only her choice to write in Arabic and then translate some of her novels herself, it is the assertiveness with which she makes her point through oral tradition, thus using the classical African tradition of tales and story telling from a female perspective. The author prioritizes the female and gives her a voice, thus reclaiming her paramount place and role in national history. The power with which Zahra or Aisha expresses herself is in opposition to a society which has relegated her status as a woman to that of a second-class citizen with little or no rights. Moreover, Abouzeid has in a sense reclaimed the Moroccan woman's right to equal treatment and justice in the implementation of the laws and rules governing the family structure and life.

As Elizabeth Warnock Farnea points out, a reviewer in the Socialist Union of Casablanca wrote, "Through her use of form in *Year of the Elephant*, Leila Abouzeid joins the ranks of modern Arab poets and writers of fiction. Her sentences are short, but they are multi-layered, thus, opening to a multitude of interpretations. However, she never loses, in her work, the flavor of classical Arabic." (March 5, 1984)

The Last Chapter: A Novel, published in 2003, is a thought-provoking semi-autobiographical story of a young Moroccan woman and her struggle to find an identity in the Morocco of the second half of the twentieth century. Shifting male/female relationships abound in the narrative, as well as clashes between traditional and modern society, Islamic and Western values, and the older classical practices of sorcery and witchcraft. These aspects join general African literary themes in which the narrative is seasoned with the mysterious and sensational for the reader to tap into the remnants of traditionalism despite the people's conversion to advertised and hegemonic universal religions such as Christianity and Islam.

The experience of Aisha in this novel is not uncommon to even developed Western European and American high school girls. At the turn of the twentieth century, when the number of high school boys greatly exceeded that of the girls, being one of the only two girls in a class of 42 students does nothing but create frustration and antagonism, especially for an exceptionally talented female student. Reading feminist writings enlightens her about the traditional perceptions and expectations of women in societies where their roles are constricted into the kitchen or the home, caring for the men and children after producing the latter. The challenges Aisha has to face during her high school experience, such as not having the means to acquire all the required books, being tricked by a friend the last day before her exams, and having to gather courage to approach her teacher for a book, are all part of modern-day school life. The heroine's personal experience led her to trust and socialize more with men than women because of the safety she finds in their mutual interaction as opposed to the hypocrisy and meanness of girls who generally have a competitive attitude. Her statement, "they did not pick at our minds, since they assumed we were born without them," does not only reflect men's perception of women in Moroccan society, it parallels the old Western Victorian ideologies of the cult of "true womanhood" and the societal misconception of women's intellectual abilities. As a student, Aisha prefers interacting with men because the widespread assumptions of girls' inferiority also provided a sanctuary for shelter and pretence. This preconceived idea about women's intelligence joins the traditional gender discrimination pervasive then in the Western European culture up until the late 1800's.

The publication of Simone de Beauvoir's "Woman as the Other" in *The Second Sex*, and later other feminist books mentioned earlier, followed to decry the injustice done to women in terms of gender discrimination, including abusive violence, which prevented them from acquiring equal rights to education, ownership of property, etc. Western European beliefs were/are articulated as "women do not have brains," or traditionally, "women are to be seen and not heard," as they were/are often silenced by social constraints. For example, in Morocco, family decisions were made about relationships and arranged marriages without consulting the girl, the worst being the writing of the Moroccan Code of Family without women's input. These testify to the masculinist and patriarchal hegemony which has subdued women and made them simple commodities, or disposable objects that could be used when needed and thrown away.

Through a series of emotional tales of different disasters, Leila Abouzeid provides the reader with a vivid awareness not only of Aisha's frustration, but also of her profound and unconditional nationalism. Her commitment to Morocco and her struggle to overcome suffering and promote justice while maintaining her self-worth and conviction in life as an emancipated woman responsible for her actions are clearly highlighted. Will she be free to make all decisions in her present life? Will Abouzeid's protagonists fit the traditional model or will there be a paradigm shift based on their self-awareness and commitment to change? In the context of her book *The Last Chapter*, Moroccan women are expected to quietly submit to, arranged Muslim marriages, and quietly bear many children, neither of which Aisha does, bringing about a number of chaotic relationships. In a society where women are still seen for their reproductive abilities as breeders or sex objects, not for their economic or intellectual assets, will it be acceptable for Aisha to live her life as a single woman? This is a query whose answers are rather rhetorically assumed in today's modern society, although now more and more women are living a relatively independent life as compared to the past. Perhaps in another novel the author will provide us with a revolutionary heroine whose life won't be full of obstacles and who will fit in regardless of her choices. Until then, *The Last Chapter* provides us with an illustration of male/female relationships in which Aisha's romantic adventures showcase the flip side of the coin, that which goes counter to the Moroccan social norms. Simultaneously, the reader is also exposed to Moroccan socio-political life where corruption is rampant in the workplace and in the struggle for women's rights. The clashes between Islamic and Western values as well as with the older practices of sorcery and witchcraft, and the conflict between French and native language use are all intertwined in a strikingly poetic narrative.

The comment by *The Cairo Times* regarding *The Last Chapter* is edifying: "With an author as talented as Leila Abouzeid and the heroine an intellectual with the tongue of a Moroccan Dorothy Parker, there is a lot of substance to the novel."[66]

Considering the caliber of Abouzeid's writing, with picturesque and enticing narratives, one would have expected her to delve further into the heroine's consciousness to highlight her emotional state. Despite this, *The Last Chapter* is a multifaceted mosaic of the contemporary Moroccan social fabric which is most likely appealing to the younger generation whose present lives are rooted in the traditional cultural heritage of the past.

The Director and Other Stories from Morocco

This book was published in 2005 by the University of Texas at Austin, with an introduction by Elizabeth Warnock Farnea and followed by 20

---

[66]Leila Abouzeid, "Time of the Writer" Festival: Centere for Creative Arts, University of Kwazulu-Natal, 22–27 March 2004.

short stories, all well–sustained, as their narratives seem to start in the middle of the plot. Referring to Farnea's introduction, the maverick literary genre, a unique and independent style, which does not follow the general trend known as the short story has become increasingly popular in the West since its beginnings in the nineteenth century.

Using the oral tradition of story telling, what critics define as a "truncated narrative," or, referring to Hortense Calisher's definition that "a short story is a tempest in a tea-cup," the writer starts the narrative right in the middle of the plot. The reader assumes that some action has taken place before the story begins. The writer proceeds with the action and brings the tale to a conclusion, a conclusion in which something has changed in the lives of one or more of the characters. However, as Farnea concludes, the definition—of vignette, unfinished novel, or truncated narrative—has never prevented writers from trying to write all sorts of forms to accomplish their story telling.

With the kind of stories in *The Director and Other Stories from Morocco*, this new book constitutes a bridge between Western culture and the East. As in her first novel, *Year of the Elephant*, the author cuts across cultural and national boundaries to offer fiction that has meaning for European, American and Middle Eastern audiences. The stories in the volume deal with traditional and modern family relations between parents and children, between husband and wives, and between citizens of newly independent Morocco and its new nationalist representative government. Independence from French colonial rule has brought many changes more or less beneficial to Morocco. Women have entered the work force in great numbers, a development which has brought them new freedom, but which has also caused problems within the traditional family. Abouzeid's goal is to help the reader understand how these apparently positive changes toward modernity have affected ordinary people's lives and how the seemingly small daily events loom large in our individual lives. Does Abouzeid support to a certain degree the Western feminist expression "The personal is the political?" This expression is often used to explain how the little things we do on a daily basis may have ramifications and lead to socio-political impact and subsequent social transformation.

Abouzeid's stories exhibit some characteristics of professional storytellers when juxtaposed with the famous Middle Eastern "Arabian Nights" stories or other universal folktales, such as the African American "The Knee-high Man" story or the African "Ananse, the Spider" stories, despite the author's dealing with historical narratives. She is able to render her characters so as to create realistic fictions through which she can confront the cultural taboos of Moroccan life. "Arabs," she claims, "do not think of praising and recommending the self." Hence, the comic and humorous portrayal of the aunt "Mrs. the great director" is highlighted in the overuse of the first person which reflects the self-centeredness in a community that is mostly collectivist: "I bought," "I traveled," "I have," and the possessive use: "My seamstress," "My hairdresser," "My dress." All these reveal the shifting social behaviors of Moroccan people in the postcolonial/independence era. The social codes and resentment toward the half-literate are shown in the town women, who love and hate the aunt for her pomposity. Though they look up to the aunt because she has become a role model of fashion, elegance, and modernity, with all the prestige that goes along with living in the capital, they also despise her. Westernized natives who would mimic the colonizer's ways, as does the director's wife, whose behavior is more ridiculous and ignorant than that of a cultural renegade, end up being rejected by their own people. The aunt's language and behavior symbolize the self-centeredness and individualistic interest in material things.

Abouzeid uses different styles to reflect the various experiences of Moroccan people: traditional families, Western education, professional occupations, marriage, poverty, tragedy and pathos. The transformation of the past collective and communal Moroccan life is well-projected through the niece's visit and the sight of a picture hanging on the wall which brought back childhood memories of the aunt's past visits to their hometown when she was a little girl of seven.

A picture of the husband on his big motorcycle, wearing boots and riding trousers, a tweed jacket, a cap molding his head with earflaps turned down, enormous spectacles pushed up on his forehead, the kind used by pilots at the beginning of the century. He looked defiantly at the camera. The aunt is riding behind him with her fair veil. The photograph brought back to the visitor's mind that scene live . . . Children crowded and followed them . . . The husband went pushing the motorcycle in the alleys right to his in-laws courtyard where it stood sparkling in its metallic attire . . . The aunt had been matched in the little girl's mind, embodying for modernity and prestige. The aunt had been the first woman in town to enter school under colonialism and had spent two years . . . The aunt thinks of herself, right up to these days, as an educated, modern, enlightened and unique, etc . . . (*The Director*).

The contrast between the memory images of the past and the present life conditions of the aunt is familiar in the disenfranchised people's experiences, having to deal with the dreamlike promises of Western modernity and being disillusioned by the reality. The striking difference resides in the aunt's ignorance of the native official language. The author puts it well: "As for Arabic, she stayed illiterate in it not knowing the difference between a stick and Alif, the first letter of the Alphabet." (p. 24) Now the image of the place the couple lives in the city: "Across the courtyard, the wall opposite had experienced humidity, its lower part mossy. Ragged shadows swing on it in the light of the setting sun and autumn breeze. The house contained two rooms, one leading to the other. The inner one, probably the bedroom, was windowless. A full length curtain, dropped on obscurity, assumed the function of a door. The furniture in the first room consisted of hard mattress on banquettes of worn wood, upholstered in a cheap old fabric. A Turkish rug mostly threadbare covered the floor under a low table . . . In the corner sat a radio in the fifties style." (p. 23) The comical part of *The Director*'s narrative is for the niece to realize to her amazement that the so-called "Director," whom her aunt continued calling "The Great Director," was nothing more than the delivery boy at her new workplace in the city.

There has not been much work done on Leila Abouzeid yet, as she is emerging from the confines of postcolonial historical and semi-autobiographical writing. "At a time when there is growing interest in the intersections between gender and war, *Year of the Elephant* provides an unself-conscious enterprise of self-affirmation,"[67] states *World Literature Today*. "Leila Abouzeid has created a new style, a mosaic of expression with which she describes her old and yet new world of Morocco,"writes Ahmed Abd al-Salam al-Bakkah, a Moroccan author.[68]

Through her stories, readers have the opportunity to assess how much the socio-historical and religious intersect with gender and political activism. The overlapping of the personal and the political is evidenced through the intentional choice of powerful female characters as protagonists whose experiences reflect those of the majority of women and whose consciousness reflects that of the rebel, or heroine whose experiences or deeds transcend the ordinary.

One of the factors that led Moroccan women to join the political action and the national struggle was the acquisition of education, leading to resistance to the violent colonial rule and the yearning for independence. One understands the motive of the writer as a social activist whose role is to tell the truth, by telling her story and that of her community. Going back to the most acclaimed of Leila Abouzeid's novels, *Year of the Elephant* (1989), the protagonist Zahra's plight is significant, as she does not have education to help her make a living as a divorced woman. Though she was a guerilla fighter for independence, and at times even

---

[67]Year of the Elephant, introduction by Elizabeth Warnock Fernea, in Modern Literatures in Translation Series, www.utexas.edu/utpress/books/aboyep.htm. Retrieved 12/4/2010.

[68]Ibid, www.utexas.edu/utpress/books/aboyep.html. Retrieved 12/4/2010.

imagined herself as one of the Qur'anic women of the Prophet Mohammed (PBH), she finds herself helpless faced with Moroccan social
reality. Her brother-in-law does not hesitate to point out the increasing
shift in the Moroccan social needs: "These days you need a high school
degree to get any work at all. Soon they will require a college degree, and
some day a college degree won't get you a job sweeping the streets." (p.
66) Though Zahra is illiterate, she gains self-confidence and gets a job
at the French Cultural Centre, while strengthening her religious faith.
As a politically-engaged Moroccan writer, Abouzeid has been involved
in the country's women's movement and concerned organizations. For
instance, in Elizabeth Warnock Farnea's *In Search of Islamic Feminism:
One Woman's Global Journey* (1998), she mentions that Abouzeid was on
a commission "investigating the current practice of family law in Morocco" that might be of important interest for her to look into (Anchor,
p. 62).

> National history is a site in which interpretation of past events
> is constantly negotiated depending on one's location. It is often
> used by national elites to justify and reinforce existing gender
> and class relationships in society. Thus, feminist authors, as part
> of their struggle to transform women's roles in their societies,
> sometimes choose to challenge dominant versions of the history
> and offer alternative versions of the national past.[69]

Is Liat Kozma's (1999) contention justified in her assessment of
Abouzeid's *Year of the Elephant?* In a research article, "Remembrance
of Things Past: Leila Abouzeid and the Moroccan National History,"
Kozma states that Abouzeid's attempts to reread and rewrite Moroccan
history from the margins, rather than from the center, as constituted

---

[69]Kozma, Liat, "Remembrance of Things Past: Leila Abouzeid and Moroccan National
History" in *Social Politics—International Studies in Gender, State, and Society,* Vol. 6 No 3
pp. 388–406, Oxford University Press, 1999.

mainly by mainstream male interpretation was perceived in *Year of the Elephant* as an endeavor to promote a feminist agenda. Abouzeid later confirms this in her open rejection of the French language, the language of the colonizer. She explains her choice to write in Arabic as a political stand, which of course pushes for a North African, and particularly Moroccan, women's standpoint. It is the expression of their voice long silenced by the patriarchal dominance based, on the one hand, on colonial rule and, on the other, on the local male objectification and violence against women. In a sense, Abouzeid has followed in the footsteps of the famous Egyptian woman writer Nawal El-Saadawi, who also chooses to write in Arabic rather than in English. All her original writings are in Arabic and most have been translated into 30 languages, including English, French, German, and Thai. These include such titles as *Woman at Point Zero* (1982), *The Hidden Face of Eve* (1980), and *Walking through Fire* (2002), just to name a few.

As we are wrapping up this entry on Abouzeid's historical accounts of the Moroccan women's struggle for freedom from male bondage at the same time that they were contributing in their nation's freedom from colonialism, it would be helpful to revisit some ideas mentioned earlier in the historical background of this paper. Both authors—Salah Moukhlis and Liat Kozma—respectively asserted that throughout her novels, Leila Abouzeid is trying to re-write Moroccan history from a female perspective. This is evidenced the choice of a political stand which validates and gives Voice to ordinary women who contributed in the multi-faceted struggle against patriarchal hegemony inside and against the French colonial domination from outside. Another query that needs touching on is whether Leila Abouzeid's writing, though largely influenced by Islamic religion, could be classified as "Third World Feminism" because of shared colonial features with other disenfranchised women in poor countries. The answer is better provided in Poon Angelia's (2000) *Re-writing the Male Text and Mapping*, in Edwidge Danticat's *Krik? Krak!* and, in Jamaica Kincaid's *A Small Place*. Chandra Mohanty, charting the critical space for a Third World Feminism and stressing the importance of women telling or writing their stories in "Replacing Culture," puts it eloquently:

> Feminist analysis has always recognized the centrality of rewriting and remembering history. This is a process which is significant not merely as a correction to the gaps, erasures, and misunderstandings of hegemonic masculinist history, but because the very practice of remembering and rewriting leads to the formation of political consciousness and self-identity (p. 30).

On June 5, 2001, Heather Tyler gave a high grading of four stars to *Year of the Elephant*, ranking Abouzeid's novel with high standards and among the best creative works, and commenting that:

> It was the first time a novel by a Moroccan woman had been translated from Arabic into English. The contents of the book were also radical: that of a female activist facing divorce in mid-life and her struggle to survive when her rights were perilously few in a society that did not accommodate her situation. Rather, it punished her for the failed marriage. Abouzeid's story touches on some similar issues: that of revolt, torn allegiances, political and personal persecution in a country fraught with power struggles. A must read for Western feminists and Western women in general. (Heather Tyler, June 5, 2001)

The novel starred a female activist faced with divorce and her struggle to survive in a society that did not accommodate her situation, divorced, illiterate, childless, and without economic resources.

PART SIX

Reflection on Arts and Women's Activism

The Role of the Writer as an Activist and Promoter of Social Change

In this last section of our discussion on *African Literature: Gender Discourse, Religious Values and the African Worlview*, the different essay selections have been geared towards not only highlighting the diversity of African writers, but also showcasing specificities that make African literary production so rich and multidimensional. Though most writers discussed in this book share more or less similar concerns regarding issues such as social justice in the distribution of wealth, poverty and national stability, the disparities between gender roles and cultural practices have been the prime target of this study. Some men have expressed interest in raising women's issues, women's writing about their experiences and sharing their stories through autobiographies or fiction narratives have opened a window on unheard voices.

The resilience with which their stories are written is profound and identifiable in ordinary people's lives. African Diaspora women writers have managed to bring the everyday life experiences into the academic realm where theory could actually be practically implemented scientifically through analysis and critical thinking. Through literature, individual and collective cultural history can be recaptured and released to the general public. It is through storytelling, or more precisely, writing, that consciousness of one's place and role in a community is determined, or reaffirmed. In addition, African Diaspora women's writings are didactic inasmuch as they also serve a therapeutic remedy for the predicaments and psychological issues women have to deal with, internally and externally.

There are many African writers, such as East African and South African writers, who constitute a huge contingent for future research. African writers whose works have been discussed here represent only a sample, the tip of the iceberg that is the African literary world. Are people born with the label "activist" at their naming ceremony or baptism? How then does an individual become an activist or promoter of social change? The discussion of Leila Abouzeid's work, including the following sections of our study, constitutes an exploration of, and an attempt to provide answers to the aforementioned questions.

In discussing Flora Nwapa as a pioneering African woman writer, and other African writers selectively, namely Mariama Ba, Buchi Emecheta, and touching superficially on the powerful young Chimamanda Adichie's *Purple Hibiscus*, one has considered the characteristics that these young writers share with first generation postcolonial male writers as well as those characteristics which make them different from one another as female writers. The focus of this study has been particularly on the analysis of a paradigm shift in traditional gender roles and male/female relationships illustrated through female character depictions in Flora Nwapa's *Efuru*. The comparative approaches allowed for expanding on other African women writers in the Francophone zone, such as Mariama Ba in Senegal and Leila Abouzeid in Morocco, both pioneers in their respective locations. The discussion of culture is based on the intersection of religious pluralism, traditionalism, Christianity, Islam and secular ritualistic practices which shaped the African social fabric. Historical external influences having strengthened patriarchal behaviors and the subsequent subjugation and annihilation of women, African women writers have been led into rewriting their own stories or creating fiction narratives that not only showcase women's perspectives but correct female images that have been distorted. African women's creativity illustrates their perceptions of reality and their yearning for a more balanced world with equal privileges and complementary attitudes towards both genders, male and female.

Molara Ogundipe-Leslie (1994) defines the feminist perspective of the woman writer as having two main responsibilities in society. First, the woman writer has to tell about being a woman. Second, she has to describe reality from a woman's view, a woman's perspective, as opposed to what men have done so far. Anais Nin (1973) made a similar point twenty years earlier: the woman artist has to create something different from man. She has to sever herself from the myth man creates, from being created by him. She has to struggle with her own cycles, storms, and terrors, which man does not understand. As mentioned earlier, most postcolonial male writers created female characters who were too subordinate, or who were not fully realized. Therefore, asking for a description of reality from a woman writer would be quite a legitimate way to correct the record. This allows the individual to better understand women's issues and be interested in doing that.

Flora Nwapa was chosen because she is one of the first Nigerian feminist writers whose works illustrate a strong sense of self-awareness, self-esteem, and female solidarity as illustrated through the questioning and challenging of gender inequalities in Nigeria. Further, she has tried to show the empowerment of women in general and particularly of Igbo women through their resourcefulness and economic independence. On another note, through *Efuru*, Flora Nwapa has depicted a woman-istic character similar to Zora Neal Hurston's Janie in *Their Eyes Were Watching God*. In the Harlem Renaissance era, a male-dominated literary world could hardly perceive the importance of the revolutionary writer that Hurston was. Though Hurston presented us with progressive female character development brought to maturity towards the end of her social experiences and especially her relationships with men, respectively Logan Killicks, Joe Stokes and Tea Cake, Flora Nwapa came up with a fully self-reliant and confident female character assertive of her choices in life and who followed through her agenda as not only respectful of traditions and the elders, but also adaptable to different situations (marriage without dowry, circumcision, pregnancy, birth and loss of her child, desertion of two husbands and loss of father), ambitious, and representative of other womanistic characteristics. Efuru's behavior in caring for her mother-in-law, Ossai, and her philanthropic gestures to her community members are illustrative of her family-centeredness and community orientation.

After grappling with the multiple socio-economic roles of women in *Efuru*, we have measured the extent to which women's responsibilities and political involvement are significant. In reference to Amadiume's book, *Male Daughters, Female Husbands*, one cannot but agree with Flora Nwapa that the African woman, in her past, has had a career more active than that of men.

The traditionally important role women have played has been revived in some recent writings, including film production. For instance, African filmmaker Sambene Ousmane's "Fat-Kine," examines the frequently forgotten and pivotal economic power African women have played throughout history without being recognized and given their political place in modern society. A movie such as "Tableau Feraille" satirizes the aftermath of male political aspirations and failure to construct solid family structures. Malian film-maker Adama Drabo's "Tafaa Fanga," or "The Skirt Power," is poignantly significant in that gender roles are pushed to their extreme with a paradigm shift in the division of labor where men are seen carrying pots full of water fetched from the river. Women's power, which is covert, is barely noticeable in the general social arena. However, though it may take the will of one to make a difference, reference to historical and anthropological studies has shown the reign of several African women leaders in different societies of the continent. In other words, if the situation is totally different in today's society, in general,

> Perhaps in almost all African societies, the woman has a "kingdom" of her own, with its obligations and its recognition. She frequently has responsibility for cultivation of land, for the preparation of food, with all its customary significance, for rituals concerned with fertility; and settling a host of questions concerned with marriage of young people and the obligations connected with it.[70]

---

[70]Hunter, Guy, 1965, "From the Old Culture to the New," *The Study of Africa*, (Methuen & Co) p. 321.

The end of Nwapa's novel finds symbolism in the choice the heroine makes to go back to her father's house and lead a life of spiritual tranquility. In terms of literary art, *Efuru*, on its surface, is a realistic portrayal of everyday Africa. Everything that is described in Nwapa's novel has been confirmed by Ifi Amadiume's anthropological work *Male Daughters, Female Husbands.* But the choice Efuru makes to be the worshipper of a traditional deity has a symbolic meaning. The symbolic representations are so significant in the African mind that the tribal memory is always what guides people's lives. Reference to Meyer Fortes and E. E. Evans-Pritchard's work, "Values to African Tribal Life" (1971) might be helpful.

> Members of an African society feel their unity and perceive their common interests in symbols, and it is their attachment to these symbols which more than anything else gives their society cohesion and persistence. In the forms of myths, fictions, dogmas, represent the unity and exclusiveness of the groups, which respect them. They are regarded, however, not as mere symbols, but as fine value in themselves.[71]

A quick comment shows that the survival of different ethnic groups in Africa and their relationships with language and the symbolic meaning of artistic creativity have helped in safeguarding their culture. This can apply to the survival of fugitive slaves in the Underground Railroad during slavery. Through songs or quilt designs, which bore symbols only recognizable to insiders, slaves were able to communicate without the masters being aware of what their intentions were.

In the Myth of the Lake or Sea Goddess Uhamiri, we see her human counterpart Efuru. She is as beautiful, kind and helpful as Uhamiri,

---

[71]Fortes Meyer & Prichard Evans E.E, "Values to African Tribal Life," *The Study of Africa*, p. 56, quoted by Nandakumar in *Africa Quarterly* July–Sept 1971, p. 134.

according to the descriptions in the novel. Flora Nwapa's use of the English language to reflect the Igbo mind is a well-known artistic technique
among Igbo writers such as Amadi and Achebe. Conversational language
is often illustrated by interactions between people and tales. As Chinua
Achebe puts it metaphorically in *Things Fall Apart*, "among the Igbo the
art of conversation is regarded very highly and proverbs are the palm-oil
with which words are eaten."[72]

Similarly in the course of the novel, *Efuru*, the elders repeatedly la-
ment the carelessness of the younger generation while conversing. They
have given up the formal greetings, respectful terms of reference and that
delicate understatement conveyed through the use of familiar proverbs.
This change in youth is due to the influence of colonization in the Igbo
social environment. Though Efuru welcomes the new medical treatment
by sending people to the hospital, she still retains all that is good from
the past, including a knowledge of proverbs and how to formally greet
elders. Let's mention a few metaphorical comparisons contained in a few
proverbs in *Efuru* and Mariama Ba's *So Long A Letter*:

> The son of a gorilla must dance like the father gorilla.
> It is well, but not very well.
> It is said that an elderly person cannot watch a goat being en-
> trapped and do nothing.
> For we don't know tomorrow, tomorrow is pregnant, as they say.
> You do not fell a tree whose shade protects you, you water it, you
> watch over it.
> Binetou like others was like a lamb slaughtered on the altar of
> affluence.
> A woman is like a ball, once thrown no one can predict where it
> will bounce.[73]

---

[72]Achebe, Chinua *Thangs Fall Apart*, p. 7.
[73]Mariama, Ba,1989, *So Long a Letter*, p. 15.

Flora Nwapa's work reflects most general characteristics of post-colonial writing, as stated by Bill Ashcroft, et al. (1989). The importance of metaphor/metonymy as distinctive of post-colonial texts is raised by Homi Bhabba (1984) who argued that "the perception of the figures of the text as metaphor imposes a universalistic reading because metaphor makes no concessions to the cultural specificity of texts."[74] Apart from the use of metaphors, the technique of selective lexical fidelity, in other words, the use of certain non-translated Igbo words are devices for conveying the sense of cultural distinctiveness, what some called "Africanisms." Moreover, such uses of the traditional language signify a certain cultural experience the writer cannot reproduce in the Western language, but whose difference is validated. The incorporation of different words and metaphors provides a cross-cultural character of the linguistic medium which in a way transcends the fragmented perception of language and the meaning given to words according to culture based on time and space. Finally, by realizing the myth of Uhamiri in terms of Efuru's life, Nwapa has created in *Efuru* a memorable character, part-real, and part-symbolic. She has also illustrated the African personality in its historical and cultural settings through characters like Nwashike and Ajanupu, because they symbolize the native dignity and basic humanity in their respect for traditional ways.[75]

Through Efuru's characterization we have a prototypical image of African womanhood, the expression of the traditional African woman's voice in a highly patriarchal society and of the African social environment. Nwapa's use of the English language is an illustration of the traditional world vision with an African context, which creates in its turn an originality of style. Though the focus is on the traditional factors,

---

[74]Homi K. Bhabba, in Nation and Narrative, from "Canadian Narrative Cinema from the Margins: 'The Nation' and Masculinity in *Goin' Down the Road*" by Christine Ramsay, p. 29 , www.Filmstudies.ca/journal/pdf/cj-film-studies223_Ramsay_margins.pdf Retrieved, July1st 2011.

[75]Ibid, p. 29.

the transitional or transformational process should not be overlooked. We notice the new cultural elements that the British or French colonization brought along with it, such as the Western school, the hospital, and other aspects that are not mentioned in the novel but are implied through the presence of White women and their behavior as compared to the native Igbo people.

Nwapa's *Efuru* embodies the crucial role of the writer in developing countries, which Mariama Ba articulates in *So Long a Letter*. Ba suggested that the "sacred mission of the writer was to strike out at the archaic practices, traditions and customs that are not a real part of our precious cultural heritage." She viewed the first educated African women to be destined for the mission of emancipation:

> To lift us out of the bog of tradition, superstition and custom, to make us appreciate a multitude of civilizations without renouncing our own, to raise our vision of the world, cultivate our personalities, strengthen our qualities, to make up for our inadequacies, to develop universal moral values in us: these were the aims of our admirable headmistress.[76]

The Western influence is important, as Mariama Ba points out in her novel by referring to the White schoolteacher who instilled in them the desire for knowledge and self-worth. The transformation is well-defined in the sense that certain traditional practices should be altered to give way for a new and different vision in the lives of the first educated Africans. Though the French colonization policy expected native Africans to assimilate the French culture, with the total transformation of Africans into people who have embraced French culture and are ready to behave like the French, the majority of colonized Africans have clung tightly to their traditional and secular cultural practices.

---

[76]Mariama Ba, 1989, *So Long a Letter*, pp. 15–16.

As Carole Boyce Davies (1986) contends in her collection of critical articles, *N'Gambika*, progressive African women perceive the women's struggle as more difficult than the obvious struggles for national liberation where the enemy is easily targeted. The complexity of our sociocultural oppression is evidenced in Gwendolyn Konie's description. She has pointed out that the struggle for Equal Rights between the sexes is going to prove even more difficult than that of colonization because in essence it is a struggle between husband and wife, brother and sister, father and mother (*N'Gambika*, p. 8). Another advocate, Annabella Rodrigues, who participated in the Mozambican liberation, identifies polygamy, initiation rites and dowry as the most difficult of traditions to eliminate and the most oppressive to women. One cannot but agree with her that it is easier to eliminate the colonial, bourgeois influences that were imposed on African women from outside than to eliminate generations of traditions from within our societies.

The study of culture and gender through Nwapa's novel, *Efuru*, and through the work of other African writers has allowed us to make connections between social history, anthropology, economy, and literature. It has also provided incentives to undertake further research on African women writers in juxtaposition to African American women writers. That study will lay the ground for discussions on the present status of women writers of African descent in the Diaspora. A scrutiny of cultural practices and historiography going back to the Kemetic era (ancient African civilization) might provide us with partial answers to questions such as why African women are where they are today. What place do they occupy in both the socio-economic and political arena from the post-colonial/independence to the present? What economic strategies do they develop to struggle, resist, and survive in a male-dominated environment where gender and other intersecting discriminations are perceived as acceptable? What kind of grass-roots projects are likely to work to boost women's socio-economic and mental health in a comfortable environment? Could such queries find answers in African literature?

Considering the various facets of the African woman's experiences, and her present situation regarding aspects of oppression that should be fought against, Molara Ogundipe-Leslie uses the poignant "mountain on the back" metaphor. She points out that African women have additional burdens such as foreign intrusion, heritage of tradition, their own backwardness and their men's domination bearing down on them. The most important challenge to the African woman, according to the writer, is her own self-perception. Since it is she who has to define her own freedom:

> The sixth mountain on the woman's back—herself—is the most important. Women are shackled by their own self negative-image, by centuries of the "interiorization" of the ideologies of patriarchy and gender hierarchy. Her own reactions to objective problems therefore are often self-defeating and self-crippling. She reacts with fear, dependency complexes and attitudes to please, and cajole where more self-assertive actions are needed.[77]

Throughout the study of various African writers of the post-independence era, patriarchal domination and the different facets of African women's oppression have been partially discussed. The depiction of Nwapa's characters in *Efuru* reflects more or less recurrent issues related to traditional life. Being one of the first African women writers in the 1960s, she has paved the way for other African women writers to further deal with contemporary complex characters and themes presenting other "faces of women" in Africa. The brief study of the Moroccan writer Leila Abouzeid has provided further explorations into African literary production by simultaneously stressing the impact of gender and culture on the main characters. The different narratives in *Year of the Elephant*,

---

[77]Molara Ogundipe-Leslie quoted by Carole Boyce Davies (1986) *N'Gambika: Studies of Women in African Literature*, p. 8, Africa World Press Inc. Trenton, NJ as refered to in "*The Journal of African Marxists* 5" (February, 1984–1989) pp. 35–6.

Return to Childhood, *The Last Chapter*, and *The Director* illustrate contemporary gender and cultural issues as a result of different patriarchal influences of colonization. Johnetta B. Cole's argument comes rightly to the point. She articulates the politics of difference as follows:

Patriarchal oppression is not limited to women of one race or of one particular ethnic group, women in one class, women of one age group or sexual preference, women who live in one part of the country, women of any one religion, or women with certain physical abilities or disabilities. Yet, while oppression of women knows no such limitations, we cannot therefore, conclude that the oppression of all women is identical. (Cole, 1988, p. 1)

Looking at the above definition and earlier treatments of African women's predicaments on different levels in Nwapa's *Efuru*, in regard to the portrayal of the traditional woman, there is a need to make some connections and conclude that she is in a transitional situation, or in mutation. That transformational process is highlighted in Mariama Ba's *So Long A Letter* in which Ramatoulaye and Aissatou's ambivalent situations affirm the educated African woman's dilemma and predicaments. Buchi Emecheta's *Second Class Citizen* is another case in which the reader witnesses the main character Adah's development and transformation throughout the plot, from Nigeria to England. The final point to make is that African women's experiences are so diverse and complex depending on the socio-cultural structures and their individual environmental socialization. As the oppression of all women is not identical, this partial study has hardly excavated the raw terrain of African women's lives. Tradition is something that must be cherished and kept jealously for the expression of our cultural identity. Let us get rid of those archaic practices that are detrimental to a category of people, namely women. It is the little contribution that opens up to other questions or domains for exploration. Let us borrow African American writer Audre Lorde's (1983) words to close this section:

Survival isn't some theory operating in a vacuum. It's a matter of
my everyday life and making decisions.
I urge each one of us to reach down into that
Deep place of knowledge inside herself and
Touch that terror and loathing of any
Difference, that lies there.[78]

The domain of gender and culture is a vast terrain for exploration
and for the purpose of introducing potential readers to African literature and the emergence and contemporary expansion of African women
writers. This discussion on *African Literature: Gender Discourse, Religious
Values and the African Worldview* is the tip of the iceberg that is wom-
en's issues viewed at regional and global levels. As it comes from one
of the pioneer African women writers, Flora Nwapa's novel, *Efuru*, is a
stepping stone and an insightful introduction to African women's concerns, concerns which were followed a decade later by her younger sister
Igbo woman writer, Buchi Emecheta, with *The Bride Price, Second Class
Citizen, The Joys of Motherhood* and others, including *Kehinde* which recently came out in 2006. While *Kehinde* deals with the current challenges and choices of African women living in the Diaspora, in *Second
Class Citizen* Emecheta talks not only about the struggle of Adah and her
survival as an individual but also about her dreams, what she calls the
"presence," while coming of age, maturing into a woman and moving
from a relatively high social status in Nigeria to the bottom of the social
ladder in a predominantly white British society.

Second Class Citizen depicts the struggle and development of women
trying to acquire education while surviving in a European environment
where racist hostility and adaptation to different cultural and religious
beliefs, coupled with misogyny and domestic violence, become daily
challenges. Negotiating these external influences while keeping one's

---

[78]Audre Lorde, *A Burst of Light*, 1988.

own cultural identity is the prototypical experience immigrants have to face in a foreign location. Here, the writer highlights the challenges and predicaments of women in general and African Diaspora women in particular. Should we think of a multiple jeopardy combination of race, class, gender, linguistic and geographical factors influencing the type of discrimination African Diaspora people have to cope with?

The interest in male/female relationships and discussion of gender differences are developed later in Flora Nwapa's last works, such as *One Is Enough* and *Women Are Different*, where the writer addresses clearly the intricacy of contemporary socio-cultural constraints and gender issues. Going back to the relational dynamics between men and women in Nwapa's and Emecheta's characters, and analyzing the latent signs of abuse and violence in Gilbert, the protagonist Efuru's second husband, or Adah's husband, Francis, in *Second Class Citizen*, one is tempted to state that the behavioral characteristics are brought to maturity in younger women writers such as Chimamanda Ngozi Adichie.

Though women have to deal with universal human issues like violence as a common social and global problem regardless of race, the extent and forms of abuse are dependent on the embedded patriarchal ideas and the sex roles expected from each gender. For example, considering Chimamanda Ngozi Adichie's *Purple Hibiscus* and Buchi Emecheta's *Second Class Citizen*, the motives behind the abusive behavior of Eugene, Kambili's father, are diametrically opposed to those displayed by Francis towards Adah. While Francis's violence might be interpreted as the result of laziness and frustration, Eugene's is perhaps driven by the instinct of domination, as well as ignorance of the new religion he apparently embraced without complying with its moral values. One may say that Papa is just an evil-spirited person who wears the mask of a prominent and good-hearted person, considering his popularity in the community.

Though a fictional work, *Efuru* has not only allowed a thematic and character study, it has helped to make connections between social history, anthropology and economy. The discussion of other African writers has opened a window on diverse perspectives and issues which pertain not only to African people but which also highlight the universality of gender and culture while focusing on the peculiarity of African literature. Briefly, this interdisciplinary approach to Nwapa's novel and the overview of Leila Abouzeid provide an incentive for further research on the work of other African women and women of African descent in the Diaspora. Such themes as gender, culture, patriarchy, oppression, marriage, religion, poverty, justice, violence, immigration, displacement, production, reproduction, and others that have been discussed in this study might open up a window for understanding the current status of contemporary African women writers' concerns in juxtaposition with those of African American women in the literary world. Nwapa revolutionized post-colonial African literature by highlighting the invisible women's social and economic contributions in an increasingly patriarchal and disintegrated society.

According to Emilia Oko (1999), Nwapa, as the first female Nigerian novelist, was defining the female self, charting her sphere like the Bronte sisters of nineteenth century England before feminism became popular. Her major works, *Efuru* and *Idu*, are celebrations of the female psyche, her consciousness, her mode of apprehending women being among a mercantile environment with trading activities. Among the Riverine Oru along the Niger Delta female genius has always been accepted. Woman is not the docile submissive unintelligent male subordinate in the patriarchal typology of the Igbo heartland such as the ones portrayed in Achebe's earlier novels. Oko continues her remarks about Igbo women in the following: woman's intellect in trade, her duplicitous serene quality and confusing love is what she celebrates as already existing and accepted among her people. Nwapa's genius is in articulating that every woman has been socialized by patriarchy into repressing her emotional self and sexuality as a human being.[79]

---

[79]Oko Emilia, 1999, " The Oguta World View and Flora Nwapa's novels" in *The Legacy of Flora Nwapa* editor: Helen O. Chukwuma, Journal of Women's Studies in Africa, Harmattan, 2000, p. 15.

In *Wives at War and Other Stories*, a testament of Flora Nwapa's foundational work is reflected in that the female characters have developed from the simple search for fulfilling the traditional female gender roles of marriage and childbirth into actively fighting political wars and surviving as human beings just as men, or achieving their personal dreams and reaching the highest level of self-actualization with or without a man in their lives. One would agree with Iniobong Uko, that in essence, Nwapa makes a realistic female portrayal, insisting that African and especially Nigerian women can transcend their traditional status to become vocal, aggressive, loving, ambitious, and courageous. Furthermore, taking a cue from Balberg:

The modern African woman of the future is not going to accept much longer a position ascribed to her by her male counterpart. The new African woman will probably wish to define the terms of her motherhood herself.[80]

In fact, a significant reflection and similarity between the above statements and Nwapa's life experience is very well documented in Maria Lanton Umeh's research work, *Flora Nwapa: A Pen and a Press*, highlighting the multi-faceted talents and life experiences of Flora Nwapa we would not have known otherwise. Unlike her fictional character Efuru, who ended her second marriage with Gilbert and went back to her father's house, Flora Nwapa bore the brunt of polygamy while finding her solace in creative activities and business through publishing and traveling in different parts of the world. She escaped the predicament of her real life and found refuge in writing and publishing books. Taking a cue from Maria Linton Umeh while quoting Paul Tyambe Zeleza:

---

[80]Uko Iniobong, "Engendering Models for Survival and Self-Actualization in Flora Nwapa's *Wives at War and Other Stories*", in (JOWSA) The Legacy of Flora Nwapa, Helen Chukwuma, Harmatta, 2000, p. 37.

Books constitute crucial repositories of social memories and imaginations containing the accumulated cultural capital of society, of its accomplishments, agonies, and aspirations. Publishers serve as indispensable midwives of the book industry, transforming private manuscripts into printed commodities for public consumption.[81]

Reference to Amadiume's value laden work, *Male Daughters, Female Husbands*, lays the foundation for discussing the complexity of a paradigm shift in traditional African gender roles and social constructs in contradiction to women's apparent invisibility in different spheres. Why do women have to work more than average to earn less than men in general? Given instances of resourceful strong women of African descent on the continent and in the Diaspora, why do they still have to bear the brunt of the work and be denied basic human rights of equality in the gender division of labor at home and pay equity in the modern workplace after bearing the brunt of slavery and colonization? Considering the plight of women and the multidimensional jeopardy that continental and Diaspora African women have to deal with in a patriarchal society, how do they negotiate these different challenges and survive in their individual or group locations? What strategies have they developed to struggle, resist and survive either in traditional societies or in transformed urban areas in Africa and Western countries with the increasingly growing digital use and tantalizing global challenges that shape our daily lives?

There is an urgent need for an investigation of the changing paradigm in African literature, from its traditional confines and nostalgic references of the past to the current shifting realities, particularly considering the number of African women writers living and writing in the African

---

[81]Paul Tyambe Zeleza, in Mary Linton Umeh, *Flora Nwapa: A Pen and A Press*, Triatlantic Books of New York, p. 105, 2010 (See Paul Zeleza's) "Introduction" to *Women in African in African Studies Scholarly Publishing*, pp. 1–44.

Diaspora (Europe, United States, South America, the Caribbean Islands, and elsewhere). Paying tribute to the first generation of pioneer African writers of the postcolonial era in the late 1950s and 1960s, and the increasingly growing number of intellectuals living in the Diaspora, what place do African women writers occupy in the African literary arena? What place will modern African literature occupy in the sophisticated digital era and the increasingly shrinking world? What pedagogical tools should be designed, and what methodologies should be implemented in broadening student and mainstream access to African literature? How have people of African Descent and particularly, women, managed to survive and start closing the inequities and inequality gaps in order to prepare the future generations for a better life? What role can women of African Descent play in educating and transforming the stereotypical perceptions of Africa and her people? The aforementioned queries constitute stimuli for a new search for answers, and as such are better left for future researchers in African Diaspora Studies to determine the impact of African literature in the world literary arena.

For those who might wonder why South African literature has not been included in this book, this restriction in the selection of our study is for the purpose of narrowing our focus down for practicality and cohesion. South African literature constitutes a huge body of work that will need attention for further studies dealing with the system of Apartheid and literary production in the recent post-independence era.

Finally, considering the historiographical locations and experiences of people of African descent the world over, African literature should be given more attention in academia, including a particular emphasis put on history. Far from pushing a propagandist agenda, one would recommend this rather for a viable and realistic grasp/discussion of common global issues such as cultural diversity, gender discrimination, violence, justice, war, isolation, relationships, and religion, just to name a few. Through their writings and artistic productions, people of African descent, while dealing with their own peculiar experiences, have crossed national and linguistic boundaries to explore our common human features in their various locations. Change in the mentality of people will only be possible if we change the basics of our informal education, and if we stop teaching the young boy that he is the master when the father is not around. If we start involving both boys and girls in the same chores, and if we stop having the young girl clean her brother's room when he is outside playing, then we will expect some possible transformation in the mentality of generations to come.

It is with humbling interests that closure is brought to this study hoping that the reader of the chapters above would find a stimulating piece of information that triggers critical thinking and adds to personal interest and knowledge. Moreover, the discussion/essay questions in the last part of the book would not only further insights in African literature, but add to a personal challenge and growth.

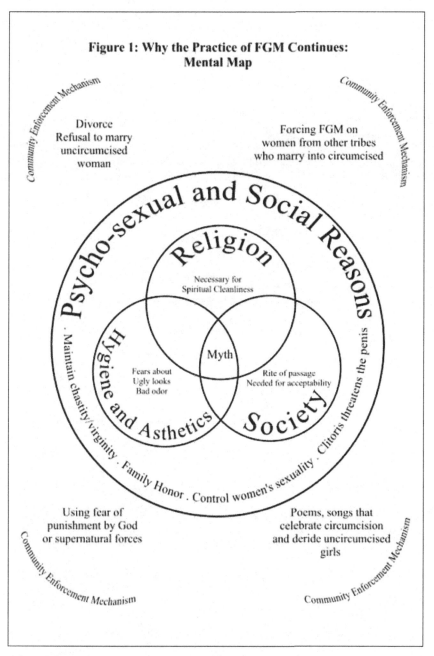

Figure 1: Why the Practice of FGM Continues: Mental Map

Department of Women's Health-Health Systems & Community Health Organization, 1999. This review was undertaken for the World Health Organization by the Program for Appropriate Technology in Health (PATH) in Washington D.C., U.S.A. The review was originally compiled and edited by Asha A. Mahamud, Nancy A. Ali and Nanvy V. Yinger. The additional support within PATH was provided by Zohra Yacoub, Dawn Sienicki, Samson Radeny, Ann Wilson, Elaine Murphy, Elsa Berhane, Kalle Makalou, TahirKhilji, Wendy Wilson, JoAnn Villanueva and Andrea Flores

Discussion & Essay Questions

Part One

1) What was the general trend of West African literature in the postcolonial era, the 1960s?

2) What historical phenomena contributed to shaping African women's social status from its original place into what it is today?

3) What triggered the writer's interest and discussion of Flora Nwapa's work? Give a few examples.

4) Comment on Prema Nandakumar's reference starting with: "They know . . . just the same" p. 21.

5) Why has it become difficult for women to participate in the political arena today? What new trends are emerging currently? Answer by using concrete examples based on the media and your own personal knowledge.

6) Find historical information and discuss its relationship to the last part of the last section of the same quote starting with "They know . . . be slaves no more."

7) What is the usefulness of studying a different culture, and specifically the Igbo society?

8) After reading this first part, how would you define gender from an African perspective as compared to the Western conception?

9) How does the concept of woman-man or "nimpi-nindja" in the Bassar people's culture (discussed in the characterization of Efuru and Amadiome's Flexible Gender role in Igbo society) appeal to you? What equivalent do we have in the Western perception of boys and girls?

10) What role did writers such as Flora Nwapa and Mariama Ba play respectively in the independence era, 1960s and the 1980s?

Part Two

1) What kind of beliefs governed men and women's behavior in traditional Igbo society? Do you think these beliefs are appropriate and applicable to contemporary society?

2) How does anthropologist Amadiume explain the Igbo gender division of labor in Nnobi? What do you think of those pre-colonial dispositions in some African societies?

3) Do you agree or disagree with the argument that European colonization was responsible for economic and social problems African countries have today?
Justify your answer with concrete examples.

4) How do you understand the process of "having one's bath" that Efuru had to go through before her first pregnancy in Nwapa's novel *Efuru*?

5) What do you think of tattooing and plastic surgery frequently practiced today? Discuss the practice considering the emotions that go along with it.

6) Choose one aspect/topic/theme in Igbo society and discuss it with regard to your own culture. Try pointing out the similarities or/and differences, and explain why.

7) What is your position on Alice Walker's remarks on female circumcision?

8) What role do you think patriarchy plays in the perpetuation of women's subjugation?

9) Do women have any responsibility and important role to play in their own alienation? Explain by giving two examples.

10) What place does the "*Dibia*" occupy in traditional Igbo society? Have you ever heard of or met any people playing equivalent roles in today's society?

11) What is the significance of breaking kola nuts in most African societies? Is there anything similar in modern day American society or your culture? Explain the ritual.

12) Comment on African American writer Alice Walker's remarks about her book *Warrior Marks*, in Boukari's "*Critical Perspectives on Gender and Culture*" (See p. 55).

13) Discuss the pros and cons of polygamy in traditional societies and modern day societies.

14) Explain the transformation and significance of the dowry. Do you agree with the institution of paying something before getting married, or not? Explain why.

15) What solution do you see for the large rate of divorce in developed countries? Is marriage worth it at all? If yes, why would people opt out?

16) What is your opinion about arranged marriages or mail-order bride practices now common among immigrants? Could you propose better ways of dealing with male/female relationships?

17) What provisions are made for today's male/female relationships and the reduction of the divorce rate in the United States?

18) What population policies are implemented in other countries you know?

19) Considering the present environmental transformation related to global warming, how could a population policy affect the present situation?

20) What implications does John Mbiti's statement have on the characters depicted in Flora Nwapa's novel *Efuru*? (Think of the protagonist and the second medicine man, who determined that Efuru was a worshipper of the "Lady of the Lake").

21) Could you give a few reasons explaining why having children should not matter anymore in our modern society?

22) How do you explain poor people's tendency to have many children?

23) What trends are observed in present-day marriage celebrations?

24) Where do you stand regarding the polemics on same sex unions?

Part Three

Explain your understanding of the book title *African Literature: Gender Discourse, Religious Values and the African Worldview?*

1) What caught your attention in the section discussing Old Ahamba and Father Higler's beliefs about God?

2) How do you understand the philosophy behind Old-Ahamba's behavior and his diverse conversations with Father Higler, the Christian priest?

3) What kind of relationship exists between the traditional priest and Father Higler? How do you explain their encounters?

4) How would you characterize Philip in the plot? What kind of relationship has developed between Father Higler and Philip? Why?

5) What impact do you think religion/spirituality has on people's lives? Do you practice any religion? How did you get involved in it? What do you draw from it? If not, why is it not worth it? In other words, what led you into rejecting or embracing a religion?

6) What difference is there between Traditional African Religion and Christianity, Islam or Judaism? Give some concrete examples from the reading to illustrate your answers.

7) What roles do the Christian cross and the Igbo "ofo" staff play, respectively, during a Christian mass and a traditional ceremony?

8) What is your definition of religion and spirituality? Comment on what you think might be more important.

9) What is a myth? What place do myths occupy in sustaining our belief systems and the choices we make in life?

Part Four

1) What kind of relationship does Ajanupu have with Efuru's maid?

2) Considering Ajanupu's character and invading presence in Efuru's private life, how would you define the social structure of Igbo people as compared to today's modern life?

3) How would Ajanupu be perceived in your social environment? Discuss any similar or different type of character you know in your family,

neighborhood, or workplace by highlighting the impact such a person has on others around.

4) Imagine the character of Ossai (Adizua's mother) in contemporary society. Select and discuss one of the following options:
  a. As a modern younger sister to Ajanupu,
  b. As a married woman with a son in American, African, Asian, Latin American, or European society. What could she have done regarding her marriage?
  c. How could she have handled Adizua's education including her household? (Make sure you discuss within cultural boundaries.)

5) Comment on African woman writer Ama Ata Aidoo's position about women's social expectations and work. How is this position regarding the idea that girls are circumcised in order to be marriageable and the Western Victorian concept of propriety and true womanhood?

6) What aspects of Ajanupu's depiction make her a postmodern woman?

7) What role do you think the extended family play in a married couple's life in Africa? Discuss this based on concrete examples drawn from the readings, internet or by any other means of information you may get from third parties.

Part Five (A)

1) What cultural or gender aspect(s) caught your attention the most in chapter five? Explain why.

2) You have been exposed to some feminist/womanist ideas on women's plight and roles in society through the image of "the mountain" on Black women's backs. Do you think other women are exempt from that burden? Explain by using concrete examples to support your arguments.

3) What aspects of African literature can you identify with? Compare or contrast those aspects with those of a book you read in American literature.

4) Discuss the theme of violence in Buchi Emecheta's novel *Second Class Citizen*, and in *Purple Hibiscus* by Chimamanda Ngozi Adichie. (Make sure you adopt a comparative approach in discussing the different aspects of violence based on concrete examples.)

5) Discuss the characterization of both Adah and Francis.

6) What role does Pa Noble play in the plot of *Second Class Citizen*?

7) What is the relevance of reading non-Western literature in a predominantly white institution?

8) What aspects of the reading covered could you identify with? Explain with concrete examples that illustrate the similarities or differences regarding today's society.

Part Five (B)

1) What is Leila Abouzeid's social background? How do you think this influenced her development into a writer?

2) Name three countries in North Africa which are neighbors to Morocco.

3) What social issues does author Leila Abouzeid often address throughout her books?

4) What comparisons could you make between Moroccan women and American women or other women in different places of the globe?

5) How would you explain activism? Find four examples which illustrate Moroccan women's activism during the resistance era against French colonization.

6) What instructions does the Islamic religion provide for women in case of divorce?

7) Explain marriage practices in your community. What comparison/parallel could you mention considering what you read in this book?

8) Explain why the protagonist in *The Last Chapter* chooses male friends rather than girls? Do you agree with the justification given in Abouzeid's narrative?

9) What helped Moroccan women to join the struggle for their country's independence?

10) What difference or similarity is there between Zahra and Aisha as female protagonists in *Year of the Elephant* and *The Last Chapter*, respectively?

11) What is Leila Abouzeid's purpose in creating the female characters in her narratives?

12) Discuss Mariama Ba's *So Long a Letter* and Leila Abouzeid's *Year of the Elephant*.

Part Six

1) What stereotypes are perpetuated about Africa and about contemporary African women activists?

2) How are outspoken women perceived by their peers, and especially in a patriarchal society?

3) List four myths about Africa and explain how you learned about them. How could you debunk those myths and discover the reality?

4) How does Efuru's portrayal transcend the mainstream male painting of women?

5) How does the following statement, ". . . a good woman does not have a brain or mouth" appeal to you? Reflect and react to it keeping in mind your grandparents' perceptions and expectations about women according to traditional gender roles in the family.

6) In Mariama Ba's *So Long a Letter*, describe the main character, Rama-toulaye, and Aissatou, her friend. What would you have done if you were in Ramatoulaye's situation?

7) Find four different themes, or issues, that Flora Nwapa raises in her book, *Efuru*, and discuss each in comparison with today's American society and social problems.

8) Are matrimonial issues peculiar to African society? Justify your opinion by using concrete examples including your own experience, or knowledge.

9) What definition does Omolara Ogundipe-Leslie give of a woman writer's role? Do you agree with that definition or not? Explain.

10) Comment on this proverb, "A woman is like a ball, once thrown no one can predict where it will bounce."

11) How does Omolara Ogundipe-Leslie represent the challenges facing the African woman? What symbolic meaning does the image of the mountain have?

12) What caught your attention in reading about African literature, and discussing different socio-cultural issues?

13) *Research Topics:* Select one or two areas from the following themes to do research in:
   a. Infanticide and bride-burning practices in India. How are these practices similar or different from female genital cutting in Africa, or body modification such as tattooing/branding to belong to a fraternity, sensitive body part piercing, and plastic surgery in modern society?
   b. Plastic Surgery (Liposuction and others)
   c. Domestic Violence
   d. Single parenthood
   e. Marriage as an Institution
   f. Singlehood
   g. Same sex marriage
   h. Transgenderism

14) What impact does culture have in the way the above situations are experienced?

15) If you had the opportunity of making a difference in your community, what would you do? What are your perceptions of an ideal society?

Endnotes

1. "Ofo" is a staff, not a stick. It's like a staff of office for the first son of a family, village head, clan heads . . . in that order.

2. See Miriam Maat Ka-Re-Monges' Kush: Jewel of Nubia: Reconnecting the Root System of African Civilization,1999

3. A journalist wrote in the *New York Times* front page headline, "Woman Plea for Asylum Puts Tribal Ritual on Trial" (*New York Times*, April 15, 1996). This is about a young woman from Togo who escaped being circumcised before marriage, traveled through Germany and finally came to the United States seeking for asylum. This young woman got imprisoned for two years, and was eventually released after feminist advocates campaigned and pleaded for Ms Kasinga to be granted asylum under the Human Rights Protection. Though some contradictory letters to the editor from some opponents were sent to refute the newspapers' rendition of Ms Kasinga's story, apparently journalists were so carried away in the sensational that they would not take into account those statements refuting the media rhetoric. While Fawuzia Kasinga was kept in detention for seeking asylum, it is impressive to see how much attention the U.S. media and newspapers gave to this case.

4. In the case of Togo, the example can apply to the Central Region of the country, particularly in Sokode, Bassar, Bafilo, Tchamba and others where coincidently the concentration of Muslims are, though the practice has nothing to do with religion, Islam or Christianity. One should also note that the perpetuation of the practice is favored by family pressure and lack of freedom of speech. Silence, due to retaliatory punishment and age-group shame for girls prevent people from speaking out and revealing the continuation of the practice. Further information can be found on: Immigration and Refugee Board of Canada (20 July 2006) Togo: Female genital mutilation (FGM); practices, beliefs, and Protection Offered.

5. A modern example is the popular TV guest Ms. Cleo, who was discovered to have ripped off thousands of people by pretending to be a Caribbean fortune-teller or psychic; mainstream society believed her until recently when her scam and her real identity were discovered. How many Ms Cleos are still out there exhibiting their pseudo-talents at different community gatherings and conferences or using online advertizing?

6. This was a two classrooms survey in AAS 281 section 1 & 2 at Western Illinois University (Fall 2009).

Bibliography

Abdullah Yusuf Ali, *English Translation of the Holy Qur'an: Meaning of the Qur'an with Notes*, Al-Minar Publishers, by Saud Arham, Churiwalan Delhi, India, 1996, 542–544.

Abouzeid, Leila, *Al-Fil*, published in episodes in Rabat, in Al Mithaq newspapers 1983, by Dar Al Maarif, then Beyrut by Dar Al Afaq Al Jadida in 1987.

Abu-Lughod, Lila, "Review: 'Orientalism' and Middle East Feminist Studies" (Review Essay,) Feminist Studies 27, no. 1 (Spring 2001):101–113.

———. *Year of the Elephant: A Moroccan Woman's Journey Toward Independence*, University of Texas at Austin, Center for Middle Eastern Studies, 1989.

———. *Return to Childhood: The Memoir of a Moroccan Woman*, University of Texas at Austin, 1998.

———. *The Last Chapter: A Novel*, Cairo, The American University of Cairo Press, 2003.

———. *The Director and Other Stories from Morocco*, University of Texas Press, 2005.

Achebe, Chinua, *Things Fall Apart*, Longman, London, 1958.

———. 1969, *Arrow of God*, Anchor Books edition.

Adichie, Chimamanda Ngozi, *Purple Hibiscus*, Anchor Books, A Division of Random House Inc., New York, NY, 2004.

Afigbo, Adiele, 1996, *Igbo Women: Why Mgbafo Philosophy Is More than Plato's* in *African People's Review*, Sept–Dec, 1996.

Afonja, S. "Women Power, Authority in Traditional Yoruba Society," *Visibility & Power Essays on Women in Society & Development* Ed, L. Dube & E. Leacock, Oxford, 1983.

Aidoo, Ama Ata, 1995, "African Women: Then and Now" in *Women: Looking Beyond*, NewYork City, United Nations Publications, 2000.

Al Qur'an: A Contemporary Translation by Ahmed Ali, Princeton University Press Surah *"Al-Fil"* The Elephants (Chapter 105), New Jersey, 1994, p. 552.

Arrington-Akorede Wanda, *The Other Wife: A Story of Courage and Strength of One Woman for the Sake of her Unborn Child*, Writers Club Press, Universe Press, Lincoln, NE, 2000.

Amadi, Elechi, *The Concubine*, Longman, London, 1996.

Amadiume, Ifi, 1992, *Male Daughters, Female Husbands* by Billings & Sons Ltd, Worcester, 1992.

Asefa, Semra, "Female Genital Mutilation: Violence in the Name of Tradition, Religion, and Social Imperative" In French, Stanley G., Teays Wanda and Purdy, Laura M., (Ed.) *Violence Against Women: Philosophical Perspectives*, Ithaca and London, Cornell University Press, 1998.

Ashcroft Bill, Gareth Griffiths, & Helen Tiffin, *The Empire Writes Back*, Routledge, London, New York, 1989.

Badran Magot, Islamic Feminism: What is in a name? Published by A-Ahram Weekly Online, 17–23 January 2002, Issue No 569.

Baker, Alison, *Voices of Resistance: Oral Histories of Moroccan Women*, Published by SUNY Press, 1998.

Beauvoir (de) Simone, Introduction "Woman as Other" in *The Second Sex* (1949), pp. 1–19. http://www.marxizts.org/reference/subject/ethics/de-beauvoir/2nd-sex/introduction.htm, retrieved 7/2/2007.

Bird, Caroline, *You're exploited, brainwashed, underprivileged if you're Born Female*, Source Book for the Women's Liberation Movement, Pocket, (1967, February 15, 1975).

Boukari, A. S. Safoura, *The Socio-Religious Factor in the Fiction of Achebe's Things Fall Apart & Echewa's The Land's Lord* (Unpublished) Master's Thesis, Universite du Benin, Lome, Togo, 1990.

Chesser, B. J., "Analysis of Wedding Rituals: An Attempt to Make Weddings More Meaningful" *Family Relations* 29:204–209, 1980.

Chukwuma, Helen, O. Journal of Women's Studies in Africa (JOWSA), *The Legacy of Flora Nwapa*, Harmattan, 2000.

Cole, Johnetta B. "Commonalities & Differences" in *All American Women*, New York, The Free Press, 1988, p. 1.

Corbett, Sara, The New York Times Magazine "A Cutting tradition." www.nytimes.com/..../20circumcision-thtml,January20,2008-. Retrieved 07/17/2010.

D'Almeida-Ekue, Silivi, *La Revolte Des Lomeennes 24–25 Janvier 1933*, Les Nouvelles Editions Africaines Du Togo, 1992.

Davies, Carole Boyce & Graves, Anne Adams, *N'gambika*, Africa World Press, Inc. Trenton, New Jersey, 08607, 1986.

Dennis, Janice Carmen, "*The Question of Power for West African Market Women*" (Unpublished) Masters of Science at SUNY Buffalo, 1992.

Dorkenoo Efua, *Cutting the Rose: Female Genital Mutilation—The Practice, and its Prevention*, London Minority Rights Group, 1994.

Durosimi, Jones Eldred, *African Literature Today*, No 13 "Recent Trends in the Novel: A Review" Editor, Heinemann Educational Books, 1983.

El Saadawi, Nawal, *The Nawal El Saadawi Reader*, London, Zed, 1997.

————. "The Struggle to End the Practice of Female Genital Mutilation" in *African Women Writing Resistance: Contemporary Voices*, Jennifer Browdy de Hernandez, Pauline Dongala, Omotayo Jolaosho, and Anne Serafin, (eds) University of Wisconsin Press, Madison, Wisconsin, 2010, p. 192.

Emecheta, Buchi, *Second Class Citizen* printed in Great Britain by William Collins Sons and Co. Ltd., Glasgow, 1974.

————. *Two Faces of Emancipation: African Women*. (No 2 Jan.), pp. 47–49, (Dec. 1975–Jan. 1976).

————. 1979, *Joys of Motherhood*, London, Heinemann, (AWS 227), 1979.

Emenyonu, Ernest N, "Who does Flora Nwapa write for?" *African Literature Today*, no 7, 1975, pp. 28–33.

Fernea, Elizabeth Warnock, *Women and the Family in the Middle East: New Voices of Change*, University of Texas Press, 1985.

Folly Anne-Laure, "Femmes Aux Yeux Ouverts: Women with Open Eyes" 1994, Video: California Newsreel.

Fortes Meyer & Prichard Evans E. E., "Values to African Tribal Life," *The Study of Africa*, p. 56, quoted by Nandakumar in *Africa Quarterly* July–Sept 1971, p. 134.

Friedan, Betty, "The Problem that Has No Name" in *The Feminine Mystique*, Jewish Women and the Feminist Revolution, jwa.org/ feminism, New York, 1963.

Goulianos, J., *A Woman's Witt*, Penguin, London, 1973, p. 291.

Gunther, John, *Inside Africa*, Unknown binding, 1955, p. 751.

Hunter, Guy, "From the Old Culture to the New," *The Study of Africa*, (Methuen & Co), 1965, p. 321.

Hunter, Eva, "Feminism, Islam and the Modern Moroccan Women in the Works of Leila Abouzeid," *African Studies*, Vol. 65, Issue 2 Dec. 2006, pp. 139–155.

Iyengar, K. R. S., 1970, "Two Cheers for the Commonwealth" pp. 28– 29 quoted by Nandakumar, "An Image of African Womanhood" in *Africa Quarterly*, 1971, p. 141.

Knox, D., and Schacht, C. Choices in Relationships, 3d edition, St Paul, MN: West Publishing, 1991.

Kozma, Liat, "Remembrance of Things Past: Leila Abouzeid and Moroccan National History" in Social Politics—*International Studies in Gender, State, and Society*, Oxford University Press, 1999, Vol. 6 No. 3, pp. 388–406.

Lightfoot-Klein, Hanny, *Prisoners of Ritual: An Odyssey into Female Genital Circumcision in Africa*, New York, NY, The Haworth Press, 1989.

Lebeuf, Annie, in *Women in Tropical Africa*, Ed. Denise Paulne, 1963.

Mbiti, S. John, *Introduction to African Religion*, Heinemann, 1975.

Miller David & Sohail H. Hashimi (eds.) "Religion and the Maintenance of Boundaries: An Islamic View," *Boundaries and Justice: Diverse Ethical Perspectives*, chapter 10, (Princeton, New Jersey: Princeton University Press, 2001).

Miriam Maat-Ka-Re Monges, *Kush: Jewel of Nubia: Reconnecting the Root System of African Civilization*, Africa World Press, 1998.

Molara, Ogundipe-Leslie, *Re-creating Ourselves: African Women & Critical Transformation*, Africa World Press Inc., Trenton, New Jersey, 1994.

Moore, Jane Ann, *Seminar Papers on African Studies the Middle-Society*: Five Orientations towards Husband-wife Roles in West African Novels, Ed. Soulayman, 1974.

Mordecai, C. *Weddings, Dating, and Love Customs in World Cultures*, Phoenix, AZ: Nittany, 1999.

Moukhlis, Salah, "A History of Hopes Postponed": Women's Identity and the Postcolonial State in *Year of the Elephant: A Moroccan Woman's Journey Toward Independence*; Research in African Literatures, Vol. 34, No. 3, Fall 2003:66–83.

Nandakumar, Prema, "Criticism: An Image of African Womanhood: A Study of Flora Nwapa's *Efuru*" African Quarterly 11 #2 (1971): 136–146.

Neslutt, Rodney, "Notes on Elechi Amadi's *The Concubine*" Nairobi, Heinemann Educational Books, 1976, p. 42.

New York Times, April 15, 1996. "Woman Plea for Asylum Puts Tribal Ritual on Trial," 1996.

N'Gambika: Studies of Women in African Literature. Ed. Carole Boyce Davies and Anne Adams Graves, Trenton, NJ; Africa World Press, 1986, p. 8.

Ngugi, wa Thiong'o, *The River Between*, London, Heinemann, 1965.

Nwapa's *Efuru*, Africa Quarterly, 11, No. 2 (July–September 1971), pp. 136–46.

Nwapa Flora, *Efuru*, Longman, London, 1966.

———. *Idu* Longman, Heinemann Educational Books, 1970.

———. *One Is Enough*, Trenton, New Jersey, Africa World Press, 1992.

Obiechina, Emmanuel, 1975, "Culture Contact and Culture Conflict" in *Culture, Tradition and Society in the West African Novel*, New York: Cambridge University Press, 1975, pp. 39–59.

Ogundipe-Leslie, Omolara, "The Female Writer & Her Commitment" in *Recreating Ourselves*, Africa World Press, 1995, p. 66.

Oko, Emilia, "The Oguta World View and Flora Nwapa's Novels" in The Legacy of Flora Nwapa, (JOWSA) edited by Helen O. Chukwuma, Harmattan, 2000, p. 15.

Okonkwo, Juliet, I. "The Talented Women in African Literature," *Africa Quarterly*, 15, Nos. 1–2 (April–Sept), 1975, pp. 36–47.

Oyeronke, Oyewumi, *African Women & Feminism: Reflecting on the Politics of Sisterhood*, Africa World Press, Trenton, NJ, 2003.

Palmer, Eustace, The Feminine Point of View in Buchi Emecheta's "The Joys of Motherhood" *African Literature Today*, Ed. Eldred Durosimi Jones, Holmes and Meir, New York, 1983, No 1, pp. 38–55.

Poon, Angelia: "Re-writing the Male Text: Mapping Cultural Spaces in Edwidge Danticat's *Krik? Krak!* and Jamaica Kincaid's *A Small Place*" *Jouvert: A Journal of Postcolonial Studies* 4, 2 (Winter) p. 30, 2000.

Saxon, L. *The Individual, Marriage and the Family*, 8th Edition, Belmont, CA: Wadsworth, 1993.

Sacks, Karen, Engels Revisited. *Women Culture & Society*, Eds. Michelle Rosaldo, and Louise Lamphere, Palo Alto, CA, Stanford University Press, 1974.

Salah Dine Hammoud, *"Arabicization in Morocco: A Case Study in Language Planning and Language Policy Attitudes"* Unpublished Ph.D. Dissertation, University of Texas at Austin, 1982.

Sartre, Jean-Paul, 1946, *L' Existentialisme est un Humanisme*, Paris: Editions Naget, translated into English by Philip Mairetunder the title of *Existentialism & Humanism*, London: Methuen & Co. Ltd., 1948, p. 30, by Assiba d'Almeida in Davies & Graves, 1986, *N'gambika*, Africa World Press, Trenton, NJ, p. 170.

Sheud, Harold, Two African Women. *Revue des Langues Vivantes*, 37, Nos 5–6; 545–58; 664–81. "A Study of Nwapa's *Efuru* and Amadi's *The Concubine*," 1971.

Soulayman Sheih, Nyang, *Three Faiths: One God, Judaism, Christianity, and Islam*, Video, Auteur Productions, (CPTV) PBS, 2005.

Sudarkasa, Niara, *Where Women Work: A Study of Yoruba Women & the Marketplace & the Home* (Ann Arbor Anthropological Paper No. 53, Museum of Anthropology, University of Michigan, 1973.

Sweetman, David, *Women in African History*, Heinemann, 1984.

Time of the Writer Festival: Center for Creative Arts, University of KwaZulu-Natal, March 2004, pp. 22–27.

Toubia, Nahib, *Female Genital Mutilation* in Peters, Julie & Andrea Wolper eds. "Women's Rights, Human Rights: International Feminist Perspectives", New York, NY, Routledge, 1995.

Tucker, Ayoka, *Minority Women in the United States—Exploring Commonalities & Differences among Women of Color* (Unpublished) Master's Thesis State University of New York at Buffalo, NY, 1992.

Tyambe, Paul Zeleza, in Mary Linton Umeh, Flora Nwapa: A Pen and A Press, Triatlantic Books of New York, p. 105, 2010. See Paul Zeleza's "Introduction" to *Women in African Studies Scholarly Publishing*, pp. 1–44.

Uko Iniobong, Engendering Models for Survival and Self-Actualization in Flora Nwapa's *Wives at War and Other Stories* in The Legacy of Flora Nwapa, p. 37.

Umeh, Marie Linton, *Flora Nwapa: A Pen and A Press*, New York, Triatlantic Books, 2010.

Walker, Alice & Parmar, Pratibha, *Warrior Marks: Female Genital Mutilation and Sexual Blinding of Women*, Harcourt Brace & Company, New York, 1993.

Warnock, Elizabeth Fernea, "Introduction to *Year of the Elephant* by Leila Abouzeid," University of Texas at Austin, 1989, p. xix.

Wardere, Abdi, "Genital Cutting in Africa: Slow to Challenge an Ancient Ritual" from HNAfricaMissions@G.PHN.MLIST@AZDW, Oct. 11, with comments by Holfeld@G.PHN.OFPS@AIDW, 1996.

Weyer, H, *LaBoda: The Wedding. POV*: Public Broadcasting System, New York: Border Picture, 2000.

http://ukzn.ac.za/cca/images/towTOW2004/Abouzeid.htm. Retrieved 6/19/2007.

http://www.amazon.com/rss/people/AJ13UBUQ25CBP/reviews. Retrieved 6/28/2007.

http://en.Wikepedia.org/wiki/Leila_Abouzeid. Retrieved 6/19/2007.

http://firstsearch.oclc.org/webZ/FSQQUERY. Retrieved 6/20/2007.

Further Readings on Female Circumcision, and Other African Women Writers

Omi K. Bhabha, in "Nation and Narrative" from Canadian Narrative Cinema from the Margins: "The Nation" and Masculinity in *Goin' Down the Road* by Christine Ramsay, p. 29. www.Filmstudies.ca/journal/pdf/cj-film-studies223_Ramsay_margins.pdf. Retrieved, July 1, 2011.

Refugee Document Centre (Ireland) Legal AID Board. Togo: Researched and compiled by the Refugee Documentation Centre Ireland on 14 December 2009. *Information on a) Prevalence of FGM; b) First Born Females Being Subjected to FGM and c) Possibility to Relocate to Avoid FGM.* Under the heading "Children" the US Department of State Country Report on Human Rights Practices States.

Immigration and Refugee Board of Canada (20 July 2006) Togo: Female genital mutilation (FGM); practices, beliefs, and protection offered (June 2006). http://www.unhcr.org/refworld/country..IRBC..TGO..45f147aba.0.html. (Accessed 14 December 2009).

Female Circumcision: www.measuredhs.com/topics/gender/FGC-CD/start.cfm. References Shelby Duncan Bettina and Yivena Herlund, 2000, Female Circumcision in Africa, Boulder, CO: Lynne Reiner Publishers, Inc.

"The Day I will Never Forget": An Unforgettable Film about Female genital cutting from Women Make Movies. www.disabilityworld.org/01-03_04/.../fgmreview.shtml. (Retrieved June 26, 2010).

Fire Eyes: Female Circumcision-Trailer-Cast. Movies.nytimes.com/movie224536/...Female-Circumcision/overview. (Retrieved June 26, 2010).

Moolaade (2004). Female Circumcision. www.imdb.com/title/tt041 6991/. (Retrieved June 26, 2010).

"Desert Flower" When Female Circumcision Goes to the Movies... Oct 12, 2009. open.salon.com/.../ desert_flower_when_female_ circumcision_goes_to_the_movies-. (Retrieved June 26, 2010).

Award-winning film on Female Circumcision. The Rivera Times Online. To raise awareness of the dangers and indignities of female genital mutilation (FGM), the Generation Femmes D'Afrique et d'Ailleurs (GFAA). www.riveratimes.com/.../award-winning-film-on-female-circum cision.html-. (Retrieved June 27, 2010).

Tariq Ramadan: www.in.com/videos/watch video-tariq-ramadan-on-female circumcision . . . www.in.com Video DailyMotion. com/video/ X7XX99 (March 30, 2009). (Retried June 27, 2010).

Busby, *Daughters of Africa: An International Anthology of Words and Writings* by *Women of African Descent from the Ancient Egyptian to the Present*, 1992.

Mernissi, Fatema, *Women's Rebellion and Islamic Memory*, Zed Books, 1996. World Health Organization, 1998, Female Genital Mutilation: An Overview, Geneva: WHO.

The Rape of Innocence by Patricia Robinett, May 25, 2010.

Movie: *As Nature Made Him: The Boy Who Was Raised as a Girl*, John Colapinto, March 2001.

Edith Wharton, *In Morocco*, Kessinger Publishing, 2004.

Sadiqi, Fatema, *Women, Gender and Language* (2003).

Henriette Celarie, *Behind Moroccan Walls* (2003).

U.S. Agency for International Development (USAID), Policy on Female Genital Cutting (FGC) Washington, DC. USAID, 2000.

LaDuke, *Africa: Art, Women's Lives* (1997).

http://digital   .library.upenn.edu/women_generateMOROCCO.html. Retrieved 6/28/2007.

http://worldviews.ige.org/awpguide/blue_lin.gif"*.

Nawal El-Saadawi, *Woman at Point Zero* (1973) *The Hidden Face of Eve* (1977), *The Fall of the Imam* (2004), *Walking through Fire* (2002).

Kitson, *Anthology: Over One Hundred Works by Zimbabwe Women Writers*, 1994.

Malti-Douglas, *Men, Women and Gods: Nawal El Saadawi and Arab Feminist Poetics*, 1995.

Russell, *Lives of Courage: Women for a New South Africa*, 1996.

Mfa-Abenyi, *Gender in African Women's Writings: Identity, Sexuality, and Difference*, 1997.

Wilentz, *Binding Cultures: Black Women Writers in Africa and in the Diaspora*, 1992.

Zenani and Sheud, *The World and the Word: Tales and Observations from the Xhosa Oral Traditions*, 1992.

Index